CANADA
and
RADICAL
SOCIAL
CHANGE

CANADA
and
RADICAL
SOCIAL
CHANGE

edited by
Dimitrios I. Roussopoulos

LACK ROSE BOOKS   Montréal

BLACK ROSE BOOKS No. D 12
First Edition 1973

Hardcover — ISBN : 0-919618-10-3
Paperback — ISBN : 0-919618-09-X

BLACK ROSE BOOKS Ltd.
3934 rue St. Urbain
Montréal 131, Québec

HN
110
.Z9R36

Printed and bound in Québec, Canada

4

CONTENTS

529172

PREFACE

This book contains some of the outstanding articles published in the radical quarterly OUR GENERATION, since its founding in 1961. The thrust of the journal's contribution to social criticism and research over the years has been one of de-mystifying corporate liberalism on the one hand, and social democracy on the other. This contribution has pioneered what has been referred to elsewhere as 'the long march through the existing institutions'. The selected articles in this book deal with the Canadian situation.

It is difficult to recall the early sixties in mood and style. It was a period of considerable experimentation. Hence the new, in new left. The sterility of the traditional revolutionaries, encouraged the new left to open up the question of both theory and practice again, in a fresh undogmatic way. Radicalism was literary taken to mean going to the root of a problem. When unemployment was discussed the very nature of work was questioned. When class was discussed the whole range of youth's involvement in politics as the avant-guard was discussed. When the crisis of the city was discussed the very relationship between town and country on the one hand and the general crisis of capitalism was investigated. Finally the impotence of our well worn political institutions, e.g. parliament, electoralism were savagely criticized.

This decade of severe social criticism and social action has permeated the thinking of the new generation in a deep sense. Alternatives were proposed to be sure. But now the period of digestion is underway. The seventies are going to be years of intense activity of a new kind, profounding rooted in the slow historical maturation of industrial/technological societies like Canada. The process of organic synthesis resulting from past experiences and present reflection are giving rise to exciting new social and political possibilities.

This book is in part a record of the bases from which the militancy of the seventies will emerge.

Dimitrios I. Roussopoulos
November 1973
Montréal

THE DIMENSIONS OF POWERLESSNESS

by Lucia Kowaluk

We live in a society of citizens who feel both powerless and alienated : powerless to effect anything important in their jobs, powerless to have any say in the product their company manufactures, powerless to put important ideas into the curriculum they are teaching, powerless to have a say in the medical care offered at the clinic, powerless to share in planning the school classes taught to their children, powerless to determine how their taxes are spent, powerless to determine the choice open to them on television. The list is endless.

This powerlessness makes people feel cut off from the world around them — alienated.

We live in huge blocks of apartments and hardly know our neighbours. If we live on a street where neighbours are friendly, this small community is only half a community — it doesn't contain the stores, clinics and schools that the citizens must use.

Each day on the bus we confront hundreds of people who mean nothing to us. And finally we have the uneasy feeling that the communities we *are* part of — the church, the street, and the bridge club — are saying and doing very little about the big things that affect our lives.

Societies find ways to deal with problems that face individuals and groups within it. Traditional authority has been just such a solution. There were times when the Church and the Government supported traditional authority as the best way to keep order and contentment. There was no support for the notions that people should have the knowledge to understand basic questions nor the means to try to solve them.

But this authority is being questioned. The last 200 years of Western thought and tradition have questioned whether an individual should remain ignorant and powerless. It has founded political, social and economic institutions through which people can have some power over their lives. We still believe in these institutions and in the philosophy behind them but this philosophy sometimes comes into direct clash with our philosophy about authority. The most obvious example is in the public chools where we tell children that people have rights and have freedom of thought, and then when children try these things out, they are "disciplined".

And what of the "democratic institutions" that have been with us for 200 years ? In a sense they have become a new "Authority", as difficult to question as the older one has been. The vote, the letter-to-the-editor, the petition, the town meeting, the individual's power with the dollar, all have become hallowed traditions with the same aura of authority that unquestioning obedience once had.

These democratic institutions still carry with them the philosophy that they give to citizens power over their own lives. But is this reality? It appears not.

The vote and the petition no longer give citizens a real say in their government, and we are back where we were 200 years ago. We are in the state of powerlessness just described in which people feel confused, not knowing where they stand and how to gain control over the bigness they feel surrounding them.

A new order must emerge. New institutions that will give citizens control over their lives.

Community organizers, both within social work and outside it (as described by Todd Gitlin and N. von Hoffman) are trying to develop knowledge and skills that will put belonging and power back into people's lives — belonging by being part of a community of common interests and common goals — that is, working together for something and better still, working for some common power.

Purposelessness:

Our society does *not* have any common goals. They are not common in the sense that nearly everyone holds the same basic values, and they are not common in the sense of being community-oriented goals. The goals, such as they are, that many people hold are values that have to do with personal gain, usually at the expense of others, and usually the most primitive sort of material gain. This value of gaining at the expense of others increases the alienation felt by most people in this society.

So let me get back to the point made above; that is, that we need to put belonging and power back into people's lives, our own lives, by working for common interests and goals, namely some control over the things that affect us.

What we need to do is to develop NEW institutions for people to use to express their rights. We have already commented that many of our traditional institutions of democracy and free enterprise have become meaningless. One person's buying power or one person's vote or one person's ownership of a few shares of stock have no power in our present day society.

At any given time in society new institutions evolve for the purpose of solving the problems presented to the society at that time. In a "natural" state this process can take generations. It is not necessary, however, for this to evolve without an awareness — a consciousness on the part of the individuals who are affected. A certain understanding of social process is possible; new institutions can be consciously and deliberately developed. If community organizers can acquire this knowledge and skill, they can be in a position to help people develop new ways of asserting their rights.

This does not mean forcing on people goals and methods they have not asked for, but instead, sensitively being aware of what, in fact, people are lacking in their lives and helping them figure out ways to achieve these goals which may be new and different.

It means consciously developing new institutions within which people will again have the power to run their own lives, and in the process will also not feel alienated. They will again begin to express their democratic rights.

But this sort of struggle requires more than a pressure group that just makes a lot of noise, and then goes home. It requires a clear understanding of the power-structure that is being challenged; that is, to what other pressures does the power structure respond, what IN REALITY are the resources at the disposal of all the parties involved?

Among other things, it means understanding that a City Councillor or a Trust Company is no longer sensitive to one person's vote or one person's rent. They now respond only to 100 people expressing themselves openly, or 100 people refusing to pay rent.

Because we are used to the old way of one vote, one man's money or opinion being worth something, we are easily caught up in the rhetoric of the old way. We're ashamed to take more decisive group action because that's force and "undemocratic"; we should use the "democratic" ways we're used to. But we forget that it is only the group action that is now democratic when we are expressing ourselves to huge City Councils, none of whose members we know personally, huge housing development owners, huge industry.

Published 1967

THOSE WHO TAKE THE MEAT
FROM THE TABLE

Teach contentment
Those for whom the taxes are destined
Demand sacrifice
Those who eat their fill speak to the
hungry
Of wonderful times to come
Those who lead the country in the
abyss
Call ruling too difficult
For ordinary men   — Bertolt Brecht.

POVERTY IN CANADA

by BRYAN M. KNIGHT

FIVE MILLION people, one quarter of the population of Canada, live in a state of poverty.[1] Why? What *is* this poverty? Can it be wiped out? How? Why has it persisted? These and other questions form the framework of the following overview.

Who Are The Poor?

To speak of "the poor" is to imply a definition at once as global as it is homogeneous. But poor people are far from homogeneous. Indeed, probably the only characteristic they all share is lack of wealth. However, we are concerned here with that portion of "the poor" who not only have low or non-existent incomes but *also feel powerless to change their situations.*

Thus, excluded from our considerations are those who deliberately seek out poverty. (For example, the provisionally poor such as university students and the serenely poor, such as cloistered nuns).

Poverty is, in essence, a state of deprivation. The essential nature of poverty is its relativeness to other segments of a particular society.

> The reconceptualization of poverty in terms of relative deprivation rather than in terms of subsistence provides a bridge between the empirical phenomenon and contemporary sociological theory. It necessitates examining poverty in a system of action. *Relative* deprivation implies a social context and a set of normative standards which serve as a basis for comparative evaluation. The systems model . . . makes it possible to examine those conditions of the system which produce relative deprivation and the consequences for other parts of the system and for the system as a whole.[2]

Whyte clarifies his definition further by differentiating between observable poverty and felt poverty. "Whereas objective poverty is relative deprivation defined by community standards, subjective poverty is experienced relative deprivation, defined in terms of individual values rather than shared norms".[3]

But what can be said to be "relative deprivation" in Canada? This poses the quantitative measure. How much is enough to live on comfortably? How much is so little that the citizen is deprived, relative to other Canadians?

The initial answer is that there is no single yardstick, — that any dividing line will be arbitrary, discriminatory and unfair to some.[4]

There are many ways of arriving at a "poverty-line". We could work out a budget to cover the barest essentials necessary to keep a family alive — this is a favourite pastime of mathematically inclined social workers and welfare officials. Or, we could look at what the Federal Government has established, by inference if not by intent, as a subsistence level in its income tax exemptions, minimum wage legislation and old age security. Or we might employ Lorrenz curves and coefficients.

Another useful method is to examine the ratio of expenditure to income. The less income a family has to spend on items other than food, shelter and clothing, the poorer it is.

Regardless of the technique employed, the minimum income needs for a family of four in an urban environment run about $2600 - $3400, for two adults $2000 - $2500, and for a single person about $1500 - $1800. Farm families probably need cash incomes of about 80 per cent of the urban level . . .[5]

No poverty line is adequate in itself to delimit poverty in Canada. The variables of geography, time, age, family size and season make a statistical nightmare out of attempts to apply an arbitrary minimum income level to Canada's poor.

Despite these problems

it is clear that we are among the few modern countries which have large numbers at this moment who are by any standards poor and who are grossly neglected by the most elementary forms of social legislation. This is a social fact of the utmost importance. In the eyes of the poor, we condone poverty by our acquiescence. And to condone it is to sanction it.[6]

Who are the poor? They are not

simply persons who have been thrown out of the normal order of economic success through some accident of frictional unemployment or personal mischoice, but rather persons who have suffered major damage in their capacities to make demands on the society.[7]

Broadly speaking, the poor can be grouped as Unemployable, Unemployed or Underemployed. More specifically they are, for example, the 95 per cent of Canada's Eskimo population living in abject poverty,[8] they are 1,400,000 old people[9] counting pennies from their Old Age pensions, they are 1,300,000 Canadians permanently physically disabled,[10] they are 38.1 per cent of Montreal's population living in "poverty, privation, and misery"[11], they are 2,949,000 wage and salary earners who earned less than $3,000 in 1961.[12]

> The problem of poverty in our present society must be understood in relationship to the realities of a wage-centered, industrialized capitalistic society, a society very different from the simple model on which much of our current social policy is based.[13].

Many causes (ill-health, recession, discrimination, to name three) initiate poverty. Some causative factors are attributable to individuals, others are beyond individual control. The significance of the poverty core is its persistence; it persists because those caught in the grip of poverty are as helpless as grains of pepper in a peppermill. Society crushes the poor ever deeper into dismal, dirty dust.

Consider the indigenous population :

> Health conditions of the Indian and Eskimo population, particularly in the North, are still among the worst in the world. The Eskimo infant mortality in 1963 was 193 per 1,000 live births against a national average of 27. The Indian death rate in 1963 was 70.4 per 1,000 against an all-Canadian rate of 26.3.[14].

Consider the physically disabled :

> In January of this year (1965), 51,671 people were qualified under the Disabled Persons Act for assistance which averaged $69.48 per month across the country. The maximum allowable income, including the Disability Assistance, for a family was $2,220 per year, and for a single person $1,260 . . . Last year nearly 10,000 people were turned away because their disablement was not assessed as total or permanent although many were nonetheless severely handicapped. Five hundred and sixty-seven applicants were not quite poor enough to qualify for the $900 a year — the maximum payable under the Act. Two hundred and twenty-three died before a decision had been made on their applications. In the same period there were 8,581 recipients of allowances for blind persons. They averaged $68.12 a month and income could reach a total of $2,580 a year without assistance being reduced below the maximum $900. Of the applicants last year, 304 were not blind enough and 68 were not poor enough to qualify.[15].

Not quite poor enough to qualify. And what *do* the poor qualify for ? First of all, the poor qualify to pay more than other people for the same, or inferior, merchandise.[16]. Second, the poor qualify for inferior housing, education and employment. Third, the poor qualify for the scorn, spite and, worst of all, pity from other Canadians. Fourth, the poor qualify to be tempted by the same tinsel as the rest of society. Fifth, the poor qualify to be unequal — e.g. over four times as many babies in "less advantaged" than in "more advantaged" areas of Montreal die before they reach one year of age.[17].

Poverty-stricken people are as alienated from society as were the lepers of old. But our modern lepers have no need of warning bells; they are not viewed as a threat to society because they are not viewed at all.

The poor are always in a subordinate role, receiving orders, but never giving them; directed but never directing; acted upon by others but unable to act. Male or female, employed or unemployed, the poor lack political, economic and social bargaining power. Deprived of opportunities to learn skills of organizing, advising, decision-making, and unaccustomed to responsibility, they are unequipped for anything but a unilateral relationship which is what they do, in fact, encounter. Through the process of child-parent identification, their habits of dependency are passed on to their children. The alienation of one generation becomes the learned behaviour of the next, and the internalized self image of the third.[18].

And so the separation of poor from non-poor is intensified.

The dependency of the poor is not primarily a neurotic need to occupy dependency positions in social relationships, but rather it results from a deprivation of those minimal social resources, at every period of their lives, which the poor need and therefore must seek. The poor are not victims of the social system in the sense that "organization men" are victims. They are rather, as Michael Harrington has emphasized, the *other* America, outsiders to the major society.[19].

But the poor, caught "in the grip of two interlocking and self-defeating forces, one sociocultural, the other psychological", cannot even "make adequate use of the admittedly meager resources available to them."[20].

Because poor people *feel* unable to control their destinies, they *are* powerless.

The poor feel inferior and incapable of improving their position in life; they feel alienated from society but their physical plight is not acute enough to encourage recourse to violent political action. Therefore, a self-perpetuating and vicious circle is often established. Society rejects the poor, holds them apart and prevents them, either directly or by its general attitude towards the change of economic and social institutions, from crossing into regions of prosperity. In turn, because of their poverty, the poor develop adjustments to their environment which contribute equally to this vicious circle and prevent them from taking advantage of opportunities for individual development.[21].

How can this vicious circle be cracked ? Little serious effort has been made in this country to wipe out poverty. One of the reasons is that,

the inherent conservatism of the very poor — to a degree that may be equalled only by the very rich — has led in many respects to an acceptance of that culture above them. The impetus to change, and demand for social action, the call to break down the social barriers come usually not from the poor, but from the conscience of the relatively well-to-do. This essential fact gives Canadian society much of its present kind of stability.[22].

Well-to-do Canadian consciences are peculiarly silent. Much muddy thinking clogs the channels of awareness of the Haves. For instance, everyone knows that Canada is becoming richer and richer. Is it not *the* land of opportunity ? It is, but not for all its people.

Over the past century, Canada's economy has averaged a growth in total real gross national product of 3.3 per cent annually and of per capita real gross national product about 1.5 per cent annually; yet despite these changes, more persons today earn less than $2000 (in constant 1951 dollars) than in 1931.[23.]

The increasing general affluence is very likely entrenching the class differential ever more firmly. The middle classes are far from anxious to share their comparative wealth. The upper classes cling cleverly and tenaciously to theirs. But it is not simply a matter of greed, or selfishness. There are fears of loss of status, of privilege, of meaning.

There is also ignorance. How many people know that "the vast amount of tax revenues that citizens contribute for welfare is largely of benefit to themselves"[24.]? Or that "a recent U.S. study showed that the "relief" and other welfare payments to low income people were more than paid back by *their* taxes"[25.]?

Insufficient Solutions to Poverty

What feeble attempts there have been to date in Canada to tackle the problems of poverty have been at best superficial and at worst, damaging. These actions were not designed to develop power among the poor. Power to have some say, some choice in their own futures. No, these well-intentioned programs were handouts — of material aid, "cultural enrichment" and counselling.

The ultimate effect of such good works has been to maintain the poor in their squalor.

Traditionally, the tried, tested and deficient approaches to eradicating poverty slip into seven slots: education, government action, middle-class citizen action, economic growth, rehabilitation, population control and housing.

Education

One of the most popular, and on the face of it, efficacious, suggestions for eliminating poverty is education. Educate the masses of poor and lo! they will be liberated to compete and consume on a par with the other educated and mobile citizens.

The incidence of little schooling in Canada is certainly cause for concern, as is the circular reinforcement of the so-called poverty culture through our present educational system. "In 1961, of Canadians aged 15 and over, there were 5,166,346 — 47 per cent — with no more than elementary schooling. These included 176,524 with no schooling and 848,261 with four grades or less".[26.]

The child from a poverty home starts school greatly disadvantaged. He is not familiar with the stories, expectations and behaviours of the middle-class. Yet the school system assumes he has values and experiences which prepare him for beginning school. Naturally, the deprived child is alienated by the strange cultural mores he is expected to abide by. The curriculum is dull and irrelevant. And thus the cycle is repeated. The child returns to his inferior housing, inadequate diet, anti-intellectual environment. Soon the temptation of early earnings and the desire to be free of a system which only forces him to repeatedly fail, encourage the child to leave. As soon as he can he becomes a drop-out.

He is more likely a push-out. His parents probably would like their child to get an education but with their own limited understanding "meager incomes and limited education (they) often do not provide appropriate or consistent encouragement for their children to make use of even the inadequate conventional opportunities present in such an environment".[27.]

And the conventional opportunities are inadequate. Schools in poor neighbourhoods are too often the ones with poorer facilities and inferior staff. The latters' attitudes towards the children are usually primed with middle-class standards. When the children fail to measure up to those standards, or when they conform to the low opinions that teachers often have toward slum children, the circle is complete. The teachers' opinions are verified, the child slips further into withdrawal from participation and the "culture" of poverty is re-enforced.

. Watkins makes an apt summary comment on the value of education in eradicating poverty : "If education, particularly higher education, was the universal panacea that some Canadians seem to think it is, then the United States ought not to have a poverty problem at all".[28.]

Government Action

In regard to the problem of *rural* poverty, as with urban, solutions are often posed as potentially practicable if they come from the higher reaches of society and work down.[29.] "Leaving it to the Government" however trustworthy, is part of society's way of maintaining the status quo, or at least of only changing it very gradually.

This is not to say that Government-sponsored programs cannot benefit citizens, and perhaps alleviate poverty. But by their very nature, Government programs have to maintain a balance. The balance is what is considered politically feasible and desirable. But only to the extent that the poor have a real voice in saying what is feasible and desirable *for themselves* can their poverty, and society, be changed significantly.

It is the "top-down" approach which spells the failure of the U.S. War on Poverty :

> The programs had to be politically clean. More than that, in many instances, by requiring approval of programs by political units below the federal level, the program was in no way to reward the wicked

(at least the wicked poor). Crucial programs that dealt with people, instead of the vague and frequently unreal entities that are "grass-rooted" community organizations, had built into them qualifications that excluded people with police records and psychological or physical handicaps. These were to be programs for the deserving and politically safe poor.[30]

Middle-Class Citizen Action

Functionally, Middle-Class Citizen Action has served to keep the poor alienated.

The recommendations have been for improved law enforcement; public welfare; public housing; social settlements; higher horizons educational programs; social work with "hard core" families; urban renewal, clean-up, paint-up, and fix-up programs; block and neighbourhood organizations . . . All these plans and programs have usually shared two characteristics:
(1) they are initiated and supported from outside the neighbourhoods of poverty and imposed on the poor, and
(2) they fail to make any lasting positive impact on neighbourhoods of poverty . . . These programs, presupposing the inferiority of the people in the area, perpetuate and exacerbate the inequality.[31]

The programs do, adds Haggstrom, serve to reduce guilt and shame in the *wider* society.

Economic Growth

Wishful thinking by concerned Haves about a general increase in wealth cannot be a long-term solution to poverty.

Economic growth — which is the only economic goal to which this country seems seriously committed — is not a sufficient solution to poverty, mostly because it creates its casualties as much as its benefactions. Notable cases in point are rural poverty in general, and the serious regional poverty of the Atlantic Provinces.[32]

Rehabilitation

Rehabilitative projects are a favourite avenue intended by the Haves to help the Have-nots. To the degree that there are jobs that can be filled and employers that are willing to hire rehabilitated poor persons, the projects have value. One of the biggest hurdles in rehabilitation or re-training programs is to decide what content for what jobs.

For many residents in America's troubled neighbourhoods the social service words should be "habilitate" and "train". Many of the government's well-intentioned programs have shot over their heads . . . You cannot retrain a man to be a computer operator if he does not have basic arithmetic and reading skills.[33]

In Canada,

The tight limitations on earned income which are a feature of the categorical assistance programs, inevitably have some disincentive effect in cases of serious but not absolute disability. Also, and of equal importance, levels of public assistance are frequently higher than could ever be produced through the earning capacity of the individual. To such individuals, it may not seem worthwhile to make full use of increased capacities developed through the services of rehabilitation agencies such as that under the auspices of the Department of Labour.[34]

Vocational training is beset with enigmas. For what occupations shall a man be habilitated when jobs are daily eliminated by automation ?

The token of existence in modern society is the word; without the word and the capacity to use language it is impossible to make an intelligible demand on the society. For those without these tokens and the capacity to symbolize in complex ways there will be little chance to use the resources of the society or to mobilize them in their own behalf.[35]

Population Control

Limiting the numbers of the poor appears to be a way of at least stopping the spread of poverty, if not of eradicating it completely. Sterilization, as a mode of limitation, is unpleasant and impractical if voluntary, and abhorrent if it is involuntary.

In Canada there is a strong reluctance in some quarters to allow dissemination of information regarding birth control.

For the poor, birth control has a valuable potential in reducing not only births, but family poverty. The obstacles are numerous : laws as mentioned above, lack of money to buy contraceptives even though their use is understood, unfounded but undispelled fears and above all, religious and cultural prohibitions against "interfering with nature".

But when the poor were given access to birth control devices it was found that "uneducated and impoverished women were the most assiduous users of the pill. They had less unexpected pregnancies than college graduates".[36]

Population control is a *limited* solution, and should only be considered within the framework of a just distribution of wealth, goods and services.

Housing

Housing is another projected solution to poverty. It has been tried both on this continent and abroad. One of the paradoxes of the effects of buildings and surroundings upon people is that dirty, unwholesome, inferior housing appears to condition people who live in those circumstances to feel dirty, unwholesome and inferior yet the converse is not automatically true. When poor people are transferred to better housing they don't become model citizens overnight — much to the distress of the ardent supporters of public and low-rental housing.

Possibly, the internalised attitudes that poor people bring with them when they voluntarily or coercively move into better housing, outweigh any advantages the improved material surroundings might have. It is clear that "We are shifting problems — not solving them. Transferring the poor from one house to another — even if it is to a solid, better-constructed public housing building — only scratches the surface".[37] That's in the United States. In Canada, where the need is for at least 300,000 dwelling units[38] experience is very limited about the effects, favourable or adverse, of public housing because there has been comparatively little.

It is true, though, of the Jeanne Mance Housing Project in Montreal, as of similar projects in the United States that "Low income limits not only guarantee that the projects will remain fortresses of poverty, but at the same time actively deny the welfare departments a free rehabilitation program in the form of the successful next-door neighbour".[39] Moving up the social scale at least in terms of income, incurs the penalty of expulsion from public housing. So the poor family which does manage to attain a higher income level has soon to expend a larger proportion of the new income on rent in the relatively expensive private sector of housing. Thus are the poor kept poor and the intent of low-rental housing frustrated.

And in Montreal, the ugly sores of slum clearance (vacant lots overgrown with wild flowers or packed with gleaming automobiles) will not offend the passers-by — because high, colourful boards shield the horror from curious eyes.

The basic puzzle is how to provide better housing for the poor and at the same time, really help the poor in the transition. Many suggestions pop up. Few have been tested. Co-op housing? Ownership by the erstwhile poor ? Rental subsides for housing in middle-class districts ?

There persists in Canada an attitude that somehow the poor are incompetent to handle their own money, that, for example, it is all right to put more and more money into the trustworthy hands of landlords, but never into the slippery hands of the poor.

People live in slums because they cannot live elsewhere (with the obvious exceptions of researchers, students and their ilk). "A slum is a dirty, miserable, diseased, human junkyard full of frustration and despair."[40] The occupants may be afraid to voice any criticisms because of the power (real or imagined) of the owners. And indeed, the resources at the command of the landlord do far outweigh those at the command of any one tenant.

An American expert on housing for the poor foretells what might come to pass :

> If we truly rebuild for the poor we shall have quite a different approach to many areas. The advice of poor people would be sought, not only as therapy for them but also because they are the clients of the architect and the city planner. (This sounds rather different from being the clients of the welfare worker). Poor people might be engaged . . . in the manual rebuilding of their neighbourhoods . . . One would consider methods to make it feasible for tenants of low-rental housing to remain in them — perhaps to purchase them — as their incomes rise. Such a program should convince poor people that they were the purpose of urban renewal, not pawns in its path.[41]

Such programs have been implemented in post-war France and pre-war England.

Potentially Effective Solutions

Poor people lack two primary essentials : money and power.

What would happen if poor people were to be given large sums of cash, *no strings attached?* No one knows for it has never been done. And until the poor have power it won't be done. But they might receive a basic, *subsistence* minimum.

In our society, people are increasingly at the mercy of changing conditions beyond their individual control, and personal responsibility for success or failure becomes more and more difficult to maintain. We know little enough yet about the possible effects of automation, but the likelihood of a serious and lasting change in our employment patterns, and therefore of income standards based on work, looms threateningly before us. Perhaps we may find the stable and impersonal device of the income guarantee the best answer to our problem . . . The income guarantee will not alone solve all the problems of poverty. Nor will any other form of financial help. But it might provide the basic "floor" below need that we are seeking, in a form more consonant with human dignity than anything we have yet devised.[42].

It is a measure of the extent of affluence in Canada that the concept of a guaranteed minimum income can even be entertained.

The corrupting effect on the human spirit of a small amount of unearned revenue has unquestionably been exaggerated as, indeed, have the character-building values of hunger and privation. To secure to each family a minimum standard, as a normal function of the society, would help insure that the misfortunes of parents, deserved or otherwise, were not visited on their children. It would help insure that poverty was not self-perpetuating.[43].

But without a voice in their own affairs, the poor would be little better off with their guaranteed income. Especially if the guarantee comes in the form of negative income tax and therefore means test, (as does the recent "generous" increase to the needy aged in Canada).

For this would be to perpetuate the inequalities of status and opportunity.

Nevertheless let us see how modest is the dollar amount necessary to bring everyone in Canada to a guaranteed minimum income. Canadian incomes[44.] at the last census were:

Income Class	Families		Individuals	
	Number	Per cent	Number	Per cent
Under $1000	163,590	4.5	530,340	37.7
1000 to 1999	302,115	8.3	273,716	19.4
2000 to 2999	382,235	10.4	216,676	15.4
3000 to 3999	557,366	15.2	195,073	13.9
4000 and over	2,251,662	61.6	191,471	13.6

To raise the lowest Canadian incomes so they exceed $3000 for families and $1500 for individuals, would cost between two and three billion dollars per year. It can be argued that even these levels are inadequate, yet in 1967 Canada expects its aged citizens to subsist on less. The total figure is only $300,000,000 more than was spent in 1961 on Family Allowances, Youth Allowances, Needy, blind, disabled Allowances and Unemployment Assistance. It is roughly equivalent to the amount spent by the Canadian Government on "National Defence".

The Poor and Power

To fully overcome poverty the poor have to shed their fatalism, well-grounded apathy and despair. To do this they have to have power to make themselves seen, heard and felt in Canada. As Niebuhr said in the 1930's :

> There is never sufficient intelligence and idealism to guarantee that the disinherited will gain an increase in rights by waiting for the privileged to divest themselves of their special advantages. Force must be used, though an intelligent society should be able to confine the use of force to those types which operate in the realm of politics, without degenerating into actual violence.[45].

How do the poor gain power non-violently ? By organising. The poor need to learn about lobbying, about citizens' rights, about legislative processes — in short, the *savoir faire* to accomplish *their own ends*.

In the words of Saul Alinsky, sociologist :

> (This is) the breaking down of the feeling on the part of our people that they are social automatons with no stake in the future, rather than human beings in possession of all the responsibility, strength, and human dignity which constitute the heritage of free citizens of a democracy. This can be done only through the democratic organisation of our people for democracy.[46].

In addition to the natural, but shortsighted fears of the middle-classes, two other factors mitigate against the poor organizing for their own interests : religion and social work.

Social work, it is almost commonplace to say, arose out of the Judeo-Christian ethic. But religion, particularly the Christian religion, has long served to keep the poor poor. Thus social work has to face an unpleasant contradiction if it wants to make any real attempts to remove poverty from Canada. So ingrained are the concepts of God-ordained society and one's proper station within that society that even today in the post-Freud era, the conventional wisdom (which embodies the Protestant ethic) has a pervasive influence.

According to this ethic, men *should* work and those who don't are either lazy or have some other character weakness.[47]. They are undeserving and receive their just desserts in poverty's deprivations.

Much of that kind of thinking has passed away but its remnants linger on. Even more influential still is the kind of philanthropic spirit encouraged by the Catholic church and which rests on a static conception of society :

it sometimes resulted in the romantic absurdity of regarding the poor as God-ordained instruments for the encouragement of philanthropy, thus placing the elimination of poverty quite outside the bounds of the Christian social spirit.[49].

Social work is largely a middle-class movement; it therefore has a loyalty to the underlying values of the middle-class, as well as to its professed values. This is why the comments of the Special Planning Secretariat are applicable to social work:

> The idea that all men had a right to a share in the benefits and responsibility of society evolved slowly. Even today the manifestations of this idea are often regarded as dangerous radicalism. While it is respectable to help the poor in their suffering, social action to remove the suffering by the adjustment of society is inevitably controversial.

Thus social workers, who generally run from controversy, sometimes attempt to mobilize poverty-stricken neighbourhoods but "without jeopardizing any existing power arrangement".[49].

Other factors besides fear of conflict are operating too: "There are four areas of confusion present in social work thinking: confusion of scope, confusion of public and professional interest, confusion in conceptual focus, and confusion in methodological priority, which must be dissipated if social work is to play a major role in dealing with poverty".[50].

Lourie details the reasons which together form the cultural lag dragging social work's heels in the dust of futility. Briefly, these reasons are: swift changes in society, agency sponsorship, concern with present programs, limited personnel, emotional investment in ritualistic way of doing things, individualism, residual concept of social work and a reluctance to advertise deficiency in quality and quantity of services provided.[51].

> To study the rich and the sources of power in society is not the kind of activity which comes easily to social workers attempting to understand the human condition.[52].

It is still true that social workers

> come to the people of the slums under the aegis of benevolence and goodness, not to organize the people, not to help them rebel and fight their way out of the muck — NO ! They come to get these people "adjusted"; adjusted so they will live in hell and like it too.[53].

In Canada, the number of social workers actively attempting to organize the poor to escape from poverty is insignificant. As Pelletier said:

> I am not among those who admire the humility, self-effacement and silence of social workers and Canadian social welfare organizations. On the contrary, I do not think they ever speak loud enough, I think they are afraid to raise their voices, and that this soft-spokenness of theirs

contributes to the comfortable self-satisfaction and the murderously easy consciences of the majority whose nests are well feathered.[54].

Drastic changes in social work training are urgently required if Canadian social workers are to leap the thirty year gap retarding them from seriously tackling the injustices facing five million second class citizens.

Social welfare here, as in the United States,

has been relegated to individual case work practice and is conducted in the context of the most degrading kinds of means tests until the relationship between the professional social worker and the client is one of constant combat and mutual manipulation.[55].

Canada entering its second century of Confederation, will probably not win *its* War on Poverty because social workers on the whole are unwilling to accept

new programs conceived in the notion that the poor are to have control over their own destiny and that they should have the right not to ask, but to demand certain rights and privileges. No longer would the interpersonal relationship between social worker and the client be one of direction from the middle-class source, however permissive and non-directive, but rather a meeting of equals in power.[56].*

"The solution then, is a two-way process. It is not only that society will change the poor; it is also that the poor will change society."[57].

---

* We are sceptical that this is possible in either the U.S. or Canada or on any meaningful scale. The Editors.

FOOTNOTES:

1. R. Phillips, Director of War on Poverty, "Country Magazine", CBC, March 14, 1966.
2. Donald R. Whyte, "Sociological Aspects of Poverty: A Conceptual Analysis" (*The Canadian Review of Sociology and Anthropology*, Vol. 2, #4, November 1965), p. 178.
3. Whyte, p. 179.
4. R. A. Jenness, *The Dimensions of Poverty in Canada, Some Preliminary Observations* (The University of British Columbia, February 1965, mimeo), p. 5.
5. Jenness, p. 17.
6. Thelma McCormack, "Poverty and Social Action", *The Canadian Forum*, Vol. VLVI, No. 550, November 1966, p. 172.

7. John H. Gagnon and William Simon, "The War on The Poor?", *Motive*, Vol. XXVII, No. 3, December 1966.

8. Jenness, p. 50.

9. "Poverty Amongst the Aged in Canada", *Profile of Poverty in Canada*, Special Planning Secretariat, Ottawa, undated, p. 1.

10. "Disability", *Profile of Poverty in Canada*, p. 2.

11. Emile Gosselin, *La Troisième Solitude*, Conseil du Travail de Montréal (F.T.Q. — C.T.C.), p. 7. Undated.

12. Jenness, p. 26.

13. Peter Katadotis, *"A Draft Proposal to Organize Welfare Recipients in a Montreal Area"*, Urban Social Redevelopment Project, Montreal November 3, 1966, mimeo, p. 2.

14. *Profile of Poverty in Canada*, p. 5.

15. "Disability", p. 1.

16. David Caplovitz, *The Poor Pay More*, Glencoe, Illinois : The Free Press, 1963.

17. *Strategy Towards Reducing Socio-Economic Inequalities In the Depressed Areas of Montreal*, Conseil des Oeuvres de Montréal, Preliminary Report October 31, 1966.

18. McCormack, p. 173.

19. Warren C. Haggstrom, "The Power of the Poor" (*Mental Health of the Poor*, ed. Frank Riessman *et al*, London The Free Press of Glencoe, 1964), p. 213.

20. Alexander H. Leighton, "Poverty and Social Change" (*Scientific American*), Vol. 212, No. 5, May 1965.

21. "The Role of Attitudes in the Development and Perpetuation of Poverty", *Profile of Poverty in Canada*, p. 4.

22. "Role of Attitudes", p. 3.

23. Jenness, pp. 24-25.

24. Patricia Godfrey, *The Sixties : Poverty in Our Society*, Canadian Association for Adult Education, pamphlet No. 2, November, 1965, p. 16.

25. Godfrey, p. 16.

26. "Education — Its Relationship to Poverty", *Profile of Poverty in Canada*, p. 1.

27. Irving Spergel, *Racketville, Slumtown, Haulburg* (Chicago : The University of Chicago Press, 1964), p. XIV.

28. Melville H. Watkins, "Poverty. What Should Be Done" (*The Canadian Forum*, Vol. XLV, No. 542, March 1966).

29. See, for example, *Rural Poverty : What Can ARDA Do?* (November, 1964 : Canadian Association for Adult Education).

30. Gagnon and Simon, p. 6.

31. Haggstrom, p. 215.

32. Watkins, p. 268.

33. Edgar May, *The Wasted Americans* (New York : Harper and Row, 1964), p. 195.

34. "Disability", p. 3.

35. Gagnon and Simon, p. 6.

36. Gregory Pincus quoted by Dr. William Shockley in "Is Quality of U. S. Population Declining?" (*U. S. News & World Report*, Vol. LIX, No. 21, November 22, 1965), p. 70.

37. Senator Hubert H. Humphrey, *War on Poverty* (New York : McCraw-Hill Book Company, 1964), p. 55.

38. "Housing Need", *Profile of Poverty in Canada*, p. 4.

39. May, p. 135.

40. Saul D. Alinsky, *Reveille for Radicals* (Chicago, Illinois : University of Chicago Press, 1946), p. 82.

41. Alvin L. Schorr, *Slums and Social Insecurity* (U. S. Department of Health, Education, and Welfare, Washington, D.C., n.d.), p. 73.

42. Godfrey, p. 14.

43. John Kenneth Galbraith, *The Affluent Society* (Cambridge, Mass : The Riverside Press, 1958), p. 329.

44. John J. Madden, "Some Aspects of Poverty in Canada", speech delivered to *Canadian Conference on Social Welfare*, Hamilton June, 1964.

45. Reinhold Niebuhr, *The Contribution of Religion to Social Work* (New York : Columbia University Press, 1932), p. 85.

46. Alinsky, p. 73.

47. "Role of Attitudes", p. 3.

48. Niebuhr, p. 8.

49. Haggstrom, p. 222.

50. Norman V. Lourie, "Poverty", *Social Work and Social Problems*, ed. Nathan E. Cohen (New York : National Association of Social Workers, Inc., 1964), p. 26.

51. Lourie, p. 34.

52. Richard M. Titmuss, *Income Distribution and Social Change* (Toronto : University of Toronto Press, 1962), p. 187.

53. Alinsky, p. 83.

54. Gérard Pelletier, "Poverty in Our Midst" Canadian Conference on Welfare, 1963.

55. Gagnon and Simon, p. 8.

56. Gagnon and Simon, p. 9.

57. *Profile of Poverty in Canada*, p. 8.

Published 1967

UNEMPLOYMENT:
A NEW ANALYSIS

by Fred Caloren

The question that our civilization is now asked to face is whether we are ready to make man the master of his social games, rather than their unwitting servant. In a post-alienated society it would be man himself who would create his own rich and playful and variegated meanings. These meanings would not be left to the automatic functioning of his social institutions, in which man is sacrificed to the blind forces of commercial-industrial economics with its high vision of the eight-hour day, the two-week vacation, the unhoped-for bliss of 'full employment.' [1]

ERNEST BECKER

THE rate of unemployment in Canada is consistently and often by a considerable margin, the highest of the industrialized capitalist societies. (See Table 1) Only four times in the last twenty years, the most recent occasion being 1966, has the annual average unemployment rate in this country dipped below 3.8 per cent, the figure now being proposed (appropriately enough ! — "to provide comparability with official U.S. potential output and GNP 'gap' calculations" [2]) as consistent, in 1975, with a fully performing economy. From May 1970 to the present (most recent figures at time of writing are for December 1971) the monthly rate of unemployment has never been less than 6 per cent, frequently closer to 7. Canadians had learned to live rather comfortably with 270, 380, 430 thousand workless in their midst ; but with these numbers running by month in the past year to 530, 570, 623, and most recently 530 thousand, the cry is up throughout the land : "Create more jobs !" Not only is the laying on of enough more "jobs" an unlikely prospect [3] in the context of our highly colonialized economy ; there are particularities of the unemployment scene hidden in the aggregates that are even more scandalous than the general situation, and that lie beyond such remedies. In any event the benefits accruing to a pumped-up free enterprise system and increased state management of the unemployed will fall essentially to those institutions and classes of people who have always reaped the harvest of working class misery, dependency and insecurity.

The Structure of Unemployment

A closer examination of unemployment as we have become accustomed to having it presented in general abstract terms reveals some startling facts about its structure that must be born in mind.

The regional disparity of the burden is, of course, well known. In terms of averages for year 1970, Québec with 27% of the employed population of the country had 37% of the unemployed ; parallel figures for Ontario were almost the reverse : with 38% and 27% respectively ; the Atlantic region shows 8% and 10% respectively. [4] By province the differences can be even more marked : in November of the past year, unemployment rates were as follows : — Saskatchewan 3.5 ; Ontario 4.6 ; New Brunswick 6.5 ; British Columbia 7.1 ; Québec 7.3 ; Nova Scotia 7.4 ; Newfoundland 11.4. [5] This pattern is habitual and often even more pronounced than these figures show. Further refinement of the gross statistics would pinpoint particular areas and communities where the number of men and women out of work is a staggering proportion of the local population and the whole community suffers, quite literally, the short and long term effects.

The duration of unemployment has been showing a very noticeable development upwards since the current critical period began to shape up in a major fashion. Since June of 1970 when Trudeau's unemployment policies really began to bite, the percentage of the labour force unemployed for 4 months or more has never been less than 2 ; in the latter half of 1971 it has been consistently closer to 3. [6] According to the seasonally adjusted figures, in November of '71, 123,000 people had been without work and seeking work for 7 months or more. That is one in five of the unemployed. The proportion of long duration unemployment has been increasing steadily over the past three years. Those out 4 months or more represented 25% of the unemployed in November 1969, 32% in November 1970 and 36% in the same month last year. [7] Even these depressing figures, because of the definition of "unemployment" used by the official statisticians, do not take full account of the hard core unemployed in the country. But one thing is sure : when these numbers grow at rates like the current ones the economic system is "creating an army of hard-core unemployed workers, who will find it difficult to nail down a job even when the economy picks up again. Many of them will never work again ; yet they are unemployed through no fault of their own." [8] Prolonged unemployment will leave its indelible marks on generations, and numbers far greater than the individuals directly implicated.

It is of utmost significance in the Canadian context that outside of the construction industry, manufacturing is the branch of economic activity hardest hit by unemployment. In 1970, construction showed an average unemployment rate of 15.3% of the labour force ; manufacturing, 6%. Construction accounted for 6% of employed persons in the economy, and 17% of the unemployment ; manufacturing involved 23% of those employed and 23% of those unemployed. [9] Between 1965 and 1970 the rate of unemployment in manufacturing rose by 76% (from 3.4 to 6), the highest rate of increase of any of the industrial sectors of the economy. [10]

The Science Council of Canada has pointed to what may be a very disturbing structural shift underlying these developments :

> Until recently, employment in manufacturing industry rose proportionately with the labour force. For most of the sixties, a constant 21 per cent of our labour force was employed in this sector. Most of our models for employment are based on the premise that this trend will continue, and that 20 per cent of the labour force will be employed in manufacturing in 1982.
>
> By mid-1971, however, manufacturing accounted for only 19 per cent of the labour force . . . . By 1971, employment in manufacturing had fallen short of expectations by 120,000 jobs.
>
> Several other sectors also fell below the employment model during this period — Canada is at present 180,000 jobs short of a 3.5 per cent unemployment rate — but the major failure was in manufacturing. (11)

The failure was particularly marked in the areas of medium - and high - technology based industry. Increased productivity and falling demand for goods produced in this area are not significant causes. What the recent stagnation of this sector reflects in relation to continued relative growth in the service and primary resource industries in Canada, is an increasing dependence on American-based multi-national corporate technology and manufacturing on the one hand, and a further reliance on resource and service industries on the other. The disastrous long-term implications for employment generally, in this country, and for employment of scientists and engineers, particularly, become evident with this prospect. Inasmuch as the high-technology manufacturing sector is crucial to the health of the economy as a whole, occupies a large part of the work force and is the critical point of leverage for the repatriation of some measure of Canadian collective control of economic activity, this development may be highly portentous.

TABLE 1

UNEMPLOYMENT RATES IN SELECTED COUNTRIES, 1960-1971

(3rd av. Q)

	1960	1961	1962	1963	1964	1965	1966	1967	1968	1969	1970	1971
United States	5.5	6.7	5.5	5.7	5.2	4.5	3.8	3.8	3.6	3.5	4.9	6.0
Canada	7.0	7.1	5.9	5.5	4.7	3.9	3.6	4.1	4.8	4.7	5.9	6.6
Japan	1.7	1.5	1.3	1.3	1.2	1.2	1.4	1.3	1.2	1.1	1.2	1.1
Great Britain	2.0	1.9	2.8	3.5	2.5	2.2	2.4	3.8	3.7	3.7	3.9	3.8
France	2.5	1.9	1.8	2.1	1.6	2.0	2.1	2.7	3.2	2.8	3.3	2.4
West Germany	0.8	0.5	0.4	0.5	0.3	0.3	0.3	1.0	1.2	0.7	0.6	0.8
Italy	4.3	3.7	3.2	2.7	3.0	4.0	4.3	3.8	3.8	3.7	3.5	3.0

Compiled from Economic Council of Canada, *Performance in Perspective*, p. 10, and *Le Monde*, le 25 novembre, 1971.

It is evident from Table 2 that Canada remains an *industrially underdeveloped* yet wealthy economy, and that our unemployment in its excessive quantity and movement is a direct amplification of unemployment on the American scene (See Tables 1 and Chart 1). Nevertheless the employment decline in the manufacturing sector is also repeated in the American economy, even more sharply it would seem. (Table 3) What may well be involved here in both cases is the evidence — seen heretofore in the obscenities of vast military and luxuriant consumer production — of the monstrous overdevelopment of the production-oriented profit-seeking "private sector," as it is modestly called, and the increasing concentration of capital in highly technological, capital-intensive manufacturing which, by design tends to reduce labour input per dollar invested and increase value-added gains per employee. [12] The U.S. "New Economic Policy" is an obvious attempt to protect and find markets for these giants of production, impaired by their own rampant growth. The extent to which these companies have monopolized the resources of the societies — human, social and natural — to their own ends, and to the detriment of the collective welfare has now become blatantly evident in the ravaging of the environment, the deterioration of vast segments of social capital and the ina-

---

TABLE 2

STRUCTURE OF ECONOMICALLY ACTIVE POPULATION
Percentage Distribution by Industry (Branches of Economic Activity)

	US ('69)	Can. ('70)	U.K. ('66)	Sweden ('65)
1. Agriculture, forestry, hunting, fishing	4.5	7.5	3.1	11.8
2. Mining and quarrying	0.6	1.6	2.3	0.6
3. Manufacturing	26.1	21.4	34.8	31.9
4. Construction	6.0	5.7	7.8	9.6
5. Electricity, gas, water & sanitary services	21.4	11.2	11.7	11.0
6. Commerce	22.4	19.4	16.0	15.5
7. Transportation, storage & communication	5.4	7.0	6.6	7.1
8. Services	29.3	30.1	27.0	22.1
9. Armed Forces	4.2	0.8	——	——
10. Unemployed	——	5.3	——	——

TABLE 3

INDEX OF
EMPLOYMENT IN MANUFACTURING — ALL INDUSTRIES

	1960	1961	1962	1963 (Base year)	1964	1965	1966	1967	1968	1969	1970	1971 (mo. of Mar.)
Canada	94.8	94.3	97.8	100	104.7	110.5	116.4	116.0	115.1	118.0	118.3	113.4
U.S.	98.8	96.1	99.2	100	101.6	106.3	113.1	114.4	116.4	118.7	115.5	109.0

Tables 2 and 3 drawn from International Labour Office, *Yearbook of Labour Statistics,* Thirtieth Edition, 1970, Geneva, 1971, and the ILO *Bulletin Of Labour Statistics, Third Quarter,* 1971.

bility of the collectivity through government expenditure on common services to keep pace with needs despite continuing increases in the sector of government spending as a percentage of GNP. Canada's record in these respects has been somewhat less harmfully excessive than the American.

To return to the specifics of unemployment in Canada, *nowhere is the problem more evident and serious than in the age distribution of the unemployed.* Those thus marginalized by the structural defficiency of the economic system are *very heavily concentrated among young people.* Roughly 50% of Canada's current unemployment falls upon the age group 14-24 years. "In the third quarter of 1971 young people who constituted some 28 per cent of the labour force, accounted for some 53 per cent of the total unemployed." [13] That figure at 11% of the labour force for that group represents about 250,000 people! Once again the geographical distribution varies. In November '71 the rates were 12.6 in B.C., 13.7 in the Atlantic Region and 11.1 in Québec. [14] Table 2 demonstrates this very clearly. When the break-down is carried even further it is found that male and female teenagers (14-19) are consistently hardest hit, with rates currently running in the ranges of 14-16% and 12-14% respectively. [15] Furthermore, the ratio of youth (both sexes, 14-24) unemployment rates to the national unemployment rates passed 1.67 in 1963 and continues to climb, in the neighbourhood of 1.85, 1.72, 1.73, 1.77 which are quarterly figures for last year. [16] The summer unemployment scene has been just as bleak with rates in the teen-age category hitting heights, in 1970, on the order of 15, 19 and 18 per cent in the specific regions of the Atlantic, Quebec and B.C. respectively. [17] (For graphic portrayal of some features of all this, see Tables 4, 5 and 6.)

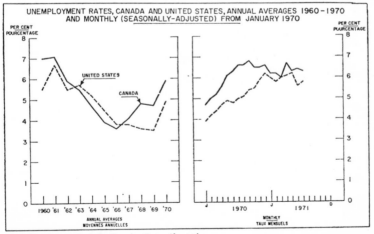

UNEMPLOYMENT RATES, CANADA AND UNITED STATES, ANNUAL AVERAGES 1960-1970 AND MONTHLY (SEASONALLY-ADJUSTED) FROM JANUARY 1970

Reproduced from Statistics Canada, *Facts About the Unemployed, 1960-1971,* Ottawa, September 1971.

31

TABLE 4

Percentage Unemployed by AGE-SEX BREAKDOWN IN CANADA

Year	National	Males All	14-19	20-24	25-34	35-44	Females All	14-19	20-24	25-34	35-44
1953	3.0	3.4	7.2	4.9	3.1	2.5	1.6	2.9	1.9	1.4	1.1
1954	4.6	5.1	10.1	7.7	4.8	3.8	2.6	5.3	2.6	2.2	1.7
1955	4.4	4.9	10.3	7.2	4.4	3.7	2.6	5.1	2.5	2.2	1.6
1956	3.4	3.9	8.1	5.7	3.4	3.0	1.9	4.0	1.8	1.9	1.1
1957	4.6	5.4	11.3	8.3	5.1	3.9	2.3	4.4	2.8	2.0	1.6
1958	7.0	8.1	16.7	12.7	7.7	6.1	3.6	7.4	4.1	3.2	2.3
1959	6.0	6.9	14.4	10.5	6.5	5.1	3.0	6.8	3.6	2.5	1.9
1960	7.0	8.1	16.4	12.3	7.6	6.2	3.6	8.6	4.0	2.7	2.4
1961	7.1	8.4	16.6	11.9	8.0	6.5	3.7	8.9	4.0	2.9	2.3
1962	5.9	6.8	14.5	9.9	6.0	5.2	3.3	7.6	3.7	2.5	2.4
1963	5.5	6.4	14.1	9.5	5.6	4.6	3.3	7.8	4.1	2.2	2.0
1964	4.7	5.3	12.2	7.8	4.5	3.7	3.1	7.6	3.3	2.3	1.8
1965	3.9	4.4	10.0	5.6	3.5	3.2	2.7	6.9	3.0	1.9	1.8
1966	3.6	4.0	9.6	5.3	3.0	2.8	2.6	6.4	2.6	2.0	1.8
1967	4.1	4.6	10.9	6.1	3.8	3.3	2.9	7.3	3.2	2.2	1.8
1968	4.8	5.5	12.8	7.6	4.4	4.1	3.4	8.3	4.2	2.3	2.2
1969	4.7	5.2	12.3	7.5	4.0	3.7	3.6	8.9	3.8	2.8	2.3
1970	5.9	6.6	15.0	10.5	5.3	4.6	4.5	11.4	5.1	3.2	3.0

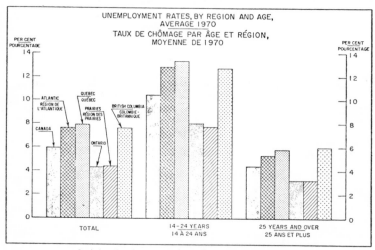

UNEMPLOYMENT RATES, BY REGION AND AGE, AVERAGE 1970

TAUX DE CHÔMAGE PAR ÂGE ET RÉGION, MOYENNE DE 1970

Statistics Canada, *Facts About the Unemployed, 1960-71.*

The Committee on Youth points to the likelihood, among this group, of statistical bias and hidden unemployment, both of which together work towards understating the real situation portrayed by the statistics by as much as 11 percentage points. [18]

That is to say, the rate of unemployment of young people is probably much closer to 22% *or up to 500,000 young people under 25 who at any given time find themselves unable to work productively by the standards of this society.* And clearly many more again are touched by this debilitating experience over a somewhat more extended period within that span of years, if you consider the frequency with which the young move in and out of jobs, dipping as they pass into the pool of unemployed.

TABLE 5

The Ratio of Selected Youth Unemployment Rates
to the National Unemployment Rates by Sex, by Year

	Males	Females	Males	Females
	14-19	14-19	20-24	20.24
1953	2.12	1.79	1.45	1.14
1954	1.96	2.06	1.50	1.03
1955	2.09	1.98	1.47	0.98
1956	2.09	2.09	1.47	0.92
1957	2.11	1.91	1.55	1.21
1958	2.05	2.04	1.55	1.12
1959	2.07	2.26	1.52	1.18
1960	2.02	2.37	1.51	1.10
1961	1.98	2.37	1.42	1.07
1962	2.12	2.30	1.44	1.11
1963	2.21	2.35	1.50	1.25
1964	2.32	2.45	1.47	1.08
1965	2.33	2.54	1.29	1.10
1966	2.40	2.48	1.31	1.01
1967	2.36	2.49	1.33	1.10
1968	2.35	2.42	1.40	1.23
1969	2.38	2.46	1.45	1.05
1970	2.31	2.51	1.60	1.13

TABLE 6

The Age Group 14 to 24 as a Percentage of Total Number of Unemployed

1953 35.8%	1954 35.2%	1955 35.1%	1956 34.5%	1957 35.2%	1958 34.7%
1959 34.6%	1960 34.5%	1961 33.0%	1962 34.8%	1963 37.4%	1964 38.8%
1965 38.9%	1966 40.0%	1967 41.2%	1968 42.6%	1969 43.1%	1970 45.2%

Tables 4, 5 and 6 drawn from The Committee on Youth, *It's Your Turn...,* Report to the Secretary of State, Ottawa, July 1971.

Statistics can put us on the track of a headcount of these staggering proportions. But statistics do not tell the story of these people who are stuck in the door-way of life's work with dim prospects of a meaningful task and a strong alternative of no employment at all. The generation whose numbers thus disturb the statisticians is the same that was born under Hiroshima's mushroom cloud, and lives in the shadow of all that it symbolises about our high technology of destruction — both of natural and cultural environment, and of human life. *Probably the seeds of social cynicism have never been sown so deeply in so many lives in this country, even considering the thirties.*

Back to figures for a moment. It is quite clear that as well as other disguising and distorting effects serving to depress the statistical picture of *general* unemployment, the Canada Manpower Training Program, operated as a contraseasonal instrument, may well absorb and hide from unemployment watchers up to 1 per cent of the labour force at peak periods of the unemployment year. [19]

The Underlying Causes

It is not hard to identify some of the major causes of this dramatic and tragic situation. One of the most spectacular is the boom in the Canadian labour force produced by the sharp rise in births following the Second World War. This heavy slug of new manpower began hitting the labour market in the very early sixties, with its loudest impact so far coming from '67 to the present when those deferring their entry through prolonged stays in educational institutions began to articulate their dissatisfaction as they encountered the world of work — or productive redundancy. Over the period 1965 - 1980 the Canadian labour force will have increased by about 3½ million, or 50%. The comparative American increase will be about 30%, and the closest European rate, that of France, about 13. [20] This means annual rates of increase on the

TABLE 7
CANADIAN LABOUR FORCE GROWTH

Age Group	1960	1970	1980	Percentage Change in Labour Force 1960-70	1970-80
		(Thousands)			
14-19	627	861	926	37.3	7.5
20-24	777	1,286	1,703	65.5	32.4
25-34	1,506	1,825	2,921	21.2	60.1
45-54	1,152	1,515	1,815	31.5	19.8
55-64	674	948	1,220	40.7	28.7
35-44	1,445	1,733	2,094	19.9	20.8
65 and over	230	206	247	-10.4	19.9
Total	6,411	8,374	10,926	30.6	30.5

Table drawn from economic Council of Canada, *Performance in Perspective 1971.* Ottawa, October 1971.

order shown in Table 7 ; with great bulges in the percentage increase in labour force appearing in the 60's in the age group 20-24 (65.5% as compared to 37% in the 14-19 and 21% in the 25-34 age groups respectively), and in the 25-34 classification in the 70's (60% as compared with 32 and 21% in the immediately adjacent age groups.) The Economic Council perceives the impact of this with a characteristic measure of cultivated moderation :

> By far the largest increase in employment requirements will occur in the 25-34 age group (in the period 70-75), and it will be especially great for males where the rate of employment growth will need to be more than double that of the last half of the 1960's. This is the age group in which most families tend to become established, with large demands for housing and durable goods and associated needs for urban services. Any significant shortfall in meeting the employment needs of this group will produce serious economic and social strains in the 1970's. [21]

A second cause we have already alluded to. The deprivation experienced by the work force in the form of such extensive unemployment is clearly related to the tenacity with which the Canadian economy hangs — and is held — upon the tits of the great American mother system. The effects of our almost organic linkage to this ebb and flow is reflected by the long standing structural underdevelopment of secondary manufacturing in this country and the recent regression in this sector. It is shown also by the waves of closures and shutdowns that rumble through this sector particularly but also in primary production, as the economy "slackens off." Reductions and lay-offs in the scores, and hundreds, and thousands are a virtual habit of our national life and account for sizeable battalions in the army of the idle. For instance, in the year June '70 - June '71 in Ontario, the manufacturing stronghold of the country, 16,224 persons lost their employment or were laid off as a result of 138 plant closures or shut-downs. The thousand three hundred of those who got notices were employees of foreign-owned plants ; and it is a safe bet that many of the others were employed in industries affected by the market fragmentation induced by foreign-controlled branch plants. [21a]

In the third place we shall not soon forget the willful work of the Trudeau government. The express and cynical use of the balance-wheel of unemployment "to reduce inflation" began clearly to take effect by the early spring of 1970 when the rates climbed over 6% and have remained there ever since. This systematic fiscal and monetary attack upon "consumer demand" was conducted to *produce* unemployment, in keeping with a well-known economic theory known as the Phillips Curve, according to which the rate of increase of wages and prices is directly related to the level of unemployment and its rate of increase. [22] In this view the most efficient method of holding prices is to allow or encourage the rise of unemployment. Canada's position as a highly trade-dependent small economy was thought to require the maintenance of high-level performance in the production-export areas of the system. (The Economic Council has since noted, and a look at comparative consumer price increases over the past few years bears it out : "The evidence does not lead us to believe that Canada's international competitive position was at any time threatened during this period." [23] What was threatened, of course, were profits in many major industries !)

A similar strategy of preserving the integrity of the fiction called the global economic system, in a trade-off for more humane goals is to be seen in the policies pursued by Canada Manpower. "The ... evidence shows that the Canadian government's strategy in the field of manpower policy is primarily a growth strategy, with the objectives of equity and stabilization clearly being secondary." [24] Of further far-reaching consequence in the current juncture, the current Manpower training program "is confined exclusively to adults" !) [25] All of this is in keeping, of course, with the underlying philosophy of political functionalism of the Trudeau technocrats. [26] In this particular case the classical encapsulation of the doctrine is to be found in Trudeau's response to a question raised in a public meeting in April 1970 by Johanna Bielowski, a high school student in Brantford. Johanna, referring to the Westinghouse shutdown that had affected her family and three hundred others in the town, suggested to Trudeau that the cure for inflation was worse than the disease. The architect of price stability replied that "this is how a country progresses economically. Everyone is forced to make greater efforts to become more productive to hold on to that position of strength. The judgement of the world is that the Canadian economy is sound." [27] The *system* will be made to thrive, even if it has to feed on the suffering of a large segment — politically insignificant, no doubt ! — of the people.

Fourthly, of course, one must mention the cyclical sags and surges that are a regular part of the picture of life in capitalist economies. ... Part of the picture in the sense that capitalist production, by the very quality of its structure, operates in this fluctuating manner, bouncing through its own waves on the shoulders of the ever-available "supplies" of wage labour, the first factors of production to be discarded when unneeded, and ever grateful for a job when one is re-offered, no matter how crummy or badly paid. Once again we are waiting in throngs upon the largess and benefactions of those *heartless institutions* upon whose creative will — to make jobs — life literally hangs !

Prospects in Store

There are some features of the current general prospect that must be noted. Indications point to the fact that since the autumn of 1970, "The Canadian economy has been expanding at a vigourous pace. [28] But while for a year GNP has been expanding at a rate of 7%, unemployment has not declined ; indeed it has increased in some areas ! The Bank of Canada analysts who have pointed this out attribute the stickiness of unemployment to the inability of the organisations of production to absorb "the larger proportion of young entrants this year." [29] This, of course explains the statistics : why in November '71 there were 262,000 young people out of work after a year of boom compared with 250,000 the previous November ; why the unemployment rate in this category has gone from 9.6 to 9.8 under the same conditions from the third quarter of 1970 to the third quarter of 1971. (See Table 8) What it does *not* explain, of course, is why production grew in this period by 7% but employment in this age group by only 4.7% ; [30] why the boom in economic production produces a *continuing boom in youth unemployment !* — why the absorptive quality of free enterprise is so unabsorbant of young workers.

The other reason accounting for continued high unemployment in the face of prosperity is "the large gain in productivity" — on the order of 4% per person employed — which is typically associated with early periods of recovery in the cycle of economic fluctuation [31] To evoke this shake-down behaviour of the free-enterprise economic system it to recognize in a genteel and harmless way the manner and degree in which labour is expendable under capitalist production : eagerly hauled out of the pools of unemployed when profitable sales-killing are to be made ; dropped when over-production sets in and profits decline ; squeezed for higher out-puts when prospects brighten and jobs are hard to find and technical innovation can produce relative advantage.

In both cases the problem lies within the structure of the economic system itself : the free-wheeling capitalist mode of production, bent above all on the survival and growth of corporations, and the seeking of profits which reward both owners and successful managers.

TABLE 8

LABOUR MARKET

	3 Q 1969	3 Q 1970	3 Q 1971
1. CANADA AND MAJOR REGIONS :			
Unemployment as % of labour force			
Canada	3.8	5.3	5.3
Atlantic	5.4	5.9	6.6
Quebec	5.7	7.0	6.9
Ontario	2.6	4.0	4.3
Prairies	2.1	3.5	3.6
B.C.	3.9	7.3	5.7
2. MAJOR AGE AND SEX GROUPINGS			
Labour Force participation rate			
Total	57.1	57.4	57.6
14-24 years	55.3	55.3	56.4
25 years & over	57.9	58.2	58.1
(Men)	85.0	85.0	84.2
(Women)	31.7	32.4	33.0
Unemployed as percentage of Labour Force			
Total	3.8	5.3	5.3
14-24 years	6.6	9.6	9.8
25 years & over	2.7	3.6	3.5
(Men)	2.8	4.0	3.8
(Women)	2.2	2.7	2.6

Table drawn from *Bank of Canada Review,* December, 1971, Ottawa, 1972.

The Report of the Committee on Youth points a finger in the same direction : "The constantly high rate of unemployed young persons coupled with the relatively fixed ratios of youth unemployed to the general population indicates that the real problem exists in the relationship of young persons to the functioning of the economic system — not in the numbers of young persons entering the labour force." [32] This source projects that even if a "desirable" 3.5% national unemployment rate were reached and maintained, high rates of youth unemployment would continue to increase. "If full employment were to be achieved in the near future, and the structure of our economy were to continue developing as it has during the 1960's, the unemployment rates of males 14 to 19 and females 14 to 24 would continue to increase." [33] The Economic Council, forecasting employment requirements for the period '70 - '75 on the basis of very conservative goals (an unemployment level in 1975 "consistent with an overall national figure of 3.8 per cent of the labour force" — levels in some age groups would still be proportionately higher !) and equally depressed initial parameters, indicates the following : for the total labour force, "employment must move up from 2.8 per cent per annum in 1965-70 to 3.3 per cent per annum in 1970-75. This is a rate well above that attained for employment over the whole of the 1960's ... In the 25-34 age group where the fastest increase in the labour supply will be occurring, employment growth will need to jump to 5.6 per cent per year in 1970-75, from 3.7 per cent in 1965-70 .... Among males in this age group, the growth rate in employment will need to more than double — from 2.4 per cent per year to 5.3 per cent. [34] The Council hints at the unlikelihood of this achievement ; we conclude that it is a patent impossibility, with ramifications far-reaching for the capitalist system in this country.

Among the latter age group, (25-34), are considerable numbers of males unaccounted for by the Council because they dropped out of the labour force in their early twenties ; [35] they will reappear with a vengence under the pressure of heavier financial responsibilities inevitably incurred in a later period, to upset "the calculations" — and, undoubtedly, "the social equilibrium." Among these also, for the period up to 1976, is a predicted supply of almost 14,000 Ph.D. graduates, only half of whom are likely, on optimistic estimates, to be absorbed into employment commensurate with their skills and expectations. In this period, in the physical sciences, universities are likely to employ only 11% on an average annual basis of those doctoral graduates available for teaching. Overall, 7,000 people qualified with doctoral degrees in various disciplines can expect to go unemployed as such in the Canadian market up to '76. [36]

The inability of "the market place" (!) to match "highly qualified" personnel with equivalent employment is likewise observable at the B.A. and M.A. levels. A study produced under the direction of the Department of Manpower and Immigration estimates that in 1971 there were 41,000 more B.A. level graduates in all fields than required by employment opportunities, and 4,900 holding M.A.'s in the same situation. [87]

All of this indicates the vast and growing, the quantative as well as qualitative, mismatch created by our production and education system between the number of young people prepared and

38

looking for useful and satisfying work and the opportunities to do such work or any work for periods which may become of marked and crucial duration. The structural inhuman orientation of capitalism is responsible for this ; and so are some of the specifics of this system as it operates in Canada : for example, the emaciated state of research and development in industry, the general underdevelopment of secondary manufacturing, and a knowledge industry at the university level that is keyed into American-based corporate life and corporation-produced culture. As a result of these specific instances of dependency, employment of engineers, scientists, academics, high-level technicians and intellectuals produced in this country has been severely restricted, and promises to become more so. [38]

Organized labour in Canada, with some notable and fairly recent exceptions in Québec, has helped to compound the plight of young workers and the young unemployed. Happily integrated into the basic assumptions and goals of business, the labour organizations in Canada have little going for young workers and even less for those who can't make it into the job structures panoplied-over by collective agreements. In fact the conduct of the unions *militates against* the aspirations of young workers. "At the present time, this huge army of unemployed youth is unorganized and lacks leadership. The older, established labour movement has shown no inclination to organize them ... If and when the young leadership of the unemployed combines its strength with a new youth leadership in organized labour, Canada will have a powerful new militant force to reckon with." [39]

A final observation needs to be made about the prospects arising from the current return to "strong expansion" of the economy. Rising prices and inflation are *still* as much a part of the picture as rising unemployment. That implies much about the continuing deterioration of the condition of the vast majority of the labour force, especially those unorganized and those who are out of work. Citing a theory cooked up in the Brookings Institution, the Economic Council attributes, in part, the ongoing "major problem" of inflation to a "labour market ... relatively tighter today *for any given aggregate level of unemployment* than it was two decades ago." [40] *"Tighter"* (!), they explain, in the supply of what they call "prime-age males." The attempt to lay blame for a fundamental contradiction in the capitalist system, in part at least, upon the "changing composition" of the labour force is both facile and mendacious in the current Canadian context. The vicious combination of inflation and booming unemployment is clearly produced by two structural properties of the corporate free-enterprise system : the pursuit of "growth" — in the sectors essential to corporate survival : production, consumption, productivity, institutional aggrandizement, profits ; and demand for goods and services that is *producer - rather than consumer -* induced, and that thrives on wars, "strategic programmes" (space projects), and other "highly desirable" industrial "development" activities that depend on the extension of technology to produce high returns on capital. Simply put, the point is that privately controlled corporate organizations run the economy, the society and the lives of individual men and women to suit *their* purposes ; in doing so, *and in order to do so,* they foster the social maladies of which we speak.

What is Being Done ?

We do not desire to discuss in the current context the merits of government measures to deal with unemployment. In the face of the dimensions of the tragic crisis as we have attempted to delineate it, it suffices to state the obvious : the federal government deliberately contributed to creating it ; whatever remedial measures are operative have been inadequate in easing the calamity beyond its current unacceptable proportions.

Just a word, however, is in order about three or four of the more spectacular programmes related to aspects of the problem of which we have spoken. Up to the fall of '71, Canada Manpower had spent about 1.4 billion dollars on manpower training since 1967. The aim of the scheme is essentially to promote the growth and efficiency of the economy by shaping up workers' abilities to meet employers' needs. The reduction of unemployment, and of poverty and interregional disparities in income distribution are only secondary objectives. Provisions of the training programme *militate explicitly against participation of young people.* Heavily oriented to "preparatory upgrading" as distinct from the acquisition of occupational skills, "in a period of high unemployment... there exists the possibility that such basic training may be used, as it were, simply as an absorbent" [41] — of up to 345,000 people per annum, which was the number placed in training in the 1970 - 71 fiscal year. [42]

The big man in the field of "job creation" — with Canadian taxpayers' money — is Jean Marchand, erstwhile trade-union leader. Since its establishment in July 1969, the Department of Regional Economic Expansion, under the authority of the Regional Development Incentives Act, has handed over 190 million dollars in grants to private corporations. [43] This encouragement is bestowed on the understanding that the companies will provide jobs after two or three years in their expanded, modernized or new facility which the hand-out helps make possible in the special zones of the country designated for "development". For expenditures to date we have been promised 44,800 jobs. Some of the worthy recipients are "good corporate citizens" like Falconbridge Nickel Mines, setting up in Bécancour ($4 million) ; and Micro-Max Products Ltd. of Kalamazoo, Michigan ($1,392,585) ; Ashland Chemical Co., Houston, Texas ($1,170,862) (grant offer subsequently declined) ; Carousel Fashions Inc., New York ($182,124) ; IBM Canada Ltd. ($6 million), all, likewise carrying employment to Québec. The conclusions to be drawn from a scrutiny of the operation of the programme are exactly what we might expect : while Québec, especially since the October Events, is getting a lion's share of the gravy ($87,130,200, or 46% of grant money awarded up to December 1, 1971) [44], within the province the patterns of regional disparity and the patterns of the industrial structure are essentially maintained if not reinforced by the grant system ; public capital offered in this fashion is following and encouraging corporate capital in its own private meanders that have already produced employment instability, over-supply and market fragmentation, especially in quick growth industries ; the number of "new" jobs created is often a fiction in that the effect of the scheme is frequently to transfer employment and unemployment from one region to another ; the continued concentration of production in the hands of foreign controlled companies ; this and other industry subsidization programmes serve, often, only to exacerbate the precariousness of our colonized economy by encouraging non-viable industry or the establishment of low-employment resource production for foreign export... [45] And, of course, in the case of Quebec where almost half of the grant money is being concentrated, the programme has a clear political design of holding Quebec in Trudeau's Confederation. [44] In a word, in exchange for the promise of 45,000 jobs we are rewarding the enterprise of a system that in the same period October '69 - November '71, has added, 189,000 more to the aggregate of unemployed !

Twenty-seven thousand eight hundred "new jobs" were "created", we are told by the glossy new hand-out describing last summer's Opportunities for Youth Program [46] What the catalogue does not say in as many words is that these jobs lasted three months and paid on an average about $800 per job [47] $24.7 million was spent on this. At the same time, 36,000 young people where channeled into militia and cadet training (a relatively small number among them in "civilian" training) programmes organized by the Department of National Defence. The total Government manna-fall to youth in the summer of '72 when 1,306,000 students, by official estimates, will be looking for work will be $85 million for 75,000 jobs : 29,000 jobs in Opportunities for Youth at $34 million; and 40,000 "jobs" in militia, cadet and "civilian" (2,300 of total) training in the DNP programme, at the bargain price of $12.8 million. [48] A large part of the $100 million being spent this winter on the Local Initiatives Program is aimed, like OFY at "high quality" young unemployed. Once again it is illusory if not deceiving to talk about *jobs*. These programmes provide high-minded *divertissement* with token remuneration. Like the Company of Young Canadians before it, but now on a mass scale, and with less delicacy, these indigenously-initiated Government-purchased "opportunities" for socially useful, meaningful work amount to a great sponging-up of the articulate and socially conscious young people languishing in the pools of inactivity and uselessness. The offer of this kind of "opportunity" is loaded with gross political intent. There is obvious potential danger to the existing order from large numbers of cynical, articulate and energetic young men and women whose ingenuity and efforts society obviously needs and whose most vital aspirations are frustrated. That pressure is being vented with the soporific of publicly financed self-made jobs. This is the perpetration by government of political drug abuse on a grand scale.

However, don't let it escape us that an important principle is at work in the tasks conceived and carried through under this programme by the people themselves in response to perceived need in the community. Even despite the minimum material recognition accorded to this work, imaginations have been fired and creative energies released in a sight of enthusiasm rarely encountered in today's world of work. The best way to depict this is to list for comparison's sake in parallel columns random pages of job activity from the catalogue of youth projects and the report on industrial jobs created by incentive grants to companies :

41

- Rebuilding electrical motors.
- Making chimney bricks, drainage tiles & flower pots.
- Producing furniture & thermoplastic parts.
- Fish processing.
- Making and bottling soft drinks.
- Working in a sawmill.
- Manufacturing metal parts.
- Producing furnace type carbon black.
- Working in a bakery.
- Manufacturing wigs.
- Manufacturing computers and components.
- Working in a print shop producing forms.
- Manufacturing electric and electronic controls.
- Manufacturing electrical equipment.
- Operative in a knitwear factory.
- Making stainless steel & cast iron parts. (49)

- Promote attendance at holiday camps by children from depressed areas.
- Educating Cape Breton youth and public in its problems.
- Construct and study advantages of geodesic dome.
- Study relationships between landlords and poor tenants.
- Attempt to interest population in cultural media and expression.
- Clearing land for recreational purposes on Indian Reserve.
- Produce puppet theatre shows for under-privileged children in institutions and hospitals.
- Research & practical projects on relationship between employment & health.
- Collect information on problems of rapid urban growth.
- Reduce pollution level of Lake Nipissing.
- Co-ordinate information and research on recycling waste products.
- Assist those in need of legal aid, Windsor.
- Provide recreational activities for children in disadvantaged rural area.
- Train students how to use a press. (50)

Of the many observations that could be made in this comparison, let us note two : the free work is aimed in great part at compensating for and rectifying the social excesses of industrial over-production, over-development, and mis-distribution ; the usefulness of the forced (wage-) work, aside from the wages, it not immediately evident, if at all, even though these enterprises may be surrounded with the aura of seriousness. In fact such work may well be felt alienating because it is useless or superfluous. The free work somehow bears the stamp of luxury and gratuitousness, although it is seen to be valuable, indeed perhaps necessary and vital by those engaged in it. The wage-work jobs are nonetheless of the category of "real", "serious" employment, basic to the economy and survival. The latter set are make-work, frills, "marginally important", to the basic achievements of the private sector.

Freely chosen work aimed at and carried out for the collective well-being of the community has been a no-no or a rare privilege in our society. However, with thousands unable to enter the gates of capitalist production, the state, under duress, has offered the taste of an experience which will have important consequences for a considerable and growing number of young people. What was considered to be a luxury has become by an ironic twist that wrenches the arm of liberalism, a necessity. Forced idleness and forced work have been traditionally the mutually reinforcing instruments of enslavement to capitalist production in the market system. Now a breach, ever so small, but officially sanctioned, has been made in the façade. Free, self-determined work has become a necessity for preserving the old system. The inevitable workings of its own dynamics have produced in the breast of capitalism *an antithetical force upon which its own continued survival will increasingly depend.* There is a paradox full of destructive portent! The official blessing of work determined by and for people, slim and controlled though the recognition be, will do one of two things. The experience will either confirm the already strong suspicion among youth particularly, that the vital and important things of their lives, in being allowed occasional free rein under strict control, are marginal to the almost inevitable social reality of the country; that schools and "opportunity" programmes and other instruments of official control are put-ons, agents of deception and self-destruction. In this case the soothing, periodic and brief interludes must continue, and the system persist, until the cynicism and the social schizophrenia reach clearly counter-"productive" proportions. Or, the experience will confirm the realization that many have known or suspected from the beginnings of capitalist societies, that another reality lies close beneath the hard carapace of that reality which is dictated by the necessities of corporate industrialism: that work need not be sterile and destructive; that it can have other goals than individual private gain and corporate advantage; that this *only* is the kind of human activity that underlies and sustains human survival and the well-being of people. In this case, the evidence is clear : a monumental social revolution spawned and nourished by capitalism itself has broken surface ; there will be no looking back.

What Is To Be Done ?

Well, what do we propose to do about unemployment ? We have nothing to add to the catalogue of measures already proposed by the fertile minds on the left in the country, and which range from state planning and management of both the production and manpower needs of the society, to the repatriation of national control of industry and the nationalization of key industries, to a basic redistribution of wealth through measures such as the guaranteed annual income. Given the dramatic proportions of this human catastrophe and the hardship and degradation to human life which it works, it would be both gratuitous and cruel to oppose *any* measure calculated to alleviate the situation.

Our analysis, however, leads us to conclude that current unemployment in Canada is endemic to a mortal impasse reached by the capitalist system of production itself. The employment crisis arises from and illuminates a profound contradiction which is tearing the social and environmental fabric apart.

The elements of the contradiction are plain enough to see. Productive work in an advanced industrial society under free-enterprise, like ours, has fallen under the almost total control of the privately controlled and privately motivated organizations of production. Work has thus been robbed, for the most part, of its satisfactions ; and men and women of their independence, by being thrown for their very sustenance upon the "jobs" offered by the

43

industrial corporations and all its supporting bureaucracies. So pervasive has this corporate control of work become, that even our perception of social reality is vitiated by it. We continue to live and act — albeit with growing doubts and pessimism — as though there were little that is socially useful to do beyond the "employment opportunities" offered by these organizations. We are bound, hand and mind. It is increasingly difficult to survive, or carry on meaningful activity, beyond the regimen they impose.

Nevertheless, this common understanding of "the way things are" is blatantly and increasingly belied by the monstrous imbalance and impairment wrought upon the social, cultural, psychic and natural elements of the fabric of life itself, by the over-development and the excesses of corporate free-enterprise. The emerging imperatives of physical survival and of the restoration of social well-being make it clear that *there is* meaningful work *aplenty* to be done ! There is only a dichotomy between the social need and popular will to accomplish this work and the hoarding up by private interests of society's means, which prevent people from doing it.

It is also clear in what we have shown, that free-enterprise industrialism has reached its fabulous achievements with increasingly proportionate numbers of people who are superfluous to the undertaking. The evidence of this is, of course, more flagrantly visible in the economically colonized part of the world than in the *métropole* of the empire. There, hundreds of millions sink in economic disutility. The state of being *de trop* becomes active exploitation when those institutions determining what work shall be "productive", by being rewarded, hold people in a work orientation designed solely to satisfying the needs of the juggernaut.

To "solve" the problem of unemployment thus depicted, three things are needed. First, there needs to be a thorough, a radical, redistribution of the means of sustaining life and well-being : of wealth, that is. In this way only, shall the implacable grip of the "job" mongers on people's lives and activity be loosened. This is a minimal first step.

Concomitant with it is the necessity of recoining the concept of work ; this, in order to make — *viable for people* — all forms of socially valuable and creative activity. Obviously this is not to be achieved by minting new *definitions* of work. It must be done by *revaluating* activity hitherto excluded from material reward. In otherwords, human *activity too,* must become the object of a redistribution of society's wealth ; and this on the basis of radically new criteria of social utility set by the community. Thus, for example, education would become a paid activity for "students", an ongoing activity in the life-time of the individual, fully integrated with "work" and with the community exigencies of material production. Activities of the sort "devised" by youth in the OFY Program would be as developed and as fully remunerated or rewarded as their necessity to the community requires. Thus a balance would be restored between the necessary work of material production, presently overdeveloped and misoriented — and dominating the field —, and the forms of work so clearly necessary to this generation but thoroughly neglected. And a balance would be created, between the share of time and effort that individuals would put into the various forms of work — goods production, social, intellectual.

Finally, and foremost, there is the need for *the democratization of the control of all work*: worker and community control of production; worker and community control of productive resources, both natural and human ; community control of community life (social organization), in order that value shall be assigned to *all* effort in proportion to its enrichment of the *whole* range of human life : both individual and social understood as of a piece, both material and psycho-social understood as interdependent.

Such prescriptions, of course, are nothing less than revolutionary. But if we take seriously the terms and the extent of the "problem" of which unemployment is but the manifestation, nothing less than a revolution of society is needed !

If this is the case, where do we start ? If the direction we suggest is necessary, there are already currents that have begun to flow in this country : movements for workers' control, struggles for community control of political, social *and economic* (for example, the attempt of the community at Cabano to establish its own pulp and corrugated paper mill) agencies and institutions — and not just the acquisition of control, but the redesigning of these institutions, and the building of new ones, to serve the needs of people. It is obvious that if youth in this country — and elsewhere, because the situation is only more pronounced here than elsewhere — were organized (not just the unemployed but all those who feel violated because they "hold" sterile and sterilizing "jobs"), if the youth were organised along the lines and in pursuit of their basic life interests, a force for revolution of no mean strength would be created. Young people should therefore be vigilant against the slumber induced by the narcotic of all the buy-off programs and marginalizing movements of their own creation which are enabled by the surplus spill-over of the production system. At the same time, they should exploit these "opportunities" and all the others they have to advance the goals of *radically changing this system.*

There is no reason on earth, except that created by powerful vested interest, why all of us can't spend all our lives in work that is necessary, useful and creative ; work that is therefore meaningful and in large measure full of pleasure.

FOOT NOTES

1. Ernest Becker, *The Structure of Evil,* New York, Geo. Braziller, 1968, p. 134.
2. Economic Council of Canada, *Performance in Perspective* 1971, Ottawa, October 1971.
3. *Ibid.,* p. 48.
4. Statistics Canada, *Facts About The Unemployed,* 1960-1971, Ottawa, September 1971, p. 33.
5. Stat. Can., *The Labour Force,* November 1971, Ottawa, December 1971. Seasonally adjusted rates.

6. *Bank of Canada Review,* December 1971, Ottawa, Jan. 1972.

7. Stat. Can., *The Labour Force,* November 1971.

8. Adams, Cameron, Hill and Penz, *The Real Poverty Report,* Edmonton, M.G. Hurtig, 1971, p. 32.

9. Stat. Can., *Facts About The Unemployed,* 1960-1971, p. 23.

10. *Op. cit.,* calculation made from figures appearing on p. 21.

11. Science Council of Canada, *Innovation in a Cold Climate,* Report No. 15, October 1971, pp. 14, 15, 16.

12. See "Getting more productivity out of capital," in *Globe and Mail,* Jan. 12, 1972. The article discusses a study directed by W.N. Hall, former president of Domtar. The article makes clear that the development of a highly productive manufacturing sector, through selective capital investment, will indeed produce an industrial base with relatively fewer jobs. "Job creation" and productive investment are not in a constant relationship.

13. *Bank of Canada Review,* December 1971, p. 8.

14. Stat. Can., *The Labour Force,* Nov. 1971, p. 50 Seasonally unadjusted figures.

15. *Ibid.,* p. 38.

16. Calculated on the basis of statistics presented in *Bank of Canada Review,* December 1971, p. S 95 and the December figures published by Stat. Can.

17. For a fuller development on this, and a very complete description of youth unemployment in its various aspects, see The Committee on Youth, *It's Your Turn* ..., A Report to the Secretary of State, Ottawa, July 1971, pp. 15-29.

18. *Ibid.,* p. 20.

19. ECC, *Design for Decision-Making,* Eighth Annual Review, September 1971, Ottawa 1971, p. 99.

20. Wolfgang Illing, *Population, Family, Household and Labour Force Growth to 1980,* Staff Study No. 19 prepared for the ECC, Ottawa, 1967, pp. 78-79.

21. ECC, *Performance in Perspective,* 1971, pp. 51-52.

21a. Jim Laxer, "Lament for an Industry," *The Last Post,* Dec.-Jan. 1971-72. For the eleven-month period ending November '71, the Ontario Government, under its legislation applying to firms employing 50 workers or more and of whom 10% or more are affected, had been notified of 47 instances of termination or lay-off which have thrown or will throw more than 7,000 employees out of work. (Press release and Year End Review issued Dec. 29 by the Department of Labour).

22. Hugues Puel, *Chômage et capitalismes contemporains,* Paris, Les Editions ouvrières, 1971, pp. 26 ff.

23. *Performance in Perspective,* p. 56.

24. ECC, *Design for Decision-Making,* p. 98.

25. *Ibid.,* p. 101.

26. For an analysis of this thinking see "The War Measures Act and the Politics of Functionalism," in *Our Generation,* Vol. 7, No. 3.

27. *Globe and Mail,* April 3, 1971.

28. *Bank of Canada Review,* December 1971, p. 3.

29. *Ibid.,* p. 9.

30. Ibid.

31. *Bank of Canada Review,* December 1971, pp. 9-10.

32. *Ibid.,* p. 18.

33. *It's Your Turn* ..., pp. 18-19.

34. ECC, *Performance in Perspective,* 1971, p. 48.

35. *It's Your Turn* ..., p. 19.

36. Max von Zur-Muehlen, "The PH.D. Dilemna in Canada", A Case Study in the supply and demand of highly qualified manpower, Ottawa, October 1971. A preliminary paper, unpublished.

37. J. Kushner, I. Masse, R. Blauer, L. Soroka, "The Market Situation for University Graduates Canada," Ottawa, Department of Manpower and Immigration, 1971. It should be noted that the figures produced in this study were projections based on previous years' experience and do not represent a sampling of 1971 graduates.

38. See, for example, Science Council of Canada, *Innovation in a Cold Climate*, and *Prospects for Scientists and Engineers in Canada*, Special Study No. 20, Ottawa, March 1971.

39. Gilbert Levine, "The Coming Youth Revolt in Labour," in *The Labour Gazette*, Vol. 71, No. 11, November 1971, p. 730. Gilbert Levine's article paints a very thorough picture of Labour's unresponsiveness to the needs of young workers.

40. ECC, *Performance in Perspective*, 1971, pp. 55-62.

41. ECC, *Design for Decision-Making*, p. 109. See chapter on manpower policy.

42. Press release issued in conjunction with Report on Canada Manpower Training Program . . . , tabled by Otto Lang, Minister, in House of Commons, December 16, 1971.

43. "Cumulative Statistics on Incentive Grants for Period Ending Nov. 30, 1971," in *Report on the Operation of the Regional Development Incentives Act and on 'Special Areas' Incentives for the Period November 1 to November 30, 1971*, Ottawa, Department of Regional Economic Expansion, December, 1971.

44. Calculation made on basis of cumulative and monthly reports up to and including November, 1971.

45. The overt abuse by industry of subsidy programmes of this kind has occasionally been documented. See, for example, articles by Ross Munro on the Ontario programme of Equalization of Industrial Opportunity, in *Globe and Mail*, April 8 and 10, 1971. By far the most thorough overall analysis to date of the federal Regional Expansion programme, as applied in Québec, is found in Fédération des travailleurs du Québec, *L'Etat, rouage de notre exploitation*, Montréal, novembre, 1971.

46. Department of the Secretary of State, *A Canadian Experiment*, Ottawa, no date; produced in January 1972.

47. See the very elusive report, "Evaluation of the Opportunities for Youth Program, 1971," prepared for the Department of the Secretary of State by Systems Research Group, Inc., (!), DSS, December 1971.

48. *Globe and Mail*, Jan. 14, 1972.

49. Pp. 23-24, "A Summary of Offers Accepted to 30 June 1971," DREE, Ottawa, October 1971.

50. Random selection, according to the major categories in which activities were divided by the DSS, from *A Canadian Experiment*.

Published 1972

YOUTH AND

CANADIAN POLITICS

by James Laxer and Arthur Pape

The nation that celebrates its centennial next year is on the way to becoming a relic. Decision-making has passed from Canada to the American head office.

The novelty of the current situation has to do with its extent. The point has now been reached where the Canadian economic elite, once the defender of national independence, has become the vanguard of the branch-plant system that is reducing this country to colonial status.

The responsibility for continental inroads into Canadian nationhood cannot be seen as American alone. The Canadian economic elite has, in large measure, willed its self-destruction as the dominant class in an independent country. Once the developer of the country's primary transportation and communications systems, the elite now heads up the American subsidiary corporations that increasingly corner the strategic sectors of our economy. Its members, no longer independent industrialists, have become managers and caretakers, living in suburbias identical to those of their counterparts on the other side of the frontier.

Hand in hand with the disintegration of Canada's traditional economic system has gone the development of government by stalemate. Our federal parliament, especially under the Liberals, has acted as a coordinator in the continued domination of the corporations.

Traditional national policy

Since the time of Mackenzie King, the substance of the traditional national policy that promoted the growth of the economy during the early years of the century, has been continually worn away. King and his successors did nothing to counter the country's drift into the American orbit. The road away from an organic relationship to Britain during this period was not to lead to independence but instead toward colonial status in a different empire.

Ironically, the regionalism and the French-English dichotomy, which very largely distinguish Canada from the United States, played a part in promoting government by stalemate. Both under Mackenzie King and Lester Pearson, the Liberals have used Canada's diversity as excuses for their failure to pursue any vigorous national direction.

The solution, of course, has neither been the unhyphenated Canadianism of the Tories nor the vapid biculturalism of the Liberals.

Canada is, in fact, formed of two nations, one of them a relatively homogeneous French fact centred on Quebec, the other a polyglot series of English speaking communities from Atlantic to Pacific. Autonomy for these groups and identity around them, is the only basis for Canadian existence. But our governments have not educated Canadians about the nature of their country; nor have they acted to evolve policies to assure the survival of its parts. Instead they have played on the fears that are natural in such divisions, and have opened the country to an external economic and cultural domination.

Merely turning from the Liberals to the Conservatives, whose policies are anchored in the country's rural or small business past, will not bring us closer to an adequate national politics. Nor do the New Democrats, usually thought of as a real alternative, offer up an electoral product basically different from the competitors. Hampered by American-dominated international unions and out to win a growing urban middle class electorate, the NDP is not likely to deal with basic issues in a new way.

The political system has failed to counter the trend towards continentalism; the provinces have resisted even less than the federal parliament, the short-run benefits of branch-plant status. The real dynamic in Canadian society is a corporate one, and it has been imported from abroad.

Educational system

Branch-plant societies have branch-plant educational systems. Not surprisingly, in a corporate society, it is the corporation men who run the institutions which supply the business community with its skilled manpower. The boards of governors of Canada's universities represent those same business interests that have failed to maintain Canada's economic independence.

The universities today have become the focal point in a clash of generations that is taking place throughout our society. The generational gap, as it exists in the universities, is the collision between young people disillusioned with today's society and the very men who built its institutions.

Curiously, although Canada's rural, northern and Atlantic regions have suffered most, economically, in recent years, it is young people in the favoured urban arena who are most disaffected with the drift to continentalism. Canada's increased affluence and technical complexity has led to a lengthened school attendance; this distinctly "preadult" world, meant for socializing and training, has developed a culture of its own. While the majority of students dutifully acquire their educational meal-tickets and complete their apprenticeships, they do so with little enthusiasm for the roles they will play in the economy. Our youth culture is increasingly dominated by a cynical discontent with the adult world as inherited, and despair and alienation in the face of the direction in which young people see society drifting.

The failure of Canada to develop an identity in keeping with our history and place in the world, compounds the problems felt by youth. Today's young people suffer from their country's incoherence as well as from their powerlessness as individuals.

The vagueness of being Canadian means we lack traditions of action in the face of problems; it means, in true colonial fashion, that we leave our fate to men elsewhere and are prepared to import already fabricated styles of life into our country. Society cannot hope to involve today's youth in a country that does not respect its own existence; it is not engaging to be a colonial.

Youth discontent exists most consciously and powerfully in the universities today. Students, together in large numbers, have time to examine their society at large, as well as the limitations of the university in particular. Many young people drop out without concern for degrees, too discouraged and personally alienated to find direction for their lives. Others, a growing minority, are beginning to work to change the society at large and the university which is its microcosmos.

Discontent: distribution of power

Protest actions such as separatist rallies in Montreal's Parc Lafontaine or Vietnam sit-ins on the steps of the House of Commons, are only the visible manifestation of today's dissent. In English Canada, organized radical youth explain the basis for their activism with a critique of Canadian life within the American "Great Society."

For them, our present style of life is basically undemocratic. In it, major decisions about the future of individuals, communities, regions, countries and even the world are made at levels of power inaccessible to those affected by the decisions.

They see the economic power centres, largely controlled from the U.S., as the main dynamic in Canadian society today. Decisions at this level set broad patterns for development of natural resources, production and consumption. In our consumer economy, individuals have no power to initiate decisions about the economy in general or the quantity or quality of goods and services produced in particular. Institutionalized elites decide what the consumer may buy, what the city he lives in will look like, and the ways available for him to make a living.

Supporting the economic system are a variety of public and voluntary institutions, which provide an ideology for society, supply its manpower and maintain its social order. The churches, the mass media, welfare agencies and the political parties are among these secondary institutions.

Parliament is the institution through which ordinary citizens are *supposed* to have power in shaping social policies. But the political parties represented in parliament are most responsive to powerfully organized pressure groups and not to individuals. Most such powerful lobbies are already a part of the mainsteam, and act politically to make sure their particular interests are looked after. They are not, for the most part, interested in asking basic questions about society. The political parties each emphasise different features of the system; they do not offer basic alternatives.

Common to all the mainstream institutions of the "Great Society" is their corporate nature. Such bodies have large and growing bureaucracies; and fitting the description of classical sociologists, these bureaucracies seem mainly geared to keeping people away from those who decide, and insulating those with decision-making power from the effects of their decisions.

Once the institutions exists, the main job for those who run it is to ensure the continuance and expansion of the corporation itself; there is seldom questioning of fundamental goals or assessment of the social implications of corporate policy.

The educational system is a vital part of the network of secondary institutions. And today's university is the epitome of the corporate institution. Controlled from the top, by men outside of academic pursuits, the university allows little power to the faculty and far less to the students. With prescribed areas for courses and arbitrary rulings for degrees, the university now is a far cry from being a community of scholars.

Involved in the major decisions of the day, the university is a profoundly political institution. This, of course, is not because the university participates in electoral politics or takes stands as an institution on community issues. Rather it is because the university's claim to neutrality in social questions serves to perpetuate the thought —and action—patterns deemed 'normal" in the dominant sectors of the community that supports it. In the university, young people serve a new form of apprenticeship. Instead of the traditional apprenticeship that trained people for jobs, the university has become a compulsory entrance requirement for professional and advanced positions within the dominant society. Primarily through its methods and life-style, the university community makes it easy and apparently attractive for young people to accept the goals of the social system, and then to go forth to take their places working in it.

Discontent: Canada and the world

In sum then, radical youth in the universities regard the co-opting of Canada into the American "Great Society" as distorting our country's internal development in the broadest sense. But such integration has wider implications still. It means we are tying ourselves part and parcel to American foreign policy around the world.

The question that faces Canada is not merely the rate of increase of our standard of living; it is whether our troops will be dragged into the war in Vietnam, should China become involved. It may even be whether our cities will be annihilated along with American cities in a world war.

By far the most foolhardy of the features of the American "Great Society" is the role it has cast for itself as the centre of a world empire. Dictating its style of life to the emerging nations, and maintaining them as raw material suppliers for its own benefit, America is engaged around the world. In seeking to defend its empire from that of the Communists, America today faces the prospects of brushfire wars, policing actions and largescale hostilities throughout the developing areas of the globe.

It is clear that the present Liberal Government is fearful of further escalation of the war in Vietnam. But a client government can only seek minor shifts in the policy of the parent empire. No matter how often Mssrs. Pearson or Martin quietly warn the U.S. of the dangers of bombing North Vietnam or of the spectacle of war with China, we will be dragged in, one way or the other, if this war goes on.

Our continued organic relation to the American empire involves the conscription of Canada's resources for the empire's international policy. Instead of giving us a voice in U.S. decisions, such a relationship makes us vulnerable to economic reprisals and frightens our government from taking public stances in opposition to the Americans.

Discontent: technology as politics

It seems likely that these trends, domestic and international, will continue. They will be enhanced still more as Canada moves with increasing rapidity into the technological era. It is not a primitive fear of machines that makes one uneasy about the advance of technology into all walks of life, from the teaching machine, through computarized newspaper copy, to cybernetically controlled industries. It is the understanding that this technology is as politically committed as is the university. It is a technology developed to serve the values and priorities of our dominant economic and social institutions. And it is capable of maintaining and enhancing itself and the order it is part of even more assuredly than the machines and bureaucracies of mere mortals. It is likely then that our continuing technological development will not only cause a host of social difficulties, but will also accentuate the undemocratic and continentalist drift of Canadian society.

In the light of this, we can expect that Canadian youth will be increasingly alienated from the society that is being built.

The first sparks

Radical action among young people in opposition to these social trends is a recent phenomenon. Since 1960 university students campaigned in opposition to nuclear weapons for Canada, and supported U.S. civil rights activists, as well as holding teach-ins and sit-ins on Vietnam, and campaigns for free university education and a student voice in determining university policy. In terms of evolving opposition politics on a significant scale and with a coherent analysis, such action has advanced only a little. But around the student activists a political and social programme is emerging.

Such a programme has as its core idea the notion of radical democracy—a search for political, social and economic institutions that give people power to make the decisions that shape their destinies. For radical youth both the creation of a relevant university and the repatriation of the Canadian economy are seen in these terms.

The university, the radicals are working toward, would be controlled by those studying within its walls—the students and the faculty. It would recognize its impact on society and would be committed to acting as a part of it, not just a handmaiden for the dominant power-centres.

A university which participated in its community would be different from our own. The sterile divisions between different disciplines could not survive an attempt to make them relevant to the world. The university would be a place more for re-examining and developing the values of our society than for the mere recanting of conventional ideas. The university and its members would involve themselves in the fate of Canada, rather than allowing the country to drift into colonialism.

If recent experience in Québec is any guide, this search for a relevant university and for broad social change will involve a re-discovery of Canada. But it will not be the traditional Canadian nationalism of John Diefenbaker with its hopelessly outdated economic policies and its failure to understand Québec. Nor will it be the nationalism that Walter Gordon has been trying to sell to Bay Street.

The fact is, of course, that today's business elite is already so much an integral part of the new continental economic structure, that it can have no interest in Canadian independence. Pathetically, Walter Gordon is wasting his time with them.

The reason why repatriation of the economy has not taken place is not because it cannot be done, but because it would not benefit those dominant in this country to do so. While there are no universally accepted plans for repatriation, many approaches have been developed. But such plans will lie dormant until an opposition movement motivated not to duplicate the American model, but to create a system without elites, becomes powerful in Canada.

In the last year radical youth connected with the Student Union for Peace Action have begun a series of community projects across the country, that are a first step in building an opposition movement. Young people have gone to live among the culturally and economically deprived, helping to organise them to have a voice in the decisions that affect them. The ideal of radical students for Canadian society is very much the same as their ideal for the university: those who are part of the community should participate in deciding how their community is to be run.

It is the Canadians under thirty years of age, who did not live through a period of accomodation to the "Great Society" and who have few vested interests in it, who will form the basis for an opposition movement. Beginning in the universities, the movement will work to create new centres of power at the base of society. Such efforts have as their goal the decentralization of power, to carve out major areas where citizens can participate directly to decide social issues. Such power in the community can serve as the basis for federal institutions that can co-ordinate economic and social policies designed to safeguard community decision-making. Of course, these goals for society will bring their supporters up against the full power of the American empire, and that is why the social movement will be a movement for Canadian independence as well.

Published 1966

A CRITIQUE OF
THE NEW LEFT

by George Grant

I speak as a Canadian nationalist and as a conservative. It is
necessary to start here for the following reason. To speak of the moral
responsibility of the citizen in general is impossible; the question
entirely depends on the kind of regime in which one is a citizen. The
United States is a world empire — the largest to date. Its life at home
is controlled by mammoth corporations, private and public, and
through these bureaucracies it reaches out to control a large proportion
of the globe and soon beyond the globe. The nineteenth century idea
of the democratic citizen making the society he inhabits by the vote
and the support of political parties must have less and less meaning.
In local matters, the citizen of an empire can achieve some minor
goals. But he cannot shape the larger institutions or move the centres
of power. Democratic citizenship is not a notion compatible with
technological empires. Now Canada moves more and more to being
a satellite of that empire. And Canadians live much of their lives
under the same imperial bureaucracies. The institutions of Toronto
are much the same as those of Detroit. Yet despite this there is a
sense in which we still have more citizenship here than in the U.S.
because we have some political sovereignty, if we fight for it. Traditional democratic means — the vote and support for political parties
have more meaning in our smaller sphere. Political choice is both
more real and more possible in Canada. This might be truly useful
to the world, if we in Canada could use it to see that North American
relations with Asia did not always simply follow Washington.

But to pass to the broader question of what it is to be a citizen
in North America in this era, let me start from the position of the
New Left in North America, that is the movement which has public
significance because of what it did in the civil rights struggle. I
find myself in agreement with the account the leaders of this movement give of the inhumanity of the institutions of North America.

55

Despite the positive changes and increasing maturity of the projects, the life of an organizer continues to be a physically and emotionally exacting one. An ERAP organizer is almost occupationally manic-depressive, as victories and defeats tend to be exaggerated to give drama to the painfully slow process of building a movement. Morale is sometimes threatened, too, by irresistible comparisons with the student movement : it is sometimes hard to keep faith in the difficult, gradual, yet solid building of a community union when the example is presented of a spectacular, though possibly more ephemeral, student demonstration.

Yet the call expressed in a letter by an ERAP organizer last February is still relevant :

> *"We are not seeking a dramatic moment of conflict, but a long series of such moments that change the balance of power... For those who want to take sides, I believe the time is at hand when real vocations exist through which we can realize our values and realize ourselves. Organizing — and many, many different skills are needed in organizing — can be a way of life if only we make it so. We ask that people join us, down here."*

"Among the young everywhere is a sense of alienation that turns even affluence and security into worthless prizes. This may prove to be the nation's critical challenge." The Berkeley Revolt, by A. H. Raskin,

New York Times Magazine, Feb. 14, 1965

"Students — middle-class youth — are the major exploited class... They have no choice but to go to college."

Paul Goodman

"We must now begin the demand of the right to know; to know the realities of the present world-in-revolution, and to have an opportunity to think clearly in an extended manner about the world. It is ours to demand meaning; we must insist upon meaning !" From a Free Speech Movement pamphlet.

When I read Professor Lynd in *Liberation* speaking of what the institutions of his society do to human personality both at home and abroad, I agree with his account of those institutions. When I hear what Mr. Savio in Berkely or Mr. Drushka in Toronto write about the inhumanity of our multiversities, by and large I agree with them. How can a conservative not feel sympathy with their outrage against the emptiness and dehumanization that this society produces?

But when the New Left speaks of overcoming these conditions by protest, I think they are indulging in dreams and dangerous dreams. The moral fervour that accompanies such dreams is too valuable to be wasted on anything but reality. When they speak as if it were possible by marching and sitting to turn North American society away from being an empire protecting its interests in the world, by violence, I just do not know how they can think this. When some of them speak as if the empires of the East were not moving in the same social direction as the United States, I think they are deluding themselves. When they propose that our modern universities can be overcome and turned into humane sources of enlightenment, I think they have not looked at our society closely enough.

Their politics of hope and of Utopia — indeed with some of them another outbreak of the traditional form of the politics of the apocalypse — seems to me a kind of dream from which analysis should awaken them. They seem to think that these massive institutions which stifle human excellence can be overcome, and I think this arises from a profound misinterpretation of modern history. For several centuries the chief energies of Western society have been directed to the mastery of nature — at first non-human nature and now human nature. We now live in the era where that process moves quickly to its apotheosis. The motive of this pursuit was that by it men should be made free. Freedom was its rallying cry. And it is in the pursuit of this dream of freedom that we have built the mammoth institutions, international and national, in which we live. This pursuit of the mastery of nature has gained men great victories over natural necessity. Who can doubt that? But at the same time as it has produced these victories, it has subjected men to the forces of the artificial necessities of the technological society. "The further the technical mechanism develops which allows us to escape natural necessity, the more we are subjected to artificial technical necessities. The artificial necessity of technique is not less harsh and implacable for being much less obviously menacing than natural necessity."[1] This is the crucial question about citizenship in this era: what is it to be a citizen in this new society ruled by its technical apparatus?

What I do not see is why anybody should believe that by some dialectical process of history there should suddenly spring out of this technological society a free and humane society. First Western men and now men everywhere in the world are driving with enormous speed to the building of this technological straitjacket. This is a society which by its very mammoth nature must destroy the idea of the responsible citizen. What evidence is there for believing that this system can by protest be turned towards the ends of human excellence ? What reason have we for believing that the vast imperial structures will act towards each other and towards their neighbours in a nobler way than empires have in the past ? The empires may restrain themselves from fright, but the small nations who are unfortunate enough to be caught between them will be ground between the millstones. And to speak about the institutions I know best — the universities — what reason is there to believe that they can be diverted from the very purpose for which they exist ? The modern universities exist above all to provide personnel to feed the vast technological apparatus. That technological apparatus is now autonomous and produces its own needs which are quite detached from human needs. Are such institutions which are of the very fabric of the modern quest to be diverted from this end ?

The supreme example of the autonomy of technique is surely the space programme. If it is possible for man to do something it must be done. Vast resources of brains, money, materials are poured out in the U.S. and U.S.S.R. to keep this fantastic programme proliferating. And it is accepted by the masses in both societies not only as necessary but as man's crowning glory. One leader of the U.S. space programme said that as we cannot change the environment of space, we will have to change man. So we are going to produce beings half flesh — half electronic organs. If it can be done, it must be done and it surely will be done. This is what I mean by the autonomy of technique. The question whether technique serves human good is no longer asked. It has become an end in itself.

There is a lot of talk among the New Left about the present system of society collapsing because of its internal contradictions. What signs are there of that collapse ? The American system with its extension into Western Europe seems to me supremely confident and to have the overwhelming majority of its citizens behind it — the same seems true of the Russian system and will be increasingly true of the Chinese system.

One immediate reason why I think the New Left is deluded about what is happening in North America is because it has misinterpreted the events which took place in the southern United States. It says today : look at our triumphs in the South; we will now carry these triumphs of citizen action into new fields of social revolution. What has been forgotten is that the powerful among the people and institutions of North America were more than willing that the society of the white South should be broken. The civil rights movement had behind it all the powerful forces of the American empire. It marched protected by federal troops, it had the blessing of the leading government figures. It was encouraged night after night by N.B.C. and C.B.S. There was violence from the white south, but the white south is not an important part of the American power elite. It will surely be a different matter when the protests are against some position which is dear and close to the American liberal establishment. We have only to think of how much is immediately accomplished by protests about Vietnam, the Dominican Republic or nuclear policy. Anyway, dissent and protest are themselves bureaucratized in our society. They are taken into the system and trivialized. They are made to serve the interests of the system they are supposed to be attacking, by showing that free speech is allowed.

I am not advocating inaction or cynicism. Nothing I have said denies for one moment the nobility of protest. Nothing I have said denies that justice is good and that injustice is evil and that it is required of human beings to know the difference between the two. To live with courage in the world is always better than retreat or disillusion. Human beings are less than themselves when they are cut off from being citizens. Indeed one of the finest things about the present protest movements in North America is that they try to give meaning to citizenship in a society which by its enormity and impersonality cuts people off from the public world. Anybody who lives within a university must know that the students who care enough about the world to protest are much finer than those who are interested in public affairs simply because they want to climb within the system and use it to gain recognition for their egos. Indeed how much finer are those who protest than those who crawl through the university simply as a guarantee of the slow road to death in the suburbs. In our monolithic society, the pressures upon the individual to retreat from the public sphere are immense. The new politics of protest have tried to overcome those pressures and to give new meaning to citizenship. Nobody should attack them for that.

What I am arguing against is the politics based on easy hopes about the future human situation. The hope, for example, that some future transformation of power in North America is going to overcome the implicit difficulties of the technological apparatus, that North American society can in the future be radically changed in its direction. Hope in the future has been and is the chief opiate of modern life. And nobody is more responsible for dipping out that opiate than Marx. Its danger is that it prevents men from looking clearly at their situation. It teaches them to dream instead of coming to terms with facts. The most dangerous quality of the politic of Utopia is that it can easily turn into despair. If people have vast expectations of hope about a society such as ours, they are going to be disappointed and then their moral fervour can turn rancid and bitter. Moral fervour is too precious a commodity not to be put in the service of reality.

If protest is to be effective in this era, if we are to be successful in creating space for human spontaneity in the iron maiden of the technical apparatus we have created, then it is essential that those who are in the forefront of protest must combine with their action the deepest and most careful thought. Action without thought will be an impotent waste of time. In this ferocious era, if we are to keep ourselves human and to be effective citizens, then our first obligation is to be free. And by free I mean knowing the truth about things, to know what is so, without simplifications, without false hopes, without moral fervour divorced from moral clarity. The central Christian platitude still holds good. "The truth shall make you free." I use freedom here quite differently from those who believe that we are free when we have gained mastery over man and over nature. It is different even from the simple cry for political liberty : "Freedom now". For in the long pull freedom without the knowledge of reality is empty and vacuous. The greatest figure of our era, Gandhi, was interested in public action and in political liberty, but he knew that the right direction of that action had to be based on knowledge of reality — with all the discipline and order and study that that entailed.

Truth seeking is of course hard to accomplish in this society. Our universities have at many points retreated from it into fact gathering and technological mastery, what is now called the knowledge industry. Most of our social scientists have used the idea of a value free social science to opt out of the battle of what constitutes the good society, and spend their time in discovering techniques for adjusting people to the system. The philosophers have often opted out to play clever professional games. Much of the religious tradition seems a worn out garment not able to help in the search for truth. Above all, what may hold people from the search for the truth is that the human situation in the totally realised mass world may be so unpalatable that we simply do not want to face it. If we do not face reality we may be able to avoid the great evils of despair and pessimism, but we also cut ourselves off from any chance of maturity and effectiveness.

I have concentrated on North America, because we in North America are inevitably in the forefront of the world. We are the society that has most completely realised the dominance of technique over every aspect of human life. Every year we are moving with prodigious speeed to the greater and greater realisation of that system. All other societies move at various speeds to the same kind of society we are creating. We are the first people who will have to learn what it is to be citizens in a society dominated by technique. Because that system is most fully realised with us, we are the first people who can look it in the face and we are called upon to see it for what it is and not fool ourselves about it. We must face the laws of its necessity — its potential to free men from natural necessity, its potential for inhumanity and tyranny. We must not delude ourselves and we must not throw up our hands. We must define our possible areas of influence with the most careful clarity. Where in this mammoth system can we use our intelligence and our love to open up spaces in which human excellence can exist ? How can we use the most effective pressure to see that our empire uses moderation and restraint in its relations with the rest of the world ? I end where I began, that our greatest obligation as Canadians is to work for a country which is not simply a satellite of any empire.

FOOTNOTES :

(1) J. Ellul, *The Technological Society*.

Published 1966

THE PROGRESSIVE
TRADITION IN
SASKATCHEWAN

by Lorne Brown

T O UNDERSTAND WHY PROTEST AND REFORM MOVE-
MENTS and even socialist parties have flourished in Saskatchewan in
what was, until very recent years, an almost totally rural environment, one
must keep constantly in mind the colonial relationship between the Canadian Prairies and the Montréal-Toronto business interests and their foreign
collaborators, at first in Britain and later in the United States. The
Canadian West, like its American counterpart, was consciously colonized
by the East to provide markets, sources for investment, and raw materials
to a limited extent for the industrial, commercial interests and traffic
for the transportation interests. In Canada, as in the United States, the
aboriginal population was reduced and the land settled by immigrants
from the East and from Britain and Europe. The "National Policy," conceived by the Macdonald Conservatives and adopted and extended by
the Laurier Liberals, developed, with the assistance of British capital,
an East-West economy designed to compete with, and not complement,
the American economy. There were three essential features to this
economy—protective tariffs, transcontinental railways, and a large
agricultural population in the West. The territory was acquired from
the Hudson Bay Company in 1870, the aboriginal population effectively
crushed and pushed aside by 1885, and Western settlement was begun
in a big way by the late 1890's.

The subjection of half a continent to the economic empire of the Toronto and Montréal capitalist was not accomplished without a struggle. Louis Riel and his Métis followers put up what turned out to be a temporarily successful resistance in 1870 when they compelled the Canadian government to grant Manitoba provincial status and guarantee the cultural and economic rights of the Métis nation. These guarantees turned out to be insufficient and, at any rate, many of them were later ignored. The Métis could not survive in the new economy; many of them moved to the Northwest and, along with Indian tribes, made their last stand on the Saskatchewan in 1885.

By 1885 the Canadian Pacific Railways (CPR), built with the assistance of huge amounts of government money, land grants and guaranteed monopolistic privilege, was completed. White settlers had been migrating from Ontario and the United States at a modest rate and were already beginning to offer resistance to their Eastern colonial masters. The Manitoba and Northwest Farmers' Union had been organized in 1883, mainly to agitate against the CPR monopoly, the ownership of the best land by the CPR and Hudson Bay Company, high protective tariffs, and the monopolistic grain companies. At the same time the Indians of the Prairies did not take kindly to being relegated to the "reserves" set aside by the federal government, and the Métis were fearful that their economy and way of life would once again be disrupted. The result was that the white settlers, the Métis and several Indian bands decided to co-ordinate their efforts to obtain their rights. A joint meeting of Indians, Métis and whites requested Louis Riel to return from exile in the United States and lead the agitation in the summer of 1884.

The agitation became more militant as crop failure and low prices in 1884 and virtual starvation among the Indians and Métis made the situation more desperate. The federal government was indifferent to the plight of the inhabitants of the Northwest. The Métis and some of their Indian allies were finally driven to armed rebellion. The rebellion was quickly crushed, the leaders imprisoned, executed or exiled and the Métis and Indians rendered economically and politically powerless. The white settlers, though most had supported the demands of the Indians and Métis, were unwilling, with the exception of a few militant leaders, to carry their protests as far as armed rebellion. [1]

What is instructive about the demands of the white settlers in 1885 is that many of them were demands which were to form part of the program of protest and reform movements in the West for half a century. They included a railway to Hudson Bay, lower tariffs and local control of natural resources (not granted by federal government until the 1930's). Their demands also included responsible government in the Northwest. Responsible government was conceded by the federal government which began a long and often bitter struggle to achieve provincial status, finally resulting in the creation of the provinces of Saskatchewan and Alberta in 1905. This struggle helped to accentuate the regional antagonism to the East and distrust of the national political parties.

1896 was a turning point in the economic development of Canada and the colonization of the West. The new Laurier government adopted the economic policy of the Conservatives and, due to favourable world economic conditions, made it a fantastic success. The accelarating urbanization of Europe, cheaper water transportation and the end of free land in the American West combined to create exceptionally favourable conditions for the settlement of the Canadian West. An aggressive immigration policy by the Canadian government and the CPR helped to assure that hundreds of thousands of immigrants would pour in from Britain, Europe and the United States. The population of Saskatchewan increased more than five fold between 1901 and 1911. [2] This rapid settlement created a tremendous market for the manufacturing of Ontario and Quebec. The entire infra-structure of a new economy, including two additional transcontinental railways, were constructed in less than two decades. Industries dependent upon agriculture like flour-milling, meat-packing and farm implement manufacturing expanded tremendously. The market for consumer goods such as textiles created a bonanza for the owners of the tariff-protected sweat shops of Montréal. The takeoff in the national economy was reflected by the rapid growth of urban centres with the creation of an industrial proletariat who would become extremely restless by the end of World War I.

The new economy was, because of boom conditions, constructed in a lopsided fashion. Railways and other public utilities as well as many manufacturing industries overexpanded with the help of a massive influx of foreign capital. They were to discover that they had more capital equipment than could be economically used. Farmers overexpanded—going into debt while prices were rising and markets were good and found themselves in trouble later. The agrarian and urban working classes were not sharing in the overall prosperity. The people of the West soon found themselves at the mercy of banks and mortage companies, railways and farm machinery manufacturers, milling and meat-packing firms, and the Winnipeg Grain Exchange—all controlled directly or indirectly by the financial interests of the East. The farmers sold their wheat in an unregulated world market over which they had no influence, and bought their equipment and consumer goods from industrial interests protected by a tariff wall. This built up a class and regional antagonism which was on the verge of an explosion when it was postponed by World War I.

Outside Agitators of Old

There were conditions less directly related to economics which helped to alienate the Prairies, especially west of Manitoba, from the national political parties and the Eastern power structure. A majority of the immigrants after 1900 were from Britain, Europe and the United States and had no sentimental ties to "old Ontario". The most politically active among the immigrants, because of their command of the language and familiarity with the political institutions, were the British and

Americans. Many of the British had come from an urban environment and were familiar with socialist ideas, some having had experience in the emerging Labour party. Many of the Americans had had experience with agrarian populism in the United States. Those who had been politically active before coming to Canada frequently obtained leadership positions in farm, labour and political organizations. [3]

Other factors differentiating Prairie society from that of central Canada included an active grass roots democracy and co-operative community institutions. Because of the sparseness of the population a much larger percentage of the people had to accept community responsibilities than was the case in an urban environment. [4] Sparseness of population and climatic conditions compelled people to do many things collectively which, in another environment, would be done individually. The fact that there was a one crop economy meant that most of the population experienced similar problems and would tend to look at the world in a similar way. Added to this was the fact that everyone had identical and easily identified enemies—the vested interests controlled in central Canada.

The years 1896 to 1911 were years of ferment in Saskatchwan with the formation of numerous farm organizations, co-operative economic ventures and political protest parties—none of which achieved immediate success but many of which contributed to disseminating ideas among the populace which gradually alienated a larger and larger proportion of the population from the existing political structures. The strongest farm organization, and one which held a hegemonic position until the 1920s, was the *Saskatchewan Grain Growers' Association* (S.G.G.A.) which was formed at the turn of the century after a number of clashes with the CPR and after the grain interests had convinced farmers that they must organize into a strong pressure group. Although the S.G.G.A. was organized along democratic lines, had active local associations, and annual conventions of democratically elected delegates, the "iron law of oligarchy" very quickly set in. The leadership at the provincial executive level seldom changed hands. [6] The leaders of the S.G.G.A. were also involved in the leadership of the Saskatchewan Co-up Elevator Company and the Saskatchewan Liberal party.

The Liberals were, with the exception of a brief interlude between 1929-1934, the dominant party in Saskatchewan provincial politics until their defeat by the Canadian Commonwealth Federation (C.C.F.) in 1944. The Saskatchewan Liberals were, until the late 1920s, considered to be the left-wing of the federal Liberal party and frequently carried on inter-party warfare against the Montréal business interests who generally dictated party policy. At home in Saskatchewan they often dissociated themselves from federal Liberal policy and poised as the champions of the Western farmer against the big interests of the East. Their social legislation was as advanced as any in Canada at the time. The provincial Liberals were exceptionally skillful at co-opting the leaders of the S.G.G.A. and other farm groups

The S.G.G.A. was, in matters of policy, schizophrenic in that it simultaneously represented *petit bourgeois* conservatism, demands for more direct democracy and the advocates of social democratic ideas. On the one hand the S.G.G.A. was obsessed with free trade and the more perfect form of free competition which was alleged to have existed in the past. This was the unrealizable dream of most agrarian protest movements in Canada and the United States. It appealed to farmers because it did not threaten their capitalistic values and generally diverted their attention from the basic evils of the system. At the same time the S.G.G.A. advocated a graduated income tax, nationalization of all public utilities and food-processing companies and the establishment of co-operatives. It also advocated political reform such as female suffrage, reform or abolition of the Senate, proportional representation and the initiative, referendum and recall. The ideas about more direct democracy were copied from American movements and could be considered radical in the Canadian context in that many of them were incompatible with the British parliamentary system.

Radical notions from abroad

The S.G.G.A. acted as an incubator of new economic and political solutions for the problems facing Saskatchewan people. The oligarchy was obliged to attract and hold members, and thus maintain an effective presure group, to appeal to class consciousness and foster a hatred of the business interests. There developed a militant minority of secondary leaders who were constantly agitating for more radical solutions and attempting to force the organization to embark upon new economic and political ventures. Every few years these people would grow sufficiently impatient that they would form political groups of their own or join a new political movement imported from the United States—none of which took real root but most of which kept the S.G.G.A. leadership nervous and helped to disseminate new ideas. [7] These groups included the Comrades of Equity, a Christian utopian socialist party organized along democratic centralist lines ; and the People's Political Association, a coalition of farmers, labour union leaders in Moose Jaw and Regina, and local leaders of the Canadian Labour Party. The most successful of these groups, and one which was active in both Saskatchewan and Alberta, was the Non-Partisan League—a populist-socialist movement imported from North Dakota during World War I. Among the speakers and organizers of the Non-Partisan League were William Irvine and J.S. Woodsworth, Labour M.P.'s in the 1920's and founders of the C.C.F. in 1932. A short-lived organization which was dedicated solely to propaganda and education was the No-Party League of Western Canada, organized by E.A. Partridge in 1913 after the S.G.G.A. had defeated a resolution which would have committed it to independent political action. The No-Party League recommended direct legislation and the single tax as instruments for accomplishing "the rescue of the natural resources and public utilities from private control and their administration for the benefit of the people". [8]

There gradually developed a militant corps of radicals who worked within the S.G.G.A. and other organizations who were never co-opted. Many of these people were to become ideological socialists and provide the hard-core of the C.C.F. in the 1930's. One reason the C.C.F. was able to survive was because it was not formed by instant radicals but by people who had moved further left over a period of years, had educated themselves politically, and had learned from their experiences, especially their mistakes, in numerous political and economic organizations.

Agitation

One of the organs instrumental in educating the farmers was the *Grain Growers' Guide,* the official weekly organ of the Manitoba Grain Growers' Association, the S.G.G.A. and the United Farmers of Alberta (UFA). The *Guide,* unfortunately, depended upon subsides from the Grain Growers' Grain Company and was consequently strongly influenced by the more conservative Manitoba wing of the farm movement. [9] E.A. Partridge, the original editor, resigned after one issue because of a dispute with his associates. Partridge had wanted to amalgamate the *Guide* with the Winnipeg *Voice,* the official organ of Western labour unions, and use it to educate Westerners about the need for radical social change. Prairie farm leaders were not about to challenge the basic assumptions of the economic system and were not ready to make common cause with urban Labour. The majority of the farmers and farm leaders, particularly outside Saskatchewan, were never to reach this stage.

Despite its handicap the *Guide* proved to be invaluable in alienating Westerners from the economic and political *status quo,* moving them in the direction of liberal reform, and encouraging a political ferment which would, in time, lead substantial numbers of farmers to embrace socialism as a political philosophy. While advocating such doubtful "reforms" as free trade and Prohibition the *Guide* also agitated for a democratization of Canadian political institutions. It advocated Senate reforms, more democracy (initiative, referendum and recall), publication or prohibition of financial contributions to political parties, female suffrage, as well as an end to political corruption, oligarchic machines and party patronage. The *Guide* also demanded greater government control of the economy, nationalization of most public utilities and several other industries, progressive taxation, an end to profiteering and, occasionally, a better deal for urban Labour and a more advanced welfare state. It built up over a period of years a distrust of traditional political institutions and a hatred of big business which helped to pave the road for socialist agitators at a later period. The terminology and rhetoric of the *Guide* helped to create a political psychology and vocabulary whereby Bay Street was synonymous with "robber baron" and a railway magnate with "bloodsucker". The *Guide* regularly carried the writings of the great muckrakers and exposed in detail a great many of the corrupt connections between business and politics in Canada. They also carried good accounts of political and economic developments in

Britain and the U.S. and, occasionally, Europe. Readers of the *Guide* were kept informed of developments in the British Labour party and American protest movements and of the co-operative movement in all countries. The works and ideas of Henry George, Edward Bellamy, Eugene Debs, the Fabian Socialists, sometimes Marx and numerous others were discussed, generally intelligently and frequently sympathetically.

By the 1920's the *Guide* had over 80,000 subcribers on the Prairies; it was the most widely read farm journal and, next to the Winnipeg *Free Press,* probably the most influential paper in the West. The *Guide* achieved such popularity not only because it appealed to peoples' frustrations and resentments but also because it was an invaluable trade journal—discussing the latest techniques in field husbandry, livestock production and agricultural methods generally. Many farmers would originally subscribe for this reason and subsequently become interested in political and economic questions. The *Guide* was extremely critical of the daily press throughout the country, continually denouncing and sometimes exposing them as paid political partisans and prostitutes to the business interests. [10] There developed in the minds of farmers a profound distrust of the press which grew into intense hatred when the Saskatchewan newspaper monopoly carried on a scurrilous and economically motivated campaign against formation of the Wheat Pool in 1923. [11] This was particularly important in that it made it more difficult for the mass media to manipulate public opinion. It also impressed upon political activists the importance of controlling a newspaper for the dissemination of information and counter-propaganda. The founders of the C.C.F. had learned this lesson well and the party in Saskatchewan usually gave high priority to the distribution of a propaganda organ.

Elections 1911

The so-called "reciprocity election" of 1911 contributed significantly to the weakening of the two party system in the West. Under pressure from farm organizations and the Western Liberal party the government negotiated a Reciprocity Agreement with the U.S. whereby there would be instituted, by concurrent legislation, reciprocity of trade between the two countries in natural products and specified manufactured products. The negotiation of the agreement was a fatal mistake for the Liberal government. The corporate power structure, upon which the party depended for funds, was alarmed that reciprocity would disrupt the East-West flow of trade, undermine lucrative markets in the West, and be the beginning of the end of the National Policy. The Canadian Manufacturers' Association, most of the Eastern press and the Conservative party launched a tremendous attack on the agreement—charging that the economy would be ruined and Canada would become economically and politically subservient to the U.S.

English Canada in 1911 was oriented towards Britain economically and psychologically, and anti-Americanism was stronger than it is today. [12] Concurrent legislation could be revoked at any time, giving the Americans an easy opportunity to threaten economic disruption as a means of political pressure.

Laurier handled the situation in a politically inept fashion. He allowed the agitation against the agreement to escalate for months and then, called an election on the issue. Businessmen, including very prominent Liberals, deserted the party in droves and threw their money and support behind the Conservatives. The press took up the cry, "No truck nor trade with the Yankees!" The Liberals lost the election, losing heavily in English Canada on the reciprocity issue and losing ground in Québec to a Nationalist-Conservative alliance on the issue of naval policy and British imperialism. [43] Only Saskatchewan and Alberta, the most agrarian and least British of the English speaking provinces, voted solidly Liberal. It was clear to any astute political observer that neither of the traditional parties could rule without at least the passive support of the business interests. The election of 1911 taught the Liberal party a lesson. Never again would they challenge the economic Establishment. It also convinced many politically aware farmers that they needed political vehicles of their own which would not be dependent upon the economic oligarchy in central Canada.

The alienation from the existing political structures grew rapidly after 1911, aided by a depression between 1912-1915. "What is needed is a new radical party with the courage of its convictions." (*Guide*, Sept. 27, 1911). Some farm leaders echoed the sentiments of the *Guide* while many became anti-party altogether and agitated for the abolition of the party system and the governing of the country by means of direct legislation and/or independent M.P.'s who would be tightly controlled by grass roots constituency associations and subject to recall. The beginning of World War I alleviated the depression but increased dissatisfaction and agitation. A militant and fairly significant minority within the farm and labour movements looked upon the war as a manifestation of European imperialism and opposed Canadian participation. The anti-war movement in English Canada was led by pacifists who espoused the "social gospel", and urban socialists. [14] Rampant corruption, war profiteering, rising prices, inept military leadership, curtailment of free speech, and persecution of so-called "enemy aliens" helped fan the flames of discontent.

By 1916 the Conservative government was under continual fire from farm and labour organizations and from the Liberal press, especially in the West. The Liberals, as usual, did the left-wing act while in opposition. On the Prairies, where the Non-Partisan League was organizing and pressure was building up within the farm organization for independent political action, the Liberal press went all out to identify with the interests of the organized farmers, warned them of the futility of independent political action, and pleaded with the federal Liberal party to reform from within before it was too late. Liberals stepped up their co-optation of farm leaders, taking Charles Dunning into the Saskatchewan cabinet in late 1916. [15] At the same time the federal Liberals made a crucial political mistake by agreeing to extend the life of Parliament by one year in the interests of the war effort. By 1917 the military and political situation was such that the Conservatives were able to split the Liberals and swamp them in a Union government

In late 1916 the Canadian Council of Agriculture, representing the main farm organizations on the Prairies and in Ontario, published the Farmers' Platform which was to form the basis for agrarian action for the next decade. In addition to the nineteenth century liberal planks demanding freer trade, the platform included such social democratic measures as nationalization of all railway, telegraph and express companies, sharply graduated taxation of personal, corporate and inherited income, taxation of unimproved land values to discourage speculation, and more government control of natural resources. It also included demands for direct legislation, abolition of political patronage, female suffrage, and publication of contributions to political parties. Most agrarian leaders were to focus the main attention on the tariff planks and lead their followers down a blind alley for years. The U.F.A., reflecting a strong American influence and the "group government" theories of Henry Wise Wood, generally emphasized populist political reforms, free trade, and unorthodox financial palliatives though a small minority among them eventually realized that basic economic changes would be necessary. [16] A somewhat larger minority in Saskatchewan was to reach a similar conclusion, adopt the socialist philosophy and combine with urban labour.

When the farm leaders published the Farmers' Platform their immediate intention was that local farm associations pressure sitting M.P.'s and Parliamentary candidates to adopt it and, failing this, that they run independent candidates pledged to the program. This was a way of channelling the demand for a third party into a more orthodox direction. The Non-Partisan League had just swept to power in North Dakota and many of the rank and file in the Western Canadian agrarian movement wanted to follow their example. As an alternative, the leadership, through the *Guide,* began to preach the desirability of sending independents to Parliament who would, like the 19th century radicals in Britain, act as a gadfly and perhaps control the balance of power and, by this method, achieve a re-alignment in Canadian politics. The idea was to force the federal Liberals to reform from within and drive all the business interests into the Conservative party. It was another of the many attempts in Canadian history to co-opt so-called radicals by having them work within or in alliance with the Liberal party.

Political Action

Local farmer associations began to nominate independent candidates to contest some federal and provincial seats in early 1917. Liberal S.G.G.A. leaders on the executive were successful in persuading the Association to stay out of politics as an official body. One of the chief arguments used was that such a step would split the association and endanger its economic activities. [17] However, the S.G.G.A. leaders could not always control events on the local level and eight Non-Partisan League and three independent farmers contested the provincial election of 1917 though only one was elected. The result was not surprising considering that the S.G.G.A. executive members campaigned extensively for the Liberals.

By 1917 most of English Canada was obsessed with winning the War and, hence, ripe for manipulation by government leaders. The Conservative government convinced that military conscription (though not conscription of wealth) was necessary, and desperately looking for means to stay in office, devised a plan whereby they could accomplish both. Since people thoughout the country had been agitating for a "non-partisan" wartime government, the Conservatives proposed a "Union Government" to carry out conscription and finish the war. English Canadian Liberals, faced with a chauvinistic electorate, had little choice but to accept. Laurier had promised the Québec people that he would never support conscription and, faced with a threat to Liberal power by the Nationalists, had little choice but to reject the proposal. English speaking Liberals were further undermined by the infamous *Wartime Elections Act* which disfranchised so-called "enemy aliens" (most of whom traditionally voted Liberal) and enfranchised the immediate female relatives of soldiers serving overseas. [18] Farm and labour leaders, many of whom had advocated a so-called "national government" anyway, had to go along with the scheme or be branded unpatriotic and effectively undermined. The organized farmers were further bought off by a nefarious deal whereby it was agreed that farmers and their sons would, in the interests of maintaining agricultural production, not be drafted. T.A. Crerar, President of the Grain Growers' Grain Company and one of the most prominent farm leaders, was taken into the Cabinet as Minister of Agriculture. The organized farmers, despite loud protests from the more militant of the rank and file, shelved the idea of immediately entering politics and withdrew their candidates. The few who remained were endorsed as Unionists pledged to back the Government for the remainder of the War.

In the election the Unionists swept English Canada and the Laurier Liberals took all of French-speaking Québec. Conscription was enforced despite widespread rioting and draft evasion in Québec and considerable discontent and evasion in the rest of Canada. Organized Labour let it be known that after the War they were going to achieve their rights. The farm leaders and their press organs had to constantly assure the farmers that they had not been sold out, especially after the government began drafting farmers' sons in 1918. A suppressed rage was building up among the urban working class and large numbers of farmers. The urban working class in the West was not benefitting economically from the war as much as their Eastern counterparts because of the concentration of war industries in the East. After the War, economic and political strife would change the face of Canadian politics, particularly in the Prairie provinces.

THE POST WAR REVOLT

The economic and political turmoil which shook Canada after the War was part of a world-wide phenomenon. The Bolshevik Revolution provided a great impetus to working class revolt and Allied intervention against the Bolsheviks was hotly resented in Canadian Labour circles.

Many people had believed Allied propaganda about the War being waged for peace, freedom and social justice, and when these things did not come to pass lost faith in the system. Widespread unemployment, rising prices and declining wages contributed to workers' militancy. In Western Canada the *Industrial Workers of the World* (I.W.W.), dedicated to the building of One Big Union and the destruction of the capitalist system, made rapid headway. Labour and socialist parties, some of which had been around since the turn of the century but had been insignificant, began to take firm root. Industrial strikes, exceptionally bitter and frequently violent, were widespread in 1918 and culminated in the *Winnipeg General Strike of 1919,* which so openly revealed the class basis of government in Canada that it acted as a catalyst in accelerating class consciousness. The leadership of the Western socialist movement, including that of Saskatchewan, was to be urban oriented.

Farmers, beset by declining farm prices and a decreasing market, embarked upon political action. Local farmer associations began to contest by-elections with outstanding success and, with each local success, pressure mounted within the farm organizations to form a third party. The more advanced among the farmers advocated a political alliance with organized labour. In Saskatchewan the S.G.G.A. leadership managed to talk the annual convention out of forming an agrarian party in 1919 but had to accept a resolution allowing local associations to take federal political action on their own initiative. They immediately proceeded to nominate candidates. By mid-1919 sentiment among farmers had so crystallized against the established parties that farm leaders elected as Unionists in 1917 could no longer afford to back Union government nor could they join the Liberal Opposition if they were to maintain political influence over the farmers. The result was the resignation of T. A. Crerar as Minister of Agriculture and the formation of "cross-benchers" under his leadership. This group, augmented by by-election winners, formed the Parliamentary nucleus of the National Progressive Party which was organized in 1920.

Progressivism

The philosophy of the main Progressive leaders and Crerar in particular, enabled the party to obtain rapid electoral successes in the West and rural Ontario, but also doomed the party to an early extinction. Crerar and his associates represented 19th century *laissez-faire* philosophy in that they believed free trade and "fair competition" would solve most of the country's problems and in this sense they were to the right of the Liberals. At the same time they were to the left of the Liberals when it came to more government control over large business corporations, especially transportation interests, and more progressive taxation policies. The Progressives represented the frustration of farmers who recognized that in an increasingly industrialized and commercialized economy their power and influence was declining. But their main solutions were to attempt to resurrect the past and this proved to be impossible. Progressive leaders like Crerar were not, in fact, dedicated to building a permanent party which could govern the country but merely wished to build up a political following which could later be merged with the Liberal party on Progressive terms and thus bring about a so-called re-alignment of Canadian politics. As it turned out the Progressives were to merge with the Liberals on Liberal terms in the late 1920's but not before they had brought about some permanent alterations in the political allegiances of numerous Prairies voters.

The Progressives, a very loose alliance of provincial and local farm organizations, with no national political organization worth mentioning, no party discipline and under inept and divided leadership, managed to elect 65 M.P.'s in the federal election of 1921. This made them the second largest national party—the Liberals having a minority government and the Conservatives about 50 MP's. Crerar and his associates immediately tried to make a deal with the Liberals for a coalition government. When this fell through, due to insufficient concessions from the Liberals and a revolt of rank and file, the Progressives refused to become the official Opposition, leaving that task to the Tories and deciding that they would vote on legislation "according to its merits". The reasons for this move were indicative of the make-up of the Progressives. The dominant Manitoba wing led by Crerar were biding their time until a favorable deal could be made with the Liberals. The Alberta wing, under the influence of Henry Wise Wood, were opposed to parties along conventional lines altogether. They favored group government and/or direct constituency control. Many Alberta members had signed recall pledges before running for office. [19] Most considered themselves accountable to their constituencies only and would often wire back for instructions from the local executive before a Commons vote. Apart from these two factions, a small group of Progressive M.P.'s were sympathetic towards socialism and usually co-operated with J. S. Woodsworth and William Irvine, the two Labour M.P.s elected in 1921. These people became known as the "Ginger Group".

The Progressives, faced with irreconcilable party splits, and subject to the clever political wooing and manoeuvring of Mackenzie King, rapidly lost what little cohesiveness they possessed. Crerar resigned as leader in 1922 and was replaced by Robert Forke, an incompetent from the Manitoba wing who generally acted as Crerar's puppet. The party declined to 24 seats, nearly all from the Prairies, in 1925 and, in the election of 1926, most of the Manitoba variety ran as Liberal-Progressives and henceforth were merged into the Liberal party. However, the Progressive period of ascendency in the early 1920's had left a permanent legacy. The so-called "Ginger Group" under Woodsworth's leadership survived the electoral extinction of the main party, partly because they were more competent and partly because they offered a more basic alternative to the traditional parties. Nearly all the Ginger M.P.'s were from the Prairies and constituted the advanced guard of parliamentary socialism. A significant number of Prairie voters, especially in Saskatchewan and Alberta, had become permanently alienated from the old parties and the Establishment generally. These people provided a base which could be expanded by new political parties should economic conditions seriously deteriorate.

In Saskatchewan the experience of the Progressives in provincial politics was different from the other provinces. In Alberta the U.F.A. swept the province in 1921 and remained in office under conservative leadership and pursuing orthodox policies until they were completely destroyed by Social Credit in 1935. The United Farmers of Manitoba gained office in 1922 ; they were later to merge with the Liberals under the Liberal-Progresive label and became the provincial section of the federal Liberal party. Due to a combination of special circumstances an agrarian party never obtained power in Saskatchewan during the 1920's and this helped to pave the way for the C.C.F. at a later date. In Manitoba and Alberta the agrarian parties gained power at a time when the farmers, though dissatisfied with the economic and political *status quo,* were still obsessed with the free enterprise ethic and unwilling to co-operate with urban labour. Any agitation against the traditional parties would thus be carried on from within a governing agrarian party and from an esentially capitalistic frame of reference. With the traditional parties retaining political power in Saskatchewan and neither farm nor labour organizations being corrupted by power, socialist ideas could be developed within both movements uninhibited by leaders faced with the task of governing within a capitalist economy. Separation from positions of power breeds radicalism. Another influence was that by the late 1920's Saskatchewan farm and labour leaders had had the opportunity to observe, in Manitoba and Alberta, the futility of building class parties with ideologies hardly different from the traditional parties. The reasons an agrarian party did not obtain power in Saskatchewan in 1921, apart from the relative popularity of the existing government, included slick manoeuvring by the Premier and nefarious deals with S.G.G.A. leaders. [20] These events and many more like them by both provincial and federal agrarian leaders, led to a profound distrust of leadership by Saskatchewan radicals which was reflected in the democratic structure and operation of the C.C.F. CCFers were usually vigilant lest their leaders sell out to the Establishment for positions of power. [21]

New development — the F.U.C.

In 1921 and 1922 there began what appears to have been another cycle in the formation of Saskatchewan economic organizations. Since the 1880's the farmers had organized pressure groups and co-operative associations which, in time, became conservative and ineffective. The more militant would form new organizations, political or economic, which, if they took root, would go through the same process in turn. One such organization, begun by men who were obviously tired of the "co-op" elevater companies which were not genuine co-operatives at all and of the cynical manipulations of agrarian political leaders, was the Farmers' Union of Canada (F.U.C.). The founders of the Farmers' Union looked upon electoral politics as futile and believed that the only way the farmers could obtain economic justice would be to build powerful producer co-operatives designed to control the entire market for all agricultural produce.

The founders of the Farmers' Union adopted their ideas directly from the One Big Union of industrial workers, including the Marxist analysis of the O.B.U. The preamble to the constitution was almost a word-for-word copy of the preambule to the O.B.U. [22]

> *Modern industrial society is divided into two classes—those who possess and do not produce and those who produce. Along side this main division all other classifications fade into insignificance. Between two classes a continuous struggle takes place.*

This was then laid out in terms of the farmer's position.

> *In the struggle over the purchase and sale of farm produce the buyers are always master — the sellers always workers. From this fact arises the inevitable class struggle.*

The preamble then draws upon Marxian economic analysis to explain that industry was concentrating in fewer and fewer hands and becoming the sole property of finance, and to combat this, farmers must combine and adapt their organization to changing conditions.

> *Compelled to organize for self-defence, they are further compelled to educate themselves in preparation for the social change which economic developments will produce whether they seek it or not.*

The Farmers' Union had, unlike most farmer agrarian association transcended the idea that free trade and more government control of the big interests of the East could solve their problems. They had accepted the realities of the modern industrial world.

The F.U.C. organized on the same basis as an industrial union. Only farmers could join and meetings were usually secret. There was a considerable degree of centralized authority and discipline. Members who refused to support majority policy could be expelled. At the same time the Union was democratically structured with members of the Executive Boards at both the local and provincial levels subject to recall. Conflict of interest was avoided by forbidding any person who was a Government official from holding office in the Union. Some of these conditions were modified in later years and the similarity to industrial unionism declined but class consciousness remained a permanent feature of the F.U.C. The Union grew very rapidly, helped by unfavourable farm prices, disullisionment with S.G.G.A. and the Progressives, and recruitment among European immigrants who had never been organized by the S.G.G.A. Within two years there were 10,000 F.U.C. members and by 1927 the Union was stronger than the S.G.G.A. and absorbed the older organization, forming the United Farmers of Canada (U.F.C.), Saskatchewan Section.

The Wheat Pool

The main achievement of the Farmers' Union during the 1920's was the popularization of the wheat pool idea and the formation, in collabroation with the S.G.G.A., of the Saskatchewan Wheat Pool in 1923-1925. To set up this organization Aaron Sapiro, the great American co-operative organizer and orator, was brought to Saskatchewan several times and toured the province spreading the gospel of co-operative marketing. The campaign became extremely bitter when the four main dailies, all owned by the Leader Publishing Company which controlled 80% of daily circulation in the province, carried on a scurrilous and hysterical campaign against the Pool and Sapiro personally. The Leader Publishing Company had a virtual monopoly of all the printing, book-binding and office supplies used by the Saskatchewan Co-operative Elevator Company which would undoubtedly go out of existence when the Pool was organized. In addition two of the six or seven shareholders in the publishing company were also principals in an insurance firm which derived a large part of its revenue from the fire and liability insurance of the elevator company.. [23] Many farmers suspected, though it was never proven, that the press was also receiving payoffs from the grain trade. The immediate result was a lawsuit between Sapiro and the Leader Publishing Company but a longer term effect was hatred for the press by the farm community which helped to undermine its influence. Another result was the founding of *The Progressive* as a weekly by the Pool advocates. *The Progressive* (later renamed the *Western Producer*) quickly became the most influential paper read in rural Saskatchewan and displaced the *Guide* which by now had become too conservative for the more socially conscious. *The Progressive,* while ostensibly independent in politics carried on an incessant war against the *status quo* and generally supported the more radical wing of the farm movement and the Ginger Group in the Commons. The Wheat Pool was not as successful as the F.U.C. had hoped, in that it did not gain control of the entire market but it became the most powerful single grain-handling agency and, through its press and local Wheat Pool committees, played a part, along with the Farmers' Union, in training the cadres who would later build the C.C.F. (Today the Pool is a very powerful and conservative institution. Its president, C.W. Gibbings, is also a director of the Royal Bank of Canada and the *Western Producer* is innocuous and reactionary).

The U.F.C. carried out an extensive educational campaign during the latter part of the 1920's, sponsoring J.S. Woodsworth and other radical reformers on speaking tours. Woodsworth was also Ottawa correspondent for the *Western Producer* and became well-known and trusted among Saskatchewanians. The U.F.C. was now the only large farm organization in Saskatchewan and while carrying on the day-to-day battle as a pressure group on behalf of farmers it was in an excellent position to disseminate information. More farmers were now willing to consider radical ideas since there was no longer a Progressive party channelling discontent in a conservative direction and the provincial Liberals, once the progressive wing of the federal party, were becoming notorious for their corrupt and vicious political machine. The Conservatives, as the only alternative party, gained power in 1929 with the help of some remaining elements of the Progressives and the Ku Klux Klan. However, they were utterly destroyed by the Depression and have never recovered as a provincial party in Saskatchewan. With both old parties unquestionably reactionary, the situation was becoming ripe for a left-right polarization of political attitudes. As it became clear that co-operative ventures like the Wheat Pool, though they alleviated the situation, did not solve agrarian problems, the organized farmers began again to consider political action but this time as a means of more basic change than that attempted by the Progressives. The attitude of the Farmers' Union and a considerable number of their followers was expressed in a resolution passed at the 1929 provincial convention. "The farmers are in favour of the abolition of the present system of capitalistic robbery and the establishment of a real co-operative social system—controlled by the producers." [24]

FORMATION AND RISE TO POWER OF THE CO-OPERATIVE COMMONWEALTH FEDERATION (C.C.F.).

In 1930 the U.F.C. abandoned its policy of ignoring electoral politics and formed the Farmers' Political Association which, in co-operation with the Independent Labour Party and left wing remnants of the Progressive, contested 13 of the 21 federal seats in Saskatchewan on a socialist platform. The platform called for the abolition of the competitive system and "the establishment of a co-operative system of manufacturing, transportation, and distribution." [25] Its specific demands included nationalization of all utilities and natural resources, state medicine and abolition of military training. The Association elected no members in 1930 but collected 23% of the popular vote in the contested ridings. The U.F.C. would concentrate more and more on politics as the Depression worsened. The drastic worldwide decline in agricultural prices and repeated drought in Saskatchewan made producer co-operatives temporarily almost irrelevant and the political avenue was all that was left. In 1931 the U.F.C. provincial convention called for the nationalization of all land and natural resources and the instituting of "use leases" whereby the government would own the land and lease it to farmers. This was seen as a way of preventing the land from falling into the hands of the mortgage companies.

The Farmers' Political Association, recognizing the need for allies, amalgamated with the Independent Labour Party in 1931 to form the Farmer-Labour Group which helped to found the national C.C.F. in 1932 and became the provincial section of the new party though it did not change its name to C.C.F. until 1935. The Independent Labour Party had been organized by immigrants familiar with British socialism and was led by M.J. Coldwell, a Regina teacher who was at that time much more radical than in later years. Coldwell became the first leader of the Farmer-Labour Group and it was generally the urban socialists, in collaboration with socialist leaders in the U.F.C., who set the ideological tone and provided the leadership for the party in the first few years. This willingness of farmers to combine with urban labour and follow their leadership was due partly to the U.F.C. experience with industrial type unionism. Other factors were that both groups had long considered large capitalists to be their common enemies and wheat farmers, since they employed little or no labour, did not feel a conflict of interest with urban trade unions. The urban connection at the provincial level was supplemented by the leadership of Woodsworth and other urban socialists on the federal scene. The urban labour leadership of what, in Saskatchewan, was essentially a rural grass roots movement was extremely important in preventing the party from declining into a *petit bourgeois* institution, though it came dangerously close to doing so between 1935 and 1938. The agrarian influence was most evident in the party structure which emphasized active participation and ultimate control by the rank and file. Provincial conventions of democratically elected constituency delegates redefined the program and elected the leadership annually. Between conventions a provincial council representative of all constituencies kept the leadership in close contact with the rank and file. At a time when the traditional parties were blatantly oligarchic and made little pretense of democratic control, this proved an important drawing card for the C.C.F. in rural areas where people had become accustomed to democratic control of local municipal institutions and co-operatives but had never been given a chance to actively participate in determining the policies of the traditional parties.

Social Credit born

The years 1931-1934 were years of consolidation and small gains for the new party with no immediate spectacular success. This was not surprising in view of their radical program and considering that a majority of Saskatchewanians were on relief and hence concerned almost entirely with their own personal survival and vulnerable to the governing authorities. The 1934 provincial election was fought on a hard-line socialist program which called for the nationalization of all private industry, land and resources. When it appeared that the Farmer-Labour Group might gain substantial support they were viciously and repeatedly denounced as Communists of the Russian variety who intended to establish state farms on the Soviet model. The Liberals and Conservatives, the Catholic Church, all daily newspapers and most weeklies carried on a campaign of villification. Economic pressure was common; Coldwell was discharged as principal of a Regina school for his political activities. The party had very little money and no regular press organ. Despite these handicaps the Farmer-Labour Group obtained 25% of the vote and elected five M.L.A.s to become the official Opposition. Though this was an exceptionally good showing under the circumstances many of the party's adherents, even some of the leaders, thought that they would win because of the severity of the Depression. They were disillusioned by the results and a further setback in 1935 when, due partly to the entry of Social Credit, the C.C.F. polled only 19% of the federal vote in Saskatchewan and elected only two of twenty-one M.P.'s. Some farm leaders talked of giving up electoral politics and concentrating on economic organizations; others began to look for a quicker road to political power.

From 1935 until 1938 Social Credit, which had just been swept to power in Alberta, threatened to dislodge the C.C.F. as the main anti-Establishment protest party in Saskatchewan. Social Credit propaganda was directed almost solely against the Eastern financial interests which had always been hated by farmers and especially so now when mortgage companies were seizing the farms. Social Credit promised to cancel interest payments on debts, pay every adult a "social dividend" of $25 monthly and put the banks under some form of government control. This program appealed to many farmers because it looked like it could solve their problems without necessitating the socialization of land. It did not threaten capitalistic values and, hence, could appeal to small businessmen who were suffering from debt and facing ruin but would not go so far as to embrace socialism. Many rank and file CCFers and some of their rural leaders favoured an alliance or merger with Social Credit which they saw as a reform party fighting the same enemies as the C.C.F. There developed a split in the party between ideological socialists and those who wanted a quicker road to power on a watered-down reformist platform. Even some of the formerly committed socialists in the U.F.C. leadership favoured alliance with Social Credit and other "progressive" elements. Coldwell won a federal seat in 1935 and was replaced as provincial leader by George Williams of the U.F.C. Williams had been a hard line socialist but now favoured compromise, and in 1936 the provincial convention, despite strong opposition from Coldwell and Woodsworth, adopted a program which made no mention of socialism, dropped the plank on socialization of land and called for co-operation with other "reform" groups.

Common Front

Between 1936 and 1933 the C.C.F. carried on repeated negotiations with the Conservatives, Social Credit, and the Communists in an effort to establish a common front against the Liberal government. [26] Fortunately no overall coalition was ever achieved but in the 1938 provincial election there were unofficial understandings or "saw-offs" in several constituencies and six Unity candidates, backed by two or more parties, contested the election. The C.C.F. in 1938 ran in only 52 of the seats ; Social Credit contested 41 and the Conservatives ran in 25. This time the C.C.F. Opposition increased to 11 members. The Social Credit elected only two and there were two Unity members. The Conservatives were no longer a factor in Saskatchewan and Social Credit soon disintegrated, helped along by the failure of the Alberta government to implement its Social Credit promises. The C.C.F. was not firmly established as the only alternative to the government and the 1939 convention dropped the policy of attempting to build alliances with other groups. The party returned to its advocacy of a socialist alternative *but it did not return to the radical socialism of 1934.* The nationalization of land was permanently dropped as a policy and the party put more emphasis on offering solutions to specific problems than on attempting to convert the public to socialism as a political philosophy. However, the C.C.F. was still essentially socialist and had escaped the fate of all other Canadian agrarian parties which had begun as protest movements and later became carbon copies of the traditional parties. Many local C.C.F. leaders had had experience in the Progressive party in the 1920's and most had been active in the Wheat Pool or the Farmers' Union. They had decided, often reluctantly, that neither liberal reformist politics nor pressure groups nor co-operatives could cure the ills of the capitalist system. Most of them have yet to recognize the limitations of parliamentary socialism.

After 1940 C.C.F. support in Saskatchewan and across the country began to increase at a phenomenal rate. In the federal election of 1940 the party elected only seven M.P.'s but five of them were from Saskatchewan where the C.C.F. had become the first party among the farmers.[27] The War had brought back prosperity to the country as a whole but conditions remained depressed in Saskatchewan. The fall of Western Europe to the Germans had destroyed the European wheat market and resulted in continued low prices. Wheat Pool committees throughout the province spearheaded a drive for higher prices and sent a mass delegation to Ottawa to demand action. The C.C.F. provincial party and the C.C.F. M.P.'s in Ottawa were the only politicians to give them full support and during the course of this struggle the party more than doubled its Saskatchewan membership. T.C. Douglas, then a federal M.P., became the provincial leader and used his oratorical abilities to great effect. The increased membership brought in enough financial support to allow the party to employ full-time organizers and operate a regular newspaper which was invaluable in propagating to supporters and, through them, the public.

The connections with the Farmers' Union and the co-operative movement now began to pay dividends for the C.C.F. The local farm union and wheat pool leaders, having been exposed to socialist ideas for several years and having a broader view of economic problems, were among the first to join the C.C.F. Lipset emphasizes that these people, having already been elected to positions of responsibility, were the natural leaders of the rural community and hence in a position to popularize a new political creed. The same could be said of the many rural school teachers and Protestant clergymen who joined the movement. They were not intellectuals alienated from their local community as has often been the case with urban socialists in North America.

Grass roots involvement and a regular press organ helped to neutralize the effects of an extremely hostile and unscrupulous provincial press and the economic power which was used to sustain the Liberal government. By 1944 one of every twelve Saskatchewan adults was a C.C.F. member and nearly all of these were farmers or urban workers— the two classes with the overwhelming majority of voters. The provincial party was also strengthened by an upsurge of C.C.F. strength across the country and by the fact that the Liberals, in a desperate attempt to retain office, extended the life of the Saskatchewan Legislature by one year beyond the legal maximum. By 1944 it was obvious that the C.C.F. would win power and, consequently, many local "respectables" who had not identified with the movement when it was struggling for survival, jumped on the band wagon. As is usual with social democratic parties the C.C.F. welcomed these people and gave some of them nominations. This development did not help to make the government any more socialist.

THE C.C.F. IN POWER

The C.C.F. won power in 1944 with 53% of the popular vote and all but five seats in the Legislature. They had been elected on a program of social reform which called for the construction of a welfare state, progressive labour legislation, protection for the "family farm" and some government owned industry. Of the 53% who voted C.C.F. probably fewer than half were committed socialists. Of the others most wanted some measure of social reform and some had voted C.C.F. merely because they were the only alternative to the reactionary and corrupt Liberal government. The government thus had a mandate to carry through extensive social reforms but not to fundamentally change the social and economic system. To attempt fundamental change would have required an extensive and intensive program of socialist education. It would also have been necessary to destroy opposition parties to the point where the C.C.F. became the hegemonic party to an even greater extent than Social Credit in Alberta. Had these things been achieved there would have been the problems of the limited constitutional prorogatives of a provincial goverment and of attempting to operate a socialist economy in one small part of capitalist North America.

The government did proceed to implement what was probably the most advanced social reform program in North America in the face of bitter and often unscrupulous opposition from the Liberal party and their friends in the press and the business community, *particularly the insurance companies.* This program included advanced labour legislation and protection of farmers against foreclosure by mortgage companies. Included were government hospital insurance, an advanced program for the free treatment of the mentally ill and cancer patients and, eventually, medicare. Auto insurance was operated by the government on a compulsory basis and the Saskatchewan Government Insurance Office (SGIO) sold insurance in other fields in competition with private firms. Most of these measures were opposed by the Liberals and very popular with the public and hence helped to keep the government in power for twenty years.

Industrialism

The government successfully expanded existing crown corporations such as the telephone and electric power companies—embarking upon a highly successful program of rural electrification which helped maintain government popularity. They also took some industries away from the private sector and established several new ones. These included a bus line, a tannery, a woolen mill, a box factory, a shoe factory, a sodium-sulphate plant, a seed-cleaning plant, fish-filleting plants, fur, fish, and lumber-marketing boards and a brick yard. A majority of these enterprises were either successful financially or provided services which were needed and appreciated by the public, but some lost money to the point where they had to be abandoned. This was used quite effectively by government opponents as evidence that socialized industry was not practical and they were successful in frightening the government out of embarking upon new "rationalization" experiments. One result was that some of the most important industries, like oil and later potash, were left in private hands though there were also other factors operating in these cases. In its later years the government, in fact, actively encouraged private industry and provided outside investors with financial and other incentives.

Civil Service

It became evident fairly early that, while the C.C.F. government was prepared to implement quite far-reaching and certainly valuable social reforms, they were unable or unwilling (really a mixture of both) to build a radical socialist society. Lipset has pointed out in *Agrarian Socialism* the fact that C.C.F. Cabinet Ministers were overly dependent on their civil servants—most of whom had been political appointees of the previous Liberal regime and many of whom actively impeded social change long after the C.C.F. assumed power. The C.C.F. did bring in a number of socialist experts from other provinces and countries to serve in policy making positions in the bureaucracy but they never carried out the wholesale housecleaning which was necessary under the circumstances. Some Ministers circulated in the same social circles as the upper bureaucracy and the professional elite in Regina and tended to take on the mores of that class. Even in the latter years of the C.C.F. government, after the carry-overs from the old regime had retired and been replaced, the bureaucracy could by no means be described as socialist. The Government boasted that it did not believe in political patronage in the Civil Service. The Civil Service Commission processed applicants for most civil service positons and chose people mainly for their technical competence. Whether or not they were socialist was generally considered irrelevant. [28] The result was that Saskatchewan civil servants developed an excellent reputation in bureaucratic and academic circles throughout Canada for competence and efficiency but, with some very notable exceptions, were not committed to building socialism.

Crown Corporations

A somewhat similar situation prevailed in the crown corporations. The purposes of the crown corporation, as seen by the government and the corporation managers, were to provide necessary services to the public, make money for the government and keep the peoples' money invested in Saskatchewan. These were desirable enough objects in themselves but they ignored workers' control over their own environment. Workers were encouraged to join unions, the closed shop was enforced, and wages and working conditions were generally at least as good if not better than in private industry. However, workers were given no effective voice in management and subsequently remained as alienated from their work as they would be in private industry. That workers should play an active part in determining the purposes, policies and structures of crown corporations seems to have occurred to only a very small minority of CCFers.

Farming

On the rural scene the C.C.F. government helped to protect the farmers against the outside commercial interests by encouraging producer co-operatives, pressing for guaranteed prices and marketing boards on the federal level, and passing provincial farm security legislation which prohibited mortgage companies from seizing a farmer's home quarter section and provided for debt adjustments and moratoriums during years of crop failure. The government also provided such services as farm machine testing, regional agricultural experts to advise farmers, etc. However, all of these things, while protecting farmers from the commercial interests, helped the larger farmers at least as much as the smaller ones. Increasing rural mechanization and its high costs created rural de-population with fewer and larger farms. In time this undermined rural community life as smaller villages disappeared and farmers did more of their business in the larger towns. Grass roots involvement declined and this in turn helped to weaken the C.C.F. The C.C.F. policy of maintaining the "family farm" did little to help defend small farmers and, at any rate, was fighting a losing battle against advancing technology. Because of the tremendous capital needed for technological farming so-called family farms have become increasingly inefficient and in recent years have been threatened by corporate farming which is directly or indirectly controlled by the corporate giants of the food-processing industry. There appear to be only two alternatives to the growth of corporate farms and the creation of a new rural aristocracy and proletariat—government ownership of land or co-operative farming. Government ownership being virtually a political impossibility in the immediate future the only solution would appear to be co-operative farming with active government assistance and intervention. The C.C.F. gave little more than moral encouragement to co-operative farming while in power and has not, since, come to grips with the problem and developed a realistic agricultural policy. The C.C.F. government fought the battles of the agrarian class against their colonial exploiters but did not really attempt to solve the problems of class division and technological change within the farming community.

Co-ops

An obstacle to building a base for radical action was that the government and the party relied almost solely upon electoral action. The co-operative movement which had once been a hotbed of social activists became bureaucratic and conservative. The co-ops had been built mainly by C.C.F. supporters but they neglected to keep them on an ideologically sound basis. Many of them forgot about co-operative principles and concentrated on increasing dividends to members. Some became worse than private employers in their treatment of employees. The Wheat Pool became outrightly reactionary in many respects. Co-op supporters could no longer be counted upon to be consistently progressive. C.C.F. supporters also failed to make concerted efforts to gain control of school boards, municipal councils, hospital boards and other bodies which could control local political decisions and influence public attitudes.

Education

In the field of education the government did not embark upon a program designed to change the social values of the people. The public school system, the universities and teachers' colleges remained essentially oriented towards capitalistic values. A few socialist civil servants in the Adult Education branch attempted to promote an activist program designed to accelerate social change but were told by the government to "cool it" because the Ministers felt that they were moving too fast and stepping on too many toes. The government made little use of the mass media as instruments for promoting socialist values. This neglect or unwillingness on the part of the government led to a frittering away of any base there may have been for radical social change. When it was almost too late the government was to discover during the doctors' strike in 1962 that they did not really rule the province—either economically or ideologically.

The Party

The internal apparatus of the party and the involvement of the rank and file were allowed to deteriorate. Cabinet Ministers retained their posts for years after they ceased to be useful and some became both reactionary and provincial. The same was true of party executive members at the local and provincial level. Internal education was sadly neglected with the result that M.L.A.'s, party officials and rank and file members were often abysmally ignorant. Grass roots activity and control within the party, though it probably remained far more pronounced than in C.C.F. parties in other provinces, declined after years of power. At times in certain parts of the province, especially in rural areas, the co-ops, the Farmers' Union and the C.C.F. (consisting virtually of the same people) had carried on such political, economic and social activities that "the movement" had become an important part of the peoples' lives. This declined with the depopulation of the rural community. Activity in some constituencies declined to the point where it involved only an annual membership canvass, an annual meeting as required by the party constitution, and an election campaign every four years. The leadership soon began to lose contact with the rank and file and this spelled doom to an organization which had to depend upon grass roots activity to offset the economic power of its opponents and a hostile mass media.

The Government

The C.C.F. government was nearly running out of ideas for meaningful social reform when it embarked upon the medicare scheme in

1960, fought one last crusade and won the election on the issue. The buildup to the medicare crisis and the crisis itself illustrated a number of things about the C.C.F. in Saskatchewan. It was obvious that when the government wanted to do something which genuinely offended the powerful interest groups of the province and the country it was operating in a hostile environment which it could not really control. The province was not genuinely committed to even moderately radical innovations. At the same time the response of the rank and file, particularly the militant minority, indicated that radicalism and resourcefulness was by no means dead in the C.C.F. The party leaders badly misjudged the determination of the medical profession and their allies in the economic elite to stop medicare at all costs. They consequently did not prepare the people and did not make adequate preparations themselves for a doctors' strike. The campaign of hysteria by the doctors, the mass media and their reactionary supporters in the Keep Our Doctors' Committees (K.O.D.) was supported by municipal councils, hospital boards and business establishment throughout the province. They generated enough pressure to nearly bring the government down and did force it to make some compromises. The government and party had been unable to respond with enough vigorous counter-propaganda and activity to crush the opposition. Their main response had to be an appeal to peoples' conservative respect for authority; i.e., mass demonstrations and direct action tactics were portrayed as undemocratic and it was emphasized that people should make their judgement at the polls when the time came. The government and the party could not take the offensive but had to "hold the fort". This they managed to do by the skin of their teeth.

On the part of the rank and file there were, especially at the local level, brave and to some extent successful attempts to counter-attack. Local pro-medicare committees were organized, propaganda was distributed and the Farmers' Union and most Labour unions came out in full support (the Farmers' Union lost a considerable number of members over the decision). There would probably have been blood on the streets if party leaders had given the word. The most significant development was the organization during the height of the crisis of Community Co-operative Clinics to be controlled by associations of medical consumers and staffed by pro-medicare doctors. These clinics were organized and financed by the hard core socialists and have become firmly established institutions in the major cities and several of the towns in the province. A significant minority had the vitality to do battle on the political and economic fronts in the face of great odds.

The C.C.F. government survived the crisis of 1962 but lost the election of 1964. The loss was due partly to the fact that medicare had unified the anti-socialist forces against the government and partly because the government fought mainly on its record and offered no new program. The party has now had four years in opposition to reflect and learn from what they did and did not do while in office. Unfortunately there are as yet few signs that they have learned significantly from their experiences. When they regain power, which they almost certainly will, by default if for no other reason, they will perhaps be less radical than they were before. They will be dealing with a radically changed environment from 1944 and even the 1950's. The province is rapidly becoming industrialized and the base of support will have to be urban. The smaller agrarian class are likely to become more frustrated as they are forced to the wall by corporate farming but it is difficult to predict whether this will force them to turn rightward or leftward; it may depend to a considerable extent upon skillful leadership. The whole province is much more attuned to the continentalist outlook of the rest of English Canada than a decade ago and this does not bide well for radical social change.

POST-SCRIPT

Since writing the above article I have spoken to a number of Saskatchewan socialists and been apprised of developments there in the past year. The situation is changing with an agricultural crisis, student unrest, labour dissatisfaction and a much more militant attitude in the ranks of the Indian and Métis minority. Students have built some links to the farm and labour movements as a result of recent campus struggles, especially in Regina. The New Democratic Youth organization is in the hands of radicals, some of whom are also active in the student movement. Red Power advocate Dr. Howard Adams has been elected president of the most important Indian-Metis association in the province. There are at least two study-action groups bringing people together who are working within and outside the CCF/NDP. Is there a possibility of an eventual student-labour-farmer-Red-Power-socialist alliance? Only time will tell.

FOOTNOTES :

1. *Two white leaders were tried for complicity in the Rebellion but were acquitted though at least one, W.H. Jackson, secretary of the Prince Alberta Settlers' Union, had definitely helped the "rebels". Jackson later became a marxist labour agitator in the U.S.*
2. W.A. Mackintosh, The Economic Background of Dominion-Provincial Relations, McClelland and Stewart, 1964, Chapter 4.
3. S.M. Lipset, Agrarian Socialism, Doubleday, 1968, Chapter 1.
4. Ibid., Chapter 2.
5. *E.A. Partridge, one of the founders of the S.G.G.A., was to have a hand in organising most of the protest economic and political groups in the province including the C.C.F.*
6. *The S.G.G.A. had only two Presidents throughout most of its 26 year history.*
7. *Partridge organized many of these groups.*
8. D.S. Spafford, "Independent Politics in Saskatchewan Before the Non-partisan League," Sask., History. Vol. XVIII No 1, p. 9.
9. *T.A. Cretar, a 19th century liberal in economic attitudes, was President of the Grain Growers' Grain Company which was strongest in Manitoba.*
10. *Up until the 1920's and probably later it was common practice for news-papers to support editorially particular political parties in return for an annual cash subsidy.*
11. S.W. Yates, "The SaskatchewanWheat Pool", *published by the United Farmers of Canada* 1942, pp. 88-89.

12. *The Alaska Boundary Dispute with the U.S. at the turn of the century was still remembered in Canada with bitterness.*
13. *Bourassa's Nationalists were challenging the Liberals for the allegience of French Canada.*
14. *J.S. Woodsworth was one of the prominent Western Canadian pacifists.*
15. *Dunning was a classical example of a sell-out. He rose to prominence through the S.G.G.A. and on through to politics. He became premier of Saskatchewan in the 1920's and then was taken into the Federal Cabinet by Mackenzie King to pacify western farmers. The distance he travelled is indicated by the fact that in 1935 King again took him into the Cabinet but this time to reassure the Canadian financial community that the government would be 'safe'.*
16. *Wood was a former American politician from Missouri who brought many populist ideas to Alberta. Alberta was settled by a much higher proportion of Americans than Saskatchewan. American populists had traditional attraction to weird financial theories. Some of these theories were to take root in the U.F.A. and sow the seeds of Social Credit.*
17. *The S.G.G.A. bought farm supplies wholesale and resold them to the farmer, thus bypassing private retailers.*
18. *Women in general did not yet have the vote.*
19. *This meant that they would resign if called upon to do so by their constituency association. This was not legally binding but a moral committent.*
20. *J.A. Mahony, president of the S.G.G.A. and a Progressive M.P., entered the provincial Liberal Cabinet as part of a deal whereby he would use his influence to keep the organized farmers out of provincial politics for the Saskatchewan Liberal government support for the Progressives federally. Premier Mortin double-crossed Mahony and backed the Liberals federally in 1921. Mahony then resigned from the Cabinet and revealed the deal to the public. Other S.G.G.A. executive members had consciously sabotaged attempts at political action so as to protect the provincial government.*
21. *Woodsworth and Coldwell, the first two national leaders, were both offered positions in Liberal Cabinets. Hazen Argue is a another contemporary example of the sell-out.*
22. *D.S. Spafford, "The Origins of the Farmers' Union of Canada", Sask. History, Vol. XVIII, No. 3, pp. 89-98.*
23. *Yates, op. cit., pp. 88-89.*
24. *Lipset, op. cit., p. 103.*
25. *Ibid., p. 106.*
26. *Ibid., chapter 6.*
27. *Ibid.*
28. *The author knows of at least one case of a trade union official whom the Minister of Labour did not wish to hire because he was a well known socialist even though he scored highest in the examination written by all applicants. He was a long time supporter of the CCF.*

Published 1969

THE SASKATCHEWAN CCF

by Arthur K. Davis

IN MORE WAYS THAN ONE, the story of the Saskatchewan Co-operative Commonwealth Federation (CCF) is like the epic journey of the hobbits through the shadow land of Mordor, so dramatically described in J.R.R. Tolkien's saga, *The Lord of the Rings.* The hobbits were little people who lived in a sunny out-of-the-way place called the Shire. They were unheroic country folk, petty burghers with a sharp eye for bargains, property values, and good food and drink. However, put to a test they did not seek, these diminutive rustics, to overcame armies of brutal orcs, underground goblins, giant cave trolls, the Nine Dark Riders of the Enemy, and all sorts of other evil forces. At critical points, to be sure, the hobbits were helped by countervailing supernatural powers ranged on the side of justice and the civilizing arts. The battles were fierce, and often lost, yet the hobbits somehow found the resources to come back and win the next round.

"The road goes ever on and on
  Down from the door where it began.
Now far ahead the Road has gone,
  And I must follow, if I can,
Pursuing it with eager feet,
  Until it joins some larger way
Where many paths and errands meet.
  And whither then? I cannot say."

(Tolkien, Fellowship of the Ring, *62)*

Organized in the depressed, drought-ridden 1930's, the CCF came to power in Saskatchewan, the Wheat Province of Canada, in 1944. For twenty years the only professedly socialist regime ever to rule a middle-level government (that is, State or Provincial) in North America presided over one of the most rural, backward, underdeveloped and ill-favoured regions on the whole continent. Ill-favoured it was, indeed, by an extreme climate, by distance from wheat markets, by lack of capital, and by shortages of trained skills. Yet this latter-day frontier backwash on the northern high plains under rarely favourable conditions could produce the best hard wheat in the world. Even more important, the Saskatchewan CCF pioneered in a long list of progressive social reforms. These included expanding and publicly financed health services, larger and therefore up-graded school units, a generously supported provincial university, inexpensive and compulsory government auto insurance, encouragement of co-operatives, and modern labour legislation that was possibly the best in North American jurisdictions. The CCF reforms also included low-cost public utilities and inter-urban bus transportation by means of crown corporations, and the bringing of modern amenities (like electrical power) to the countryside and the small towns — no small achievements for a sparsely populated, poor province. In the impoverished far northern Metis and Indian settlements, for the first time new schools were built, all weather roads were constructed, a government-operated air service was set up, and a chain of government trading posts was established to break the Hudson Bay Company monopoly. Such were the high-priority goals of the Saskatchewan CCF government, 1944 — 1964.

In 1962 came medicare.

Saskatchewan medicare meant universal, compulsory, tax-financed, prepaid health insurance. Compared with other health plans over the previous three generations in North America, the Saskatchewan plan — though conservative when contrasted with European programmes — was a tremendous break-through. It was a fitting climax to nearly two decades of health-service pioneering. Universal, compulsory hospital insurance in Saskatchewan dated from 1947 — after two generations of accumulating experience limited in local and provincial medical health efforts. And in the summer of 1962, medicare came to stay in Saskatchewan, despite an unsuccessful, last-ditch stand by a doctors' strike that created an international uproar.

Almost everywhere else in North America after World War II, conservative and at times reactionary governments prevailed, with a few exceptions. Yet the Saskatchewan CCF after its landslide victory in 1944 won four more general elections. Then in 1964 it lost a hair-breadth contest to the Liberal Opposition, which conspicuously lacked both positive ideas of its own and well-founded criticisms of the CCF. Indeed, the immediate cause of the overturn had little to do with either the CCF or the Liberals. The immediately critical factor seems to have been the collapse of the provincial Social Credit party: the Liberals inherited enough Socred votes to win. The CCF defeat was confirmed in 1967 by a somewhat wider margin than in 1964, but with no significant change in the peevish character of Premier Thatcher's Liberal government.

How can we explain these paradoxes? Is the CCF era in Saskatchewan an example of the modern tendency of socialism to emerge in backward rural economies, like Czarist Russia and Mandarin China instead of in the advanced industrial countries of western Europe as originally predicted by Karl Marx? Or is it a unique phenomenon that baffles comparative analysis? Is the CCF finished in Saskatchewan, or merely dormant? Something can be said for each of these interpretation. But a different view will be offered here. We shall argue that the CCF in Saskatchewan was populist or petty-bourgeois, never socialist; that it was simply a new phase of "the farmers' movement" which has loomed large in the province ever since the turn of the century; that its similarities to Social Credit in Alberta outweight differences; and that the farmer's movement — though subject to alternating phases of ebb and flow is deeply rooted in persisting economic and social relationships on the Canadian high plains.

Let us look first at the voting results of the nine provincial general elections in which the CCF has participated. For our purpose the popular vote is more revealing than the legislative standings, which we will ignore. It is important to note, however, that in Saskatchewan as everywhere else in North America the rural population is over-represented in the Legislature.

TABLE I
SASKATCHEWAN PROVINCIAL ELECTIONS :
POPULAR VOTE BY PARTIES, IN PERCENTS
1934-1967

	CCF	Lib.	Socred	Conserv.	Other	Total	% Eligible voters Who voted
1934	24.4%	48.5%	——	27.1%	—	100.0%	84.9%
1938	18.3	45.5	16.0	12.3	7.9	100.0	83.8
1944	53.6	32.5	——	11.2	—	100.0	80.3
1948	47.6	31.2	8.1	7.6	5.5	100.0	83.4
1952	54.0	39.3	3.9	2.3	.5	100.0	82.9
1956	45.2	30.3	21.5	2.0	1.0	100.0	83.9
1960	40.8	32.7	12.3	14.0	.2	100.0	84.1
1964	40.3	40.4	.4	18.9	—	100.0	81.6
1967	44.4	45.5	.3	9.8	—	100.0	77.8

Sources : Chief Electoral Officer, Govt. of Saskatchewan
and G.A. Jupp., "Implications of Political Participation for
Social Change," unpb. ms., 1967.

How extraordinary the voting participation in Saskatchewan Provincial elections has been may be seen by looking at the extreme right-hand column in the accompanying table. Jupp found, for eight Saskatchewan elections between 1929 and 1960, inclusive, an average voting turnout of 83 per cent of the eligible voters. For Alberta's nine provincial elections, 1930 — 1963 inclusive, the corresponding figure was only 67 per-cent — a significantly lower turnout (ibid, p. 12). Indeed, only once in the past generation have Alberta voters attained a Saskatchewan level of participation. That was in the landmark 1935 election whan Aberhart's Social Crediters first swept to power. We should also note that after the peak medicare election of 1960, voter participation in Saskatchewan has moved slowly but steadily downward from about 84 to 78 per cent. Even so, the latter figure is well above the national norm. F. Engelmann and M. Schwartz show an average voter turnout of 71 per cent for provincial elections in seven provinces from the 1920's to the early 1960's: Saskatchewan led with 83 per-cent, while Alberta lagged at 67 per-cent, and Manitoba trailed with 63 per-cent. (*Political Parties and Canadian Social Structure*, Prentice — Hall, 1967, p. 40).

Looking now at the left-hand columns of the table, the record shows that the CCF achieved two peaks, 1944 and 1952, the only two occasions during this period when any party won a majority (over 50 per-cent) of the votes cast. Government in Saskatchewan since 1930 has typically been established by plurality decisions in multi-party elections. During the generation we are discussing the CCF and the Liberals have been the major contestants, year in and year out; the Conservatives and the Socreds have functioned as minor parties. But the latter have been important monetheless.

In 1938 the protest vote was more or less evenly divided between Social Credit and the CCF. Differences between these two groups were still not clearly defined; joint candidates were run in four constituencies. However, the Social Credit tide which swept Alberta in 1935 had not produced the promised monetary reforms or the monthly Cash dividends, and voter discontent in Saskatchewan began to coalesce in favour of the CCF. The 1944 CCF landslide followed. But Social Credit resurfaced in Saskatchewan in 1948, when the CCF, the Liberals and the Progressive Conservatives all experienced losses. The Socreds picked up two-thirds of these losses. About one-third went to four independent candidates (usually Liberal — Conservative coalitions) and one Labour-Progressive (Communist) in the heavily ethnic (non-Anglo) far northern and eastside rural constituencies and in Moose Jaw city. Here are the net gains and losses of each party in percentage points, comparing 1948 with 1944. For example, the table shows that the difference between the 1944 CCF popular vote (53.6%) and the 1948 share of the vote (47.7%) was 6.0 percentage points.

Losses (1948/1944)		*Gains* (1948/1944)	
CCF	6.0	Socreds	8.1
Libs	4.0	Others	5.5
Pcs	3.6		13.6
	13.6		

(Source : calculated from Table I, above.)

If we consider per-cent change instead of arithmetic percentage-point shifts, a similar but sharper picture emerges. The CCF loss of 6.0 percentage points in 1948 compared to 1944 was 11.2 per-cent of the 1944 CCF share of the popular vote (53.6%). The corresponding Liberal figure was 11.4 per-cent; the PC figure, 32.2 per-cent. From this standpoint, the two major parties (the CCF and the Liberals) suffered small and equal losses, while the PC's took a much heavier set-back. But if we add most of the "other" vote to the Liberals and the PC's (say 3 and 2 percentage points, respectively) then it appears that the CCF and PC losses in 1948 compared to 1944 were approximately equal (about 11 per-cent of the 1944 share of the popular vote), while the corresponding Liberal loss was only two-thirds as much.

The main Socred surge came in 1956. In that year Social Credit won over one-fifth of the province-wide vote, concentrated in the far northern and northern fringe-of-settlement, east-central and southwestern constituencies. In those areas live relatively larger proportions of small farmers, many village pensioners and certain ethnic groups like the German Mennonites. The Socreds exceeded their province-wide share of the popular vote (21.5%) in 21 of 46 rural constituencies. As in 1948, the Socreds hurt the Liberals much more than the CCF.

Province-wide Voting Changes, 1952 — 1956					
	CCF	Lib	PC	Socred	Other
1. Change in % points	—8.8	—9.0	—0.3	+17.6	+0.5
2. Line I as % of share of popular vote in 1952	—16.3	—22.9	—13.0	+450.	+100.

(Source : Calculated from Table I, above)

The other minority party, the Progressive Conservatives (PC's), went through a surge in 1960 that peaked in 1964, mainly at the net expense of the Socreds. In 1964 the Liberals were also surging, and they continued to show gains in their share of the popular vote in 1967, though at a much lower rate. The CCF gained almost as much in 1967 as the Liberals. Minor-party activity, then, has been very significant in the electoral fate of the two Saskatchewan major parties.

Let us look more closely at percentage-point gains and losses, 1958 — 1967. The following figures show these changes for six provincial elections, each compared with the preceding. Thus, for example, the CCF in 1948 dropped 6 percentage points below its 1944 share of the popular vote, and the Liberals lost 4 percentage points.

Percentage — Point Changes in Share of Popular Vote, Six Provincial Elections, by Parties, 1948 — 1967			
	CCF	Lib.	Combined SC/PC
1948	—6.0	—4.0	+4.5
1952	+6.4	+8.1	+9.5
1956	—9.2	—9.0	+17.3
1960	—4.4	+2.4	+2.8
1964	—0.5	+7.7	—7.0
1967	+4.1	+5.1	—9.2

Source : Derived from Table I

Some interesting facts emerge from this table. In four of these six elections (excepting only 1960 and 1964) the CCF and the Liberals gained or lost shares of the popular vote in concert. That is, they both went up or they both went down, although not equally. And in the same elections, the combined minor-party vote, of course, moved in the opposite directions : when both major parties gained, the combined minor-party share the vote decreased, and vice versa. However, a temporary aberration seems to have occured in the 1960 and 1964 elections. In those contests, the major parties moved in opposite directions, while the minor-party vote fell sharply. Finally over these two decades, combined minor-party gains seem to have cut into the CCF more than into the Liberal vote. Conversely, combined minor-party losses have tended to favour the Liberals, especially in 1964.

More specifically the big CCF drop in percentage points occurred in 1956, when the combined minor-party vote leaped from 6.2 to 23.6 percent of the popular tally. Yet the Liberals lost almost as much. That year the minor-party combination drew about equally from each major party. In 1960 the CCF experienced another loss in percentage points, but only half as much as in 1956. The Liberals gained slightly (2.4 percentage points), and the minor-party vote peaked at 26.3 of the total votes cast. Yet the CCF won substantial victories in terms of Legislature seats in both 1956 and 1960. In 1964, however, the minor-party share fell sharply, mainly to the Liberals, who took over the government. An even greater minor-party decrease in 1967 was translated into almost equal gains for each major party. Judging by the last two elections, the Liberal rate of gain has slacked off, while the CCF is still rising.

WHO VOTED FOR WHOM

Let us now consider what kinds of people voted for which party in Saskatchewan provincial elections. Our main source is Lipset, *Agrarian Socialism,* Berkeley, 1960, and Silverstein, ch. 5 of Part II, *Agrarian Socialism : Twenty Years Later* plus certain studies and impressions of my own. The hard data is sketchy : strong on the side of survey and quantitative census and voting studies, but weak in terms of personal and depth interviews properly sampled.

The record clearly suggests that the CCF from 1944 and ever since has stood on two power bases : the upper-middle and middle-income farmers (especially the grain farmers, less so the mixed grain-and-dairy-or-cattle farmers), and the urban blue-collar workers. The Liberals have relied upon three bases of social power : the mercantile and professional oligarchies in the villages and small towns and cities ; the city white-collar groups ; and the Roman Catholics in town and country. (These three categories overlap in part.) The poorer farmers have been ambivalent : some have opted for the CCF, more have gone for the PC's, the Socreds, and the Liberals.

Secondary to class divisions are those based on religion and ethnicity. Overlapping again is significant. The CCF in rural Satkaschewan was primarily a WASP movement: United Church members, with their emphasis on applied Christian ethnics, have consistenly been over-represented among CCF voters. Anglicans and Lutherans, the next largest Protestant denominations, have leaned toward the rightist PC's-Socreds-Liberals. The Ukrainians (Greek Catholics and Greek Orthodox) have been divided between anti-Soviet and pro-Soviet viewpoints, reflected in pro-CCF and pro-Liberal voting behavior, with lesser deviations toward Social Credit. Roman Catholics have bent heavily toward the Liberals.

In ethnic terms, the predominant British-origin group has split between CCF and PC. The small French enclaves have voted Liberal ; the Dutch and Germans (especially Mennonites) have gone Socred first, and Liberal second. Speaking generally, the Scandinavians are CCF ; the Indians, initially CCF, have switched to the Liberals. (Nothing much having changed since the Liberal victory of 1964, the Indians and Metis could switch again in the near future. But they are important only in two Northern constituencies.)

What about urbanization ? This is a key process in Saskatchewan. Paradoxically, although rooted mainly in rural populism, the CCF has always run higher in the two largest urban areas (Saskatoon and Regina : 1966 population 116,000 and 131,000 respectively) than in most of the rural constituencies. From 1946 to 1966, the province's urban population practically doubled from 25 per cent to 49 per cent of the total ; the farm population fell from 53 to 29 per cent; and the rural non-farm sector (small towns and villages below 1000 people) remained constant at about 22 per cent. The flow of people toward the cities might the CCF in its union labour support, but this does not necessarily detract from its farmer appeal. The village mercantile oligarchies have always been prone to vote Liberal (with large PC and Socred minorities) mainly, I suspect, because of latent resentment against the local social supremacy of the larger farmers rather than because of Liberal ideological ranting. This is not likely to change. Neither is the ranting, however wasted.

Another key long-run trend is age : the population is showing an increasing proportion of younger people. A study of voting in Saskatoon in the 1964 election by Courtney and Smith indicated that the CCF lost out to the Liberals among the younger adult voters. (Silverstein, *op. cit.,* 469.) This is a potentially serious trend for the CCF. On the other hand, the current revolt among students and young people could more than offset this development, provided the CCF takes a turn or two for youth. It is no longer possible in Canada to assume that younger voters have been captured by affluence for the conservative parties, as appeared to be the case in the early 1960's.

A realistic theoretical view of the Saskatchewan CCF is indispensable both for understanding what happend and for guiding future political action in the Shire. While the Shire now means mainly Saskatchewan, the trends in the North American economy are such that Canada itself is becoming another shire. As George Grant has shown, the national business elite in eastern Canada since World War II has — without public debate — opted for inclusion in the affluent American economic empire. Branch-plant capitalism has operated politically through the Canadian Liberal party; it has recently recaptured the Progressive-Conservative party after a decade of Diefenbaker's renagade populism. (See Grant, *Lament for a Nation,* Toronto, 1965.) What really happened in Saskatchewan during the CCF era? The answer may provide a clue as to how the hobbits of North America may deal with the cave trolls that rule the Dark Tower in Washington.

In previous studies, two views of the CCF have predominated. One has emphasized indigenous agrarian unrest; the other, the impact of leaders and ideas imported to the rural hinterlands from urban labour and other metropolitan radical sources outside the high plains. Examples of the first are P. Sharp's *Agrarian Revolt in Western Canada* (Minneapolis, 1948) and D. McHenry's *Third Force in Canada* (Berkeley, 1950). The second approach is best represented by S. Lipset's well known *Agrarian Socialism* (Berkeley, 1950; expanded Anchor edition, 1968). Similarly oriented is L. Zakuta's *A Protest Movement Becalmed* (Toronto, 1964). But the latter study is limited to the CCF in Ontario, where urban labour groups and middle-class intellectuals have always dominated the party.

In our judgment the first perspective is much nearer the truth, for the region west of Winnipeg. In the 1968 edition of *Agrarian Socialism,* the insightful papers of John Bennett and John Richards support this view.

A wider frame of reference is required to include both the rural and the urban CCF movements. We suggest "metropolis versus hinterland." In essence, metropolis dominates its hinterlands politically, and exploits them economically. Hinterlands are sooner or later impelled to fight back: the initial dominance of metropolis is inherently unstable. In North America the main goal of exploited groups has typically been to improve their relative position within the prevailing system. And they usually succeeded — there has been enough affluence since World War I to substitute business unionism for radical unionism, and to subsidize the discontented commercial farmers — more clearly so in the United States than in Canada.

Examples of metropolis-hinterland relationship? For one, the small town and its surrounding market areas in the nearby countryside, so well described by Thorstein Veblen in "The Country Town" (*Absentee Ownership,* 1923, ch. 7). For another, the relationship now prevailing between southern Canada and its far north. Or between eastern industrial Ontario and the less developed Prairies and Maritime hinterlands. Perhaps most significant of all is the metropolitan-hinterland symbiosis which has emerged since World War II between the American empire and Canada.

However, *metropolis* and *hinterland* must not be confused with territorial referents. Every metropolis contains within its boundaries large exploited groups. *Upper-class* and *under-class* are interchangeable terms with *metropolis* and *hinterland,* respectively. In brief, the modern world can be viewed as a hierarchy of overlapping metropolis-hinterland, or upper-class and under-class relationships. The core of the upper class consists of the larger entrepreneurs and corporation managers, along with upper-level government policy-makers and a wide fringe of professionals — advisory lawyers, chartered accountants, and so on. The heart of the under-class is the wage-labour category, especially if organized into unions; together with a fringe of lower-level white-collar employees and of small entrepreneurs. The latter would ordinarily orient toward big business, provided they could make it into that club. When they find themselves excluded, they are sometimes available for anti-establishment stances.

From this standpoint, the CCF in Ontario was an urban under-class movement appealing mostly to trade unions and a few middle-class non-conformists. On the prairies, supporters of the CCF were overwhelmingly the middle and upper-middle farmers uneasily allied with a few trade unions and a handful of professional and middle-class reformers motivated mainly by the "social gospel" — applied Christianity.

Though we shall come back to the "social gospel" later in this paper, let us acknowledge here its prime importance in the Western populist, hinterland reaction against the impact of unbridled laissez-faire capitalism. This reaction was rooted in fraternal and egalitarian sentiments harking back to primitive Christianity, generated by similar conditions of rural scarcity vis a vis urban plenty — by the New Testament rather than by the Communist Manifesto of 1848.

> *"The social gospel of Christianity is difficult to define... Its central purpose was to work for "the Kingdom" in this world. It laid heavy emphasis upon the doctrine of love and proclaimed the principle of co-operation as opposed to that of competition... All across the Canadian West these men helped prepare a fertile ground for the progressive movement, the Social Credit party, and the Co-operative Commonwealth Federation."* (K. McNaught, A Prophet in Politics : a Biography of J. S. Woodsworth: *Univ. of Toronto Press, 1959, pp. 48-50, and ch: IV.)*

But there were other, more important socio-economic developments. They had started earlier, and they stayed later.

A century ago in Canada, the "National Policy" was emerging. Confederation and western agricultural settlement was a competitive response by Montréal and Toronto business interests to the immense industrial expansion of the United States that began in the 1850's and was greatly stimulated by the American civil war, 1861-65. Though absorbed by domestic hinterlands till the end of the 19th century, American economic expansion was potentially a major threat to Canadian enterprise, for all capitalist complexes require expansion in order to survive. As finally crystallized, Canadian National Policy focussed on settlement of the West as the new hinterland cushion for eastern business and finance. Public capital would be made available for private business expansion by means of a heavily subsidized transcontinental railroad (the CPR, completed in 1885), a low-cost homesteading land policy, encouragement of immigration to the West, federally financed research farms to adapt farming technology to the semi-arid western plains, replacement of the Hudson's Bay Co. imperium in Rupertsland by public government (accomplished in 1870), and above all a protective tariff to reserve this vast developmental undertaking for British and Canadian capital against the Americans. (See V. C. Fowke, *The National Policy and the Wheat Economy,* Toronto, 1957; also Ch. 3 *The South Saskatchewan River Project,* Report of the Royal Commission, Ottawa, 1952; and C. Schwartz, *The Search for Stability,* Toronto, 1959.) Fowke neglected to mention another essential policy : shunting Indians onto reserves.

But eastern metropolitan expansion into western Canada by means of the National Policy contained the built-in seeds of a counterattack. Prairie settlement in large part (excepting mainly certain religiously-motivated colonies from central and eastern Europe) was a migration of profit-minded petty-bourgeois Anglos from Ontario, England and the U.S.A. — bent on realizing some fast bucks. These settlers brought with them a cultural heritage of achievement-motivation, of representative government, and of self-help through voluntary organizations. They moved into an isolated region and an unbelievable climate. No words can convey to unbelieving outlanders the extremes of the Saskatchewan landscape and seasons. For a recreation of the epic of prairie settlement, turn to the writings of W. Mitchell, S. Ross, E. McCourt, Jim Wright, R. Stead, F. Grove, Kerry Wood and James Gray — among others ; or see the National Film Board's "Drylanders" and "A Lake for the Prairies." *

POPULISM NOT SOCIALISM

Lipset errs in describing the Saskatchewan CCF as "agrarian socialism". Nor was it an offshoot of the great depression of the 1930's; at best the incredible ordeal of the "dirty thirties" was an accentuating factor. It was an integral part of the "farmers' movement," generated by the regional conditions of family-farm production in a comparatively homogeneous hinterland fighting back against two or three generations of metropolitan exploitation. Its chief ideological orientations was not Marxism, nor even Fabian socialism, but the "social gospel" of

---

* *For a historical background see "The Progressive Tradition" by Lorne Brown in this book.*

Protestant Christianity.

The social gospel movement, though never sharply defined, generally held that what counted in religious life was not only Sunday theological ritual but everyday ethical practice as well. The Industrial Revolution brought great riches for a few, especially in the mushrooming towns and cities. But not everyone accepted the laissez-faire philosophy of the survival of the fittest: that the rich were rich because they deserved to be, and that the poor would prosper likewise if they would just stop drinking, work hard and save their money. The growing contrast between upper-class luxury and mass poverty, and the links established by the muckrakers in the United States between big business and municipal corruption — such tendencies convinced many religious leaders that the gap between pristine Christian values and modern life was becoming uncomfortably wide.

Primitive Christianity, like the Jewish prophets of still earlier times, emerged from an economy of chronic and often acute scarcity. Underclass small farmers, shepherds and artisans necessarily inclined toward sentiments of egalitarianism, brotherhood and self-help through mutual sharing. Were things going badly for the little man because of pressures from rich property owners and urban merchants? Then drive the money changers from the temple. This situation has repeated itself many times. On the Canadian prairies the secular version was, chase the eastern monopolists and their political henchmen from the seats of government; make democratic government work for the common people. Most of the key leaders of Social Credit and the CCF on the prairies were originally preachers in Methodist, Baptist or other evangelical denominations: J. S. Woodsworth, T. C. Douglas, W. Aberhart, and E. Manning — to name but a few.

Calls to build the New Jerusalem in the western hinterlands were numerous and inherent in the regional order of small entrepreneurs. The CCF slogan of "Humanity First" was just another example. There will doubtless be others.

DECLINE OF CCF AND AFTER

In this final section, we face two questions. Why did the CCF lose in 1964? What is likely to happen? Our answers are speculative, like the other attempts to answer this type of question. So far, the best effort is that of John Richards (in Lipset, 1968). However, this needs systematic checking.

The usual explanation of why the CCF lost in 1964 focuses on urbanization and the resulting increase of white-collar occupations, the decrease in the number of farms, the medicare battle in 1962, and the bureaucratization of the CCF government and party — successful protest movements become fat and conservative. These are not satisfactory, although not irrelevant. They largely ignore the voting shifts in the province, and the upsurge of CCF voting in 1967.

We suggest that the Liberal core of power in the upper and middle white-collar classes is likely to grow. Its village core, on the contrary, is likely to be undercut by the urban drift of population, and this sector is vulnerable to right-wing populist appeals by Social Credit and the PC's. The CCF should retain the middle-sized farmers, whose numerical decline may be offset by the growth of labour unions as the new potash and other industries are unionized. The spreading revolt of youth — a new factor — should damage the converative parties considerably more than the CCF. A link-up between (moderately) radical youth and university types, as an idea group, and labour and farm grass-roots could ring the starting bell, provided the university types learn to do their organization homework and to get ride of some of their middle-class blinders. The provincial Liberals should suffer increasingly from their association with a federal administration increasingly identifiable with big-business, pro-American and elitist policies.

The central political fact òn the high prairies is still populism. However relative, deprivation persists among the urban and rural under-classes of the western hinterlands. There are still acute housing short-ages, a tightening cost-price squeeze for farmers and other small pro-ducers, and rising costs for all services, especially education and health. And the gravest questions about the worth or quality of middle-class life are being raised by youth. Radical appeals to the common man should become more potent, not less.

The persistency of western populism has been obscured by party labels. That Alberta and Saskatchewan voters supported Socred or CCF in provincial elections and PC in federal contests, during the last decade, is only superficially paradoxical. Diefenbaker, the prairie lawyer, was a populist through and through. He captured the PC party on the wave of nationwide underclass revolt against the arrogance of eastern metropolitan elites led by the Liberal Party. When the eastern big business interests outsted Diefenbaker as PC party leader in 1967, Sas-katchewan swung back to its local populists, electing six of eleven CCF MP's in June, 1968.

Did the spreading affluence of the last decade undercut the CCF? Did the CCF, by bringing services to the countryside, preside over its own devise? We think not. True, the strongest impression of my first tour of the province in late 1958 was one of "embourgeoisement." The larger towns were seeking and getting all sorts of new services, from dry-cleaning firms and paved streets, to new schools and dentists. Farmers were installing indoor plumbing. Cocktail lounges and mixed drinking places came next year. But affluence is relative — and not all that widespread. The smaller farmers and the urban underclass were not involved.

Was the 1962 medicare ruckus an issue in 1964? I doubt this. The 1960 election was fought specifically on the medicare issue and won by the CCF. By the 1964 election, the 1962 doctors' strike had been long lost by the rash and out-of-touch medical leadership. Medicare was not an issue in 1964. Indeed, the Liberals promised to extend its benefits.

Did the CCF succumb to Michel's "Iron law of oligarchy"? No doubt there was a certain hardening of the arteries in the government

— and the party — but probably no more — less rather — than in other parties. Richards indicates that in the CCF provincial council of 80 members — mostly non-politicians — the party had a built-in defence against bureaucratization, at least to some extent.

My own hunch is that what hurt the Saskatchewan CCF in the early 1960's was the party's federal alliance with organized labour. The farmer entrepreneurs can team up with labour unions in the province mainly because farmers and workers are not directly linked in common economic enterprises. Where labour strikes or costs affect farmers, as in railroads or in grain terminals, sharp conflicts of interest appear. From field experience in the Saskatchewan countryside I obtained a vivid impression of the latent antagonism of CCF farmers toward labour unions. This explains why I have used *CCF* rather than *NDP* as a label in this paper.

The role of the middle-class intellectuals and professionals in the CCF has been ambivalent. On the other hand, they supply the indispensable ideas and social analysis. On the other, they tend to be out of touch with the populist rank-and-file. Leadership by university people in Saskatoon in the early 1960's "put off" many lower-class activists. No grey-flannel image can win. Neither can a straight labour man. Least of all, an Easterner who can be tagged as a Labour henchman or a city slicker with creased pants and polished shoes.

In short, the Saskatchewan CCF, unless it is seduced by "concensus politics" seems certain to rise again. Its main hope lies in polarizing (within limits) the political spectrum, not in offering something for everybody.

But now let us consider a wider perspective. Canada has willynilly become an annex of the American empire. The Shire is national, as well as maritime or western. How can the hobbits recapture their domain? How can they link up with the underclass hobbits in the United States heartland? Perhaps even more important, how can they relate to the underclass hinterlands abroad — in Latin America and Africa and southeast Asia? To answer these questions, the homework has not been done. The essential workings of the economic and political systems have not been sufficiently researched, let alone made plain.

A generation ago, the CCF and Social Credit surged to power in the western high plains by means of local study groups, rooted in a social movement from below, and led by alienated middle-class professionals (mainly preachers and teachers) and by middle and upper-middle farmers. In both cases, a world-view was successfully established. The similarities and differences — behaviorial and ideological — between these two social movements have yet to spelled out. It is my hunch that the similarities significantly outweight the differences. Why did Saskatchewan go CCF while Alberta went Socred? This key question I still cannot answer. Meanwhile, the world has changed during the past fifteen years. New study groups and study kits are needed. *Above all, a new people's movement.* The latent popular basis is already there. But social movements are not generated by professorial papers like this one. They come from the people and from people-rooted leaders.

This raises the leadership question. As in Alberta, the people's movement in Saskatchewan was led by a charismatic leader. When preaching the social gospel on the high plains, Tommy Douglas could roll up his audiences with his vision of the New Jerusalem. He was doubtless the greatest orator in North America — given the context of the prairie farmers movement. Greatness is a result of a special empathy between the leader and the led.

Douglas' successor, Woodrow Lloyd (a former teacher and officer of the Saskatchewan Teachers Federation, and CCF Minister of Education for a decade and a half in the Douglas cabinet) — became Premier of Saskatchewan in November, 1961, when Douglas resigned to become national leader of the new-born New Democratic Party. It was a bad time to leave, and there were critical waverings in the Saskatchewan CCF government. But the medicare crisis of 1962, precipitated by the blind refusal of the Saskatchewan College of Physicians and Surgeons to accept the people's 1960 election verdict in favour of prepaid, universal and compulsory health insurance, — this crisis resulted in a resounding defeat of the medical dinosaurs. The doctors' strike in the summer of 1962 was a dead loss. Lloyd's government stood like a rock. Yet it refused to take off the gloves with the misguided doctors, despite immense provocation. Perhaps this was a mistake. The doctors, who make a very fat living from other people's misery, were sitting ducks for an all-out attack on "blood-suckers and leeches." Mistakenly or not, Lloyd took a conservative line. He saved the doctor's collective face, not in their interest but in the public interest.

continued upper part of next page

COMMENTARY

by Lorne Brown

Although Professor Davis' article presents us with some useful insights into the CCF in Saskatchewan he is, I feel, in error when he claims that there were more similarities than differences between the CCF and Social Credit. Davis is largely correct in his metropolis-hinterland analysis and in depicting the two movements as part of a revolt against the colonialism of the Toronto and Montréal capitalists but he exaggerates the socio-economic similarities of Alberta and Saskatchewan. There were significant economic differences, with Alberta being a much more diversified economy and not nearly so dependent upon a one-crop economy. There was more mixed farming and ranching in Alberta and much less dependence upon grain as a cash crop. There was more business and industry and hence a larger and stronger business-oriented bourgeoisie. The religious and social

Despite two lost elections (1964 and 1967) Lloyd has grown in stature in Saskatchewan. As much as Tommy Douglas, he is like Gandalf the ageless wizard in Tolkein's saga. There is no one in sight to challenge his party leadership. Urban business and professional types wearing polished shoes? A Madison-Avenue image in Saskatchewan is doomed. Allienated young people? The over-30 and under-30 cleavage is a misleading split, though not entirely irrelevant.

Such categories are insufficient. Douglas and Lloyd were only parts of the people's movement in Saskatchewan. The movement generates leaders; leaders mold the movement. In a period of downswing, someone from the rank and file may jump up and say, "Let's go." And a new surge starts. It's as simple as that — and as unpredictable. (For a good example, see J. McCrorie, *In Union is Strength*, pp. 48-49, on the 1948 meeting in Saskatoon, which saw a rebirth of the Saskatchewan Farmers' Union.)

After a lost battle, calls inevitably arise for new strategies, new leaders, new tactics, new images. This is understandable, but not necessarily valid. Looking back on prairie development, and viewing it in a nation and continental context, much has changed — yet (after allowing for counter-actions) much remains the same. Prairie farmers and prairie labour unions and working people are still relatively deprived categories. Young people have greatly changed. Hinterland still confronts metropolis.

---

outlook of the people of the two provinces was strikingly different. Alberta had a much larger proportion of American settlers who brought with them an individualistic and rightwing fundamentalist outlook in religion. Saskatchewan by contrast was much more influenced by British immigrants, many of whom were aware of Labour party ideas. The Protestant Christianity which was dominant in Saskatchewan was, as Davis points out, of the liberal "social gospel" variety and not a personalist fundamentalism with the over-riding emphasis on individual salvation.

Social Credit and the CCF had some similarities in that both denounced the Eastern capitalists in the 1930's and both took the side of the debtors against the creditors. For a few years there was even limited co-operation between the two movements in some areas. But the two parties were, for the most part, radically different in structure, leadership, ideology and practical policies. Social Credit (See J.A. Irving, *The Social Credit Movement in Alberta*, U. of T. Press, 1959) was exceptionally authoritarian in structure from the very beginning and dependent upon a charismatic leader, Aberhart, who controlled the party

continued next page

even to the point of personally choosing all candidates for public office. The leadership of Social Credit has always been in the hands of conservative fundamentalist Christians with an extreme authoritarian bent. The partys main ideology has consisted of a 'Back to the Bible' emphasis plus the lunatic financial theories of Major Douglas. The party has consistently been opposed to socialism, the welfare state and organized labour and frequently turns election campaigns into anti-socialist crusades. Party spokesmen quickly forgot about the Eastern capitalists and developed a demonology revolving around the threat to Christian civilization from world Communism. Sometimes the "international Jewish conspiracy" was included for good measure. Even the early party was supported by small town merchants and a significant section of the urban *bourgeoisie*. In a very few years Social Credit had completely sold out to the business community, were financed by Big Business, and supported by the Establishment press including the Edmonton *Journal,* which must be the most right-wing daily in Canada. Today Social Credit is in the hands of more orthodox conservatives, and in recent years E.C. Manning has been attempting to bring about a new conservative alliance. (See E. C. Manning, *Political Re-alignment,* McClelland and Stewart, 1967.)

The CCF, while its membership consisted mainly of farmers, was undoubtedly social democratic (with a strong populist influence) in theory and practice. The populist influence made the CCF more internally democratic than most socialist parties and does not appear to have made it less radical than it would otherwise have been. The Saskatchewan CCF was consistently to the left of its Ontario counterpart on most issues and was at least as socialist as the mainstream of the Labour Party. The leadership of the CCF, including the secondary leadership, consisted mainly of urban socialists and the socialist wing of the farm movement. Many Saskatchewan farm leaders had had experience in the urban labour movement, some in the O.B.U., and were ideological socialists. (See Spafford's article in *Politics in Saskatchewan,* edited by Ward and Spafford, 1967.) The CCF government, of course, implemented many social welfare but few socialist policies. This does not prove it was not a social democratic party. It is merely another example of the results to be expected when social democrats achieve parliamentary power.

What one should be attempting to understand is why, even given some dissimilarities in the socio-economic make-up of the two provinces, the people of Alberta and Saskatchewan attempted to solve their problems by electing radically different protest parties. This is an area where a great deal more hard information is badly needed. How much was due to historical accident, errors of strategy on the part of the Left, and other factors which have little relation to sociological conditions. Could the CCF have been more radical given the socio-economic circumstances and the limitations of provincial power or would viable socialist alternatives to the CCF have been possible? What is to be done by radical socialists in Saskatchewan at the present time?

SOCIALISM
AND THE N. D. P.

by Richard Thompson

Aspects of Social Democratic Parties

Social democratic 'movements' in neo-capitalist countries in the contemporary world have very sharp limits built into their policies and party organization. The Saskatchewan NDP, as such a party, faces the same limitations. At the same time there are *individuals* within the NDP (as in other social democratic parties) who consider themselves 'socialists' in the sense that they believe in and/or espouse changes that transcend the welfare state. It is the contention of this paper that as individuals they can do little more than make minimum quantitative changes in the policy of the party. It is actually unnecessary to look beyond Saskatchewan to see that this is the case and to confirm the thesis that social democratic parties, once in power, are unable to enact even the limited reforms that they put forward.

A reformist party in power faces two choices: it can help to administer neo-capitalism so as to make it run more smoothly or it can attempt to bring in new welfare measures. If it does the latter it must find a source of funds for redistribution. If these funds are taken from taxing the surplus value of neo-capitalist corporations it will result in the stagnation of the economy which in the long run will wipe out the gains made through extended welfare. If these funds come from the more 'affluent' members of the working class (or the farmers) electoral support from these groups will be undermined. If the reformist party chooses the former of the two paths, administering neo-capitalism, then it must drop its most meaningful welfare reforms from the very start. Thus social democracy has *a priori* limits on its ability even to maneuver reforms.

André Gorz, in considering the difference in strategy between Reformist and socialist parties states that:

> It is the difference between granting reforms which perpetuate the subordination of the working-class in factory and society; and reforms imposed, applied and controlled by the masses themselves, based on their capacity for self-organization and their initiative. [1]

In other words it is a qualitative difference which goes beyond such partial and quantitative measures as the redistribution of wealth under a reformed capitalism. It is unlikely that social democrats could make major social reforms but even if they could it would not necessarily bring into question the quality of life under capitalism and how this is effected by the relations of production. It is possible to enact certain limited and fragmentary changes in this area via legislation (e.g. the elimination of cigaret advertising or controls on planned obsolescence) but the rationality of profit still remains and its logic will continue to determine, among other things, the quality of life in neo-capitalist society. It is a top-down logic (in the same sense that any reforms of it are imposed from the top) and as such it must necessarily tend to *pacify* subordinated classes and repress any autonomously emerging needs before they can be fully articulated.

It is precisely because certain needs are smothered (and new needs created) within advanced capitalism that reformist parties must always gravitate towards the position of *administering* the bourgeois *status quo*. [2] Not only is this the case at present but it is becoming increasingly true. Profits constitute a smaller and smaller portion of an increasing economic surplus as time passes which means that while the modes of control over the subordinated classes increase both quantitatively and in their degree of sophistication there is simulataneously a decrease in the rate of profit under capitalism, [3] a decrease which undercuts reformers' attempts to implement redistribution.

The most common argument used against any proposed 'radical' change in the program of the NDP defends 'gradualism' on the basis that: "We must get the voter's support before we can do anything." Such an argument — one which calls into question methods rather than ends — should be met first on its own ground, the *method* is inadequate.

Votes give men the right to rule, noted Marx, but not the power to do so. The logic of the ballot is a logic tightly locked within the confines of the existing social order. At best it can mobilize, in a *passive* and not an active way, the votes of a section of the population with a common political consciousness. Only secondarily (or incidentally) does it attempt or effect any development of consciousness. Because its primary goal is the mobilization of votes for *its* ends rather than the mobilization of people for their collective end(s) then it is unable to mobilize anyone (with the exception of some of its own bureaucrats [4]) if it comes to power.

Social democratic parties are bureaucratic. Gramsci remarks that bureaucracy within a political party "is the most dangerous habitual and conservative force; if it ends up by constituting a solid body, standing by itself and feeling independent of the masses, the party ends by becoming anachronistic, and in moments of acute crisis becomes emptied of all its social content, like an empty shell." [5] The feeling of being independent of the masses, and subsequently not feeling responsible to them, derives from the actual objective separation from the masses with which the NDP is faced. Within the NDP major policy decisions are

105

not made by the general membership (to argue otherwise in the present situation is to extrapolate formalism to the ridiculous). Thus the paradox, if indeed it is a paradox, of a party which 'represents the people' by consistently ignoring the people.

This is not being particularly unfair. The techniques of the reformist party, techniques which can in no way be abstracted from other facets of the party such as structure and program, *have to be* primarily empirical and survey-like. The parallel with advertising technique, although it is often overdrawn, is not inapplicable in this situation. Thus, fairly recently, an NDP committee discussed, among other things, the pros and cons of building up certain 'charismatic' candidates in the next provincial election. It appears that certain of the NDP's "hidden persuaders" are not unwilling to learn from the Trudeau experience. There is little point in harping on this particular point except to note in passing that it is indicative of the predominant political methodology of the party. [6] The people are effectively being ignored because all that can be expected from public opinion techniques (whether they be ballots, polls, or cruder methods) is a regurgitation of the forms of consciousness (ideology) generated by bourgeois society within its media, its institutions and within the alienated labour upon which it rests. Lipset noted before 1950 that "the Saskatchewan CCF is sowing the seeds of opposition to socialist change" [7] and although he may have been stating only part of the case it is a part that cannot be ignored.

Bureaucratization

The bureaucratization of the party stems from its inability to maintain a politically active and conscious base among the population. Thus the party, initially a *mass party* [8] with fairly firm roots in the major sectors of the subordinated classes, has become transformed into a bureaucratic *electoral party*. The essential dialectic operative between leadership and the base (members and supporters) has been undermined and thus the once organic nature of the party is being constantly superceded by fragmentary and individualistic styles of organization. [9]

The changes (and inadequacies) of the NDP's program, which constitute the most common target of criticism from the left, are more than casually related to party organization and to 'political method'. The alienation of the party from the masses (which is institutionalized within every aspect of party organization) also separates the party from the masses in terms of program. Party policy tends increasingly to be formed out of abstractions rather than out of concrete societal relationships. This is repeatedly demonstrated in the way reformist parties deal with questions such as poverty which is transformed into a thing-in-itself, into an abstraction, and hence there is a failure to situate the specific problem in its general context. The resulting party policy, based on an abstraction, is a reflection of the isolation of the party from the masses. It is extremely fallacious, given the dialectic operative between party organization and party program, to repeat the mistake of the social democrats and criticize them only on the basis of policy. To do so is to fail to understand the problem in its totality : to do so is to understand policy as a thing-in-itself, as an abstraction.

Socialist Strategy in Saskatchewan

Almost all neo-capitalist countries have produced social democratic parties which operate within the electoral arena to effect reforms within the context of neo-capitalism. They act as a vehicle whereby the most glaring social evils become exposed and acted upon (whether by the reformist party itself or as a result of its having articulated the problem to the public at large). The question which plagues socialists the most is the problem of their relationship to these social democratic parties. There exist two clear alternatives in this situation : to act in an organized manner within the reformist party in order to transform it or to build towards a new party. Unfortunately there is usually no clear strategy at all and the result is that many socialists dissolve themselves (rather uncritically) within the reformist party or that they become ineffective cynics. In either case they reduce themselves to isolated individuals and thereby preclude the possibility of developing an organic and coherent alternative.

It is precisely the emergence of a coherent alternative (which must exist at all levels of the party in an integrated manner) for which socialists must work if any fundamental change is to be brought about. The elevation of policy into a thing-in-itself is *de facto* the very same error that is made by ardent social democrats whose almost sole concern is with 'organization' in the abstract, organization without content. But this does not answer the question in the short term, it merely states the prerequisite harmony between theory and practice that must exist for the evolution of an effective mass socialist party. What must be raised is the problem : under what conditions can a new party come into being ? Further, perhaps, we can ask whether or not the contradictions inherent within social democratic parties are such that it can realistically be supposed that they will *in themselves* participate in laying the groundwork for an explicitly socialist party. This latter question is crucial in deciding what relationship socialists are to have to the NDP in Saskatchewan.

The former question, that of the requisite conditions for the energence of a mass revolutionary party, can only be dealt with generally in the scope of this paper. We can, however, note that historically we are entering a new stage of revolutionary activity which cannot be understood on anything but a global scale. The breakdown of the tight bipolar system (of the cold war) by the early sixties, which followed on the heels of a series of nationalist movements in sections of the third world (notably Africa) and the subsequent, and parallel, development of revolutionary anti-imperialist movements throughout the whole of the third world, is one of the most important factors internationally. The Black movement in the U.S. (which is not without its tangible effects on both Black and Indian people in Canada) and the student

107

movement internationally also find their major historical roots in the late fifties and early sixties. Similarly we can point to the crisis in international currency (which is ultimately irresolvable within international capitalism) and the accompanying mild stagnation of the North American economy(ies), the primary brunt of which is borne by the working class and, on the Canadian prairies, the farmers.

It is necessary to specify conditions to a much greater extent than is done in the above paragraph. In the agrarian-based Saskatchewan economy (where the small farmer faces the ever-growing effects of monopoly in the sectors of the economy on which he depends most directly: in production inputs and also the output market) the squeeze of international capitalism is paving the way for corporate land-holding and the subsequent transformation of the small 'independent' farmer into a wage-worker (whether on a corporate-owned 'farm' or in the city). The decisive factor in this process is the political response it engenders and the resultant change in consciousness that it brings to the farm population. The second factor, in considering Saskatchewan, is the satellite-like nature of the other primary sectors of its economic base (e.g. potash, with an unstable international market; mining in the North, which is an exclusively extractive process; and pulp and paper, which is subsidized by cheap labour and indirect forms of Provincial government aid). The urban service sectors are, of course, almost totally dependent on the above-mentioned economic determinants. [10]

The role of the State

It is crucial to any party which recognizes and attempts to come to grips with the growth of monopolization (and the concurrent satellization of 'peripheral' sectors of the economy) that that party fully understand the role of the state in this development. To a greater and greater degree the state plays the role, as Lenin put it so well of being the servant of the bourgeoisie. Mandel notes that:

> The state ... becomes to an increasing extent an indispensable instrument for the monopolies. The realization of profit — and not just average profit, but the superprofit which they regard as their right — can no langer depend on the mere working of "economic laws"; the state's economic policy must, when necessary, render these very "laws" harmless, when their operation threatens the profits of the monopolies. [11]

The Canadian federal structure of government provides for a 'division of labour' in this respect. The provincial governments (for both historical and economic reasons) play a major role together with the federal government of promoting the interests of the monopolized sector of the corporate world. Two blatant cases in Saskatchewan being, under the Liberal government, potash and pulp.

All of this is not to suggest that the realm of choice available to the government was large in scope and that it (the provincial government in this instance) could have realistically done anything else. Quite the contrary, as long as capital formation occurs almost exclusively within the private monopolized sector, then the government, lacking any realistic autonomous source of development capital, must *of necessity,* opt for a policy which can do nothing but promote the continued aggrandizement of the monopolies via super-profits. It is essential that any socialist party understand this point: social democratic parties do not fail simply because they are co-opted (in the limited sense of the word) but because it is virtually impossible to find any ground on which to maneuver.

It is clear out of all this that the objective economic reality of Saskatchewan has changed dramatically since the twenties and thirties. The *Regina Manifesto,* the initial and most radical expression of social democracy in Saskatchewan, was born in an era when the 'frontier' society of the West was being consolidated within the North American economy. The Co-ops, the various Farmers' Movements, the CCF and so on were, primarily, the radical expression of this consolidation. Organizations such as the Wheat Pool provided the farmer with collective protection of his needs in a manner which could at least partially counter the position of power held by companies like the CPR and the independent wheat dealers. It was also possible, within the early, agrarian-dominated Saskatchewan, for the provincial government to maintain a *relative* autonomy vis a vis the corporate world. The so-called 'history of compromise' of the CCF in power is, in fact, primarily a history of changing conditions. The social democrats, even in their most radical policy formulation, had neither a theoretical understanding of the new emergent problems nor a vehicle with which to tackle them. The major reason for this has been that the changes in the province have not been merely quantitative ones (e.g. an increase in the power of 'Eastern business') but qualitative : the old frontier was at first consolidated and integrated into the mainstream North American economy, now it is being systematically exploited by the integrated and highly monopolized institutions of advanced capitalism.

What is clear, given the change in the social relations of production, is that the objective basis for the emergence of a new radical socialist party is developing. This is due, not only to the afore-mentioned changes in the economic fabric of the province and country but also to the new wave of socialist thought which is sweeping the paraphenalia of cold war mythology into the waste basket of history, where it belongs. The national and local expressions of the growing global change in consciousness still remain in relatively primitive forms and are restricted (in terms of their major implications) to a relatively small number of people. The past year has amply demonstrated, on a number of fronts and in particular among students, that this embryonic development is historically irreversable (except in the unlikely case of fascist repression).

Social democratic parties, whose origin coincides roughly with the end of the compitative stage of capitalism, are structurally and ideologically incapable of coping with the new problems. This is the main source of the difficulties of social democracy which I dealt with in the first section of this paper. The question still remaining, however, is whether or not the internal contradictions of reformist parties merit socialists working within those parties, in this case the NDP. The major internal contradiction is between the electoral base of support (the most politically conscious sectors of the oppressed classes) and party policy and organization. Without attempting a definitive answer to the question at hand it is possible to outline two alternatives for active socialists at this time.

The ideological insight

One of the most important insights of Mannheim, in *Ideology and Utopia,* is that "the opportunity for relative emancipation from social determination, increases proportionately with insight into this determination." [12] It is for precisely this reason that young socialists must have an understanding of the nature of social democratic parties if they are to *consciously* build towards any alternative. For a socialist the "relative emancipation" of which Mannheim speaks is in fact the relative power to make history. It is possible only when organically constituted socialist forces are able to retain at least a relative *autonomy.* [13] The two alternatives, building a socialist movement outside the NDP or acting as an open and organized caucus within that party, both imply the retention of autonomy vis-a-vis ideology and organization for socialists.

The latter alternative, that of acting as an organized caucus within the NDP, presupposes that the degree of autonomy will permit relatively independent political action (non-electoral action, organizing a mass base, etc.) *as well as* the advocating of a coherent socialist program. The criticism of the Party as it is now constituted, would be a criticism of both its policy and of its organizational structure but more important, it would be expressed not merely verbally but concretely and in every instance through the practical action of the socialist caucus. The key to the practicability of this mode of organization is the *recognition* that it constitutes *merely a short-term-strategy.* The initial forms that the organization assumes and the kinds of political projects it adopts will be constantly superceded as its strength and understanding grows. At some stage the 'caucus' must deal with the irreconcilability of its aims and organization with those of the social democrats. The response to this form of crisis will, of course, depend on the matrix of political conditions at that time.

The second alternative, that of laying the groundwork for a socialist party outside the NDP, would not radically differ from the first alternative in its major implications. It has several advantages, for example, the problems of 'Provincialism'* could be dealt with more easily. The major argument for total autonomy would appear to be the concern about co-option. The assumption that socialists working within social democratic parties must necessarily be rendered ineffective (and end up by integrating themselves into the structures of the social de-

---

* *i.e., the tendency to restrict political perspectives to the provincial arena due to the balkanization of the Canadian political economy.*

mocratic party) is *absolutely* true if working within the reformist party is to mean doing so as individuals and without any long term socialist strategy. It definitely *need not* be true for a caucus. The main argument against attempting to establish a new party at this time is fairly obvious : there does not yet exist a sufficient base upon which to build. It is possible, within the next several years, to build that essential base for a socialist movement and if an effective caucus can be established there seems little doubt that this goal can be achieved more quickly.

1. *Gorz, "Reform and Revolution" in* The Socialist Register : 1968, *Merlin Press (London,* 1968), 124.

2. *The dismal failure of the British Labour Party is summed up by social democrat Michael Lipton's disillusionment when he asks : "How did the Labour Government, with its many able men and its great initial impetus, come to sacrifice ends to means ... ?" (See* Matters of Principle : Labour's Last Chance, *Penguin,* 1968, 17). *An indication of the Labour Party's 'dilemma' is reflected in the 'nationalized' sector of the British economy. Mandel notes that : "Out of 272 seats on the boards of Britain's national- ized enterprises, 106 were occupied in 1956 by directors of private firms (of whom forty-nine were directors of private insurance companies and thirty-one were bank directors)." (In Ernest Mandel,* Marxist Economic Theory, Volume II, Merlin Press, London, 1962, 502.) *This type of situation could only exist because the originally dynamic view of 'national- ization' of enterprise has been reduced and maintained only in legal form just as British 'socialism' has likewise been reduced to mere appearance. Lipton's "sacrifice of ends to means" is in fact the total abandonment of socialism and its replacement by a watered-down rhetorical facade.*

3. *The accumulation of 'super-profits' within the capitalist economy during its monopoly stage does not contradict Marx's view (in* Capital) *that the rate of profit declines within the capitalist economy. First of all, the number of capitalists is reduced in the monopoly stage and, secondly, mo- nopoly super-profits are by-and-large tied to monopoly re-investment and expansion. The* realized *rate of profit, for the capitalist class as a whole, still declines.*

4. *Even on this score it is not well off. Two decades ago S.M. Lipset argued that : "The fact that extensive participation in the Saskatchewan CCF is not a result of the growth of a new political movement or of some characteristic inherent in the CCF becomes clear if the organization is compared with the party elsewhere in Canada where it has been successful."* (Agrarian Socialism, *Anchor Books, N.Y.,* 1968, 259.) *He goes on to argue that the ratio of elected posts to members (in agrarian organizations such as the Wheat Pool, etc.) was very low. The great numbers of respons- ible officials (and petty-officials) during the early phases of the farmers' movement allowed for much better contact with the 'grass roots' supporters. This phenomenon has diminished in quantity and quality. The ratio is higher but also real power has shifted almost totally to the top bureaucrats in organizations such as the co-ops and the NDP.*

5. The Modern Prince and Other Writings, 175.

6. *In a Saskatchewan NDP document titled "Evaluation of the* 1968 *Federal Election Campaign" there is not one mention of the NDP's program during the campaign (this is generally consistent with all the literature circulated by the party). The survey questions (asked, of course, of MLA's, campaign managers etc.) are indicative of the predominant political methodology of the party, e.g. "Question 1. What were the most beneficial practices carried out in the campaign in your constituency ?"*

7. Op Cit., 278.

8. *i.e. a radical social democratic party not socialist. However, it was a mass party.*

9. *The so-called 'pluralist' structure of electoral parties in liberal democracies, when applied to social democratic parties, is catastrophic, " ... demands for individual consumption and wages which remain of primary importance for poor regions and categories cannot serve as a unifying theme for the workers' movement. The political unity of the working class ... can only be constructed around themes which transcend immediate interests towards a synthesis at a higher level. Thus ideological and political work, the critique of the 'consumption civilization' and the elaboration of a model of change become determinate." (Andre Gorz, Op Cit., 127. Emphasis added.)*

10. *The service sector itself is, of course, far from 'being free of monopolistic structures.*

11. *Mandel, Op Cit., 507.*

12. *Harcourt, Brace & World, Inc. (N.Y., 1936), 47-48.*

13. *Lenin's insistance, between 1903 and 1917, on retaining an autonomous bolshevik party speaks less to the specific democratic centralist features of that party than to the fact that it retained organizational and ideological autonomy within the milieu of socialist and social democratic forces. It was thus able to pursue, within the context of pre-revolutionary Russia, what Marx referred to as his favorite motto : "the ruthless criticism of all that exists."*

Published 1969

THE N. D. P. SINCE ITS FOUNDING

by Evelyn Dumas and Edouard Smith

> *"This party is approaching the responsibility of power. It has responsibility and great influence. If we are to be responsible we have to forego the luxury of extreme stands."*
>
> Andrew Brewin at the 1967 N.D.P. Convention

The New Democratic Party was a stillborn child of Canada's old left. Canada's social democrats retained their virginity however, longer than their West European counterparts. But in 1956, at its Winnipeg convention, the C.C.F. caught up with the times and rejected the most radical aspects of the Regina manifesto of 1933. It played down references to socialism and did away completely what was left of both its pacifist heritage and its commitment to collective ownership of the economy.

The Regina manifesto would not appeal to contemporary radicals. It was highly centralist (favouring concentration of power in Ottawa), and this despite the fact that Canadian socialism made its first major advances in a provincial context. It privileged state ownership despite the fact that its popular basis was largely in the Prairie co-operative movement, as witnessed by the name of the party, the Co-operative Commonwealth Federation.

But the C.C.F. had genuine appeal through its spirit and the vital relationship it achieved between a grass roots movement and its leaders. In federal politics, the party was foremost the conscience of the nation, and never really aimed at power. In the one province where the C.C.F. held power, Saskatchewan, the leadership of the party channelled a popular protest movement against big capital and Eastern financial power into a British labour party model while a similar movement in the neighbouring province of Alberta was directed to ultra-conservative social creditism.

Outside Saskatchewan, the C.C.F. appealed to radical reformers, people who believed profoundly in the extension of the welfare state and to middle-class liberals concerned with civil liberties, peace, defence and foreign aid. But the failure of the C.C.F. to ever develop, much less promote an indigenous ideology based on the radicalism of its constituency (which it actually restrained) made it very weak before the onslaught of welfare statism in the mainline Canadian politics of the late fifties.

The rise of John Diefenbaker, the so-called red Tory who became Prime Minister of Canada in 1958, was the downfall of the C.C.F. The C.C.F. had nursed a generation of anti-Liberals, who opposed the central government and the Eastern establishment; but it had not raised a generation of socialists, because it had refused to politicize the population even in the one province it controlled. So when Diefenbaker came, and offered much of the vehicle for protest of the populist appeal, plus the assurance of power, the C.C.F. had had its day in federal politics.

At the very moment the C.C.F. was declining, the Canadian labour movement, recently merged as the American movement on which it models itself was also crossing a desert of ideas and militancy. What better time for a marriage between the lame and the blind? Out of this came the New Democratic Party.

The Marriage and After

Leaders of the Canadian Labour Congress point to their tie-up with the New Democratic Party as proof of their independence from the official American trade unions movement represented by the AFL-CIO. Their claims to independence are justified only insofar as they challenged simplistic management views about a sheep-like working class quietly following the counsel of outside agitators. But in spirit and principles—or lack of them—and in methods, there is no difference worth mentioning between AFL-CIO chiefs and their Canadian counterparts. The kind of U.S. domination over Canadian policies that sometimes occurs in unions is no different from the repression union leaders in the U.S. exert on dissenting elements within their ranks. And there are cases to prove that all-Canadian unions can be as obtuse in their approach to social problems and militancy as any American labour boss.

The mainstream North American labour movement has had no injection of new life since the thirties and the CIO. Pockets of militancy still exist of course, notably among California's farm workers, in British Columbia and in Québec. But generally the movement is suffering from the artereosclerosis that fits aging views and aging leaders.

Thus the labour movement has settled down in its self-defined role: managing the material welfare of that fraction (a third) of the work force that it represents. Not only does it manage interests instead of representing people, but it makes little effort to break through to the new working class (poor unskilled workers, the white collar and intellectual workers) that it does not include in its ranks.

Having such a strong stake in the status quo, how could the leaders of the Canadian Labour Congress possibily produce a political movement that would in any way put forward a programme of radical change? The C.L.C. did not come to politics as British unions came to Labour, on the crest of a wave of grass roots fervour; it did not even come to the N.D.P. with the spirit that drew many unions members to Roosevelt's New Deal. In the N.D.P., the C.L.C. brass saw a convenient equivalent of the U.S. Democratic Party of the sixties.

From time to time, N.D.P. officials complain that the labour movement, despite its affiliation, has not delivered working class votes. This should not come as a surprise. The unions could not deliver something that they did not have. *The N.D.P. did not address itself to the working class but to its fossilized leadership.* The leadership could at best provide election funds. It was hoped that it would also offer organizers, but when the crunch comes, the unions will invest in collective bargaining and its derivatives rather then political education: as was said of the French voter, its heart many be on the left but its wallet is on the right.

Thus, far from bringing a broader constituency to Canadian social democracy, as had been hoped, the C.L.C. brought the leaden weight of an additional bureaucracy. The price that was to be paid for this in the following years was hardly worth the money added into party coffers, even from the party's point of view.

The Fabian Failure in Québec

Besides organized labour, there was another constituency Canadian social democracy wanted to win, and that was the predominantly French province of Québec. It had long been an article of faith among social democratic thinkers that if Québec had never voted for the C.C.F., it was because of the economic, intellectual and social backwardness of the province. It does not seem to have occured to them that the radical streams of that society did not fit neatly into polite British-type fabianism, or that left-wing colonialism is in no way preferable to other brands of the same phenomena—as everyone will agree after Czechoslovakia.

The N.D.P. thought it would resolve all its problems with Québec by recognizing in principle the existence of two nations within the Canadian state. It was the first Canadian party to do so, and was thus the first to cash in on the resurgence of nationalist feeling in the French-speaking province. It did so when the Canadian Prime Minister, Tory John Diefenbaker, was in power, and he was not only opposed to any hyphenation of the word Canadian, he moreover had a bunch of idiots in the Québec wing of his party. The N.D.P.'s policy on French Canada drew a short-term harvest of increased support in opinion polls in Québec.

But between having a party convention adopt a two-nation policy —partly by seducing diehards with prospects of electoral gains—and acheiving a true partnership between the reform elements of two quite different societies, there was a chasm that the N.D.P. never breached. It never overcame the obstacles to such a marriage that stemmed from the party's bureaucracy and its old attitudes on nationalism and Québec, from the state of the labour movement, and from the nature of Québec politics itself. Today, with the Conservative party's acceptance of a special status for Québec, the Liberal party's program for a bilingual, bicultural Canada, and with the anti-Québec elements of the N.D.P. once more coming out of the woodwork, Canadian social democracy is even more irrelevant to Québec that it was prior to 1960.

There were obstacles to true co-operation within the party leadership. Many high-ranking social democrats could not rid their mind of their notions about Québec's backwardness, nor of their distaste for nationalism. Be the issue a national pension fund or medicare, Québec's demands to run its own show were more often than not interpreted as a conservative reaction, rather than the expression of a desire to shape social policies according to the fundamental inclinations of an autonomous society.

The trade union movement did not help ease the tensions. The C.L.C. and several of its major affilaites were having their own problems with unruly Québécois. A new generation of union leaders in the Québec Federation of Labour was seeking to increase the Federation's power and revamp some of the cobweb-ridden structures of the labour movement. They were up against entrenched bureaucracies in Ottawa and Toronto, as well as against more traditional elements inside the Q.F.L., those elements whose fights against the reactionary nationalism of the Duplessis era in Québec had estranged them forever from nationalist aspirations.

Then there was the rivalry between C.L.C. unions and the Confederation of National Trade Unions, the latter an indigenous product of Québec. The C.N.T.U. refused affiliation to any particular party for a combination of reasons : part gomperism, part syndicalism, part sympathy amongst some leaders for the Liberal parties in Ottawa and Québec, but most of all a reluctance to proclaim commitments at the top of the organization without regard for the feelings and convictions of the membership.

Both the reform elements of the Q.F.L. and segments of the C.N.T.U. could have been drawn into the N.D.P. and seemed at times to be about to jump in. But the party as a whole allowed itself to be identified with the conservative brass of the C.L.C. The moment of truth came in 1963, at a policy convention of the Québec N.D.P.

At that meeting, two sets of commitments clashed : the nationalists versus the federalists, and the reform social democrats versus the more radical—albeit traditional—socialists. The federalist—social democrats won insofar as they succeded in quashing the idea of an entiriely autonomous Québec wing. The dissenters went off to form the Parti Socialiste du Québec, of brief and unhappy memory. The N.D.P. had lost its chances of becoming a viable political alternative in Québec.

It lost these chances because after the 1963 convention, it had little to differentiate itself from the reform Liberals who held power in Québec. Some dreamt for a while of an alliance between the Liberals and the N.D.P., the former occupying the provincial field, and the latter the federal. In fact, both parties drew voters from the sames classes. But the weakness of this strategy was double-barrelled: on the one hand the conservative, dominant streaks within the Liberal party were not about to foster in their bosom a possible rival; on the other, the reform elements were very much Québec-oriented, and many would eventually follow René Lévesque into a independentist party; though they may have been—and are still—willing to favour the N.D.P. on an election ballot, they were not about to put the necessary energies in the building up of a strong provincial wing of the federal party.

As for the radical elements of Québec politics, those of them in the N.D.P. who had had some chances of winning in the late fifties and early sixties were lost forever. The Québec N.D.P. quickly became identified with English-speaking Québec reform, as the location of its electoral gains bore out.

The constant in the evolution of the social democratic programme has been the progressive rejection of all those elements which have traditionally separated socialists from liberals and conservatives: public ownership; anti-militarism and anti-colonialism; abolition of special, especially economic, privileges, etc.

As we have already noted, this process began in Canada, not with the founding of the NDP in 1961, but with the repudiation by the CCF in 1956 of the Regina Manifesto. The old socialists prepared for their union with a tough and conservative trade union bureaucracy by divesting themselves of any programmatic elements that might possibly cause the controllers of the C.L.C. coffers to have second thoughts.

The process has been completed at succeeding conventions in '63, '65 and '67, although with occasional foot-dragging and the odd cry of wounded socialist conscience.

In 1961 British Labour chief Hugh Gaitskill was brought over to remind them of the need to support NATO as, said he, did all European social democratic parties (he forget the most sucessful, the Swedish SDP, which does not). When some of the natives became restless during the ensuing two years, George Brown, Gaitskill's and later Wilson's strong right arm, visited to remind the party in 1963, that social democracy required Canadian boys to guard civilization against Eastern Europe's alien hordes. In 1965 at Toronto, things were better. Fenner Brockway, whose new title of Lord so impressed the convention chairman that he kept repeating it, much to the embarassment of that old socialist and fighter for colonial freedom, represented the mother-party and along with Tommy Douglas, still a man of conscience, opened the flood-gates to more serious and more radical discussion of foreign affairs than the party had heard since the forties. Strong resolutions were overwhelmingly passed condemning US imperialism in Viet-Nam and the Dominican Republic. The Toronto union brass glowered on the platform. Later they explained to Douglas, through their representatives in the caucus and on the party executive, men like David Lewis and Andrew Brewin, that that "kind of thing" was not helpful to the party in getting support from "responsable" elements in the population. Things became quiet again except in the occasional speech by Douglas when he was out of hearing distance of Brewin. NDP members of the recent Common's committee considering continued Canadian membership in NATO voted *for* continued membership while favouring some modifications in its orientation. This position is substantially the same as Trudeau's.

A similar degradation is evident in the party's positions on domestic issues, especially those dealing with economics and power. With virtually no policy regarding the economic orientation of this country, except for a Canada development fund and some references in regard to the localization of new industries in areas of chronic high unemployment such as Cape Breton, the party was faced with two conflicting approaches at the 1967 Convention. A paper emanating from Québec and authored by Charles Taylor, brought some of the traditional socialist tools for public control of the economy together with an essentially Galbraithian analysis of Canadian society. Although criticized at the Québec convention by a large minority as too mild—albeit the criticisms were mainly from young old-leftists—the paper was substantially rejected at Toronto largely because of fears by trade union technocrats of anything smacking of economic nationalism and by party poll-watchers panicky at anything which might alienate potential voters by being identifiable with socialism.

The Convention did go along with proposals by MPs Cameron (now deceased) and Saltsman (a likely contender for Douglas' post) that outlined the way the party could better administer the Canadian branch plant economy so as to offend practically no one and demonstrate to the electorate how responsable and efficient the New Democrats were.

On the question of the distribution of power in our society, it would appear that the NDP simply sees no problem. It has never discussed it as such and no statement appears to be on the horizon. That workers do not control their own unions much less controlling industry; that farmers are powerless before government boards that control everything but guarantee nothing in the agricultural sector; that students and younger teachers feel alienated from the educational industry into which we pour billions of dollars each year; that the poor are acted upon by dehumanizing agencies and dependent upon them for their very physical survival; that native peoples feel betrayed and are being destroyed as communities by an insensitive federal bureaucracy, in all these areas, having to do with the very essence of our life in society, the NDP is mute or if it speaks, it mouths pious good wishes. It seems incapable of responding with passion, with a programme or a strategy for profound change.

What remains of the N.D.P. in 1969 ?

There are three schools within the party now: the so-called "new left" (the Toronto group around Renwick and Stephen Lewis), the Cameron/Saltzman line which is official policy; and the followers of

Charles Taylor.

The "new left" can be dealt with briefly. It aims at replacing the old foggies who now run the party by a new generation of 'swingers'. It feels that the over-sixty crowd in the N.D.P. caucus and its pre-occupation with the old age pensions are not exactly the right men to attract the votes of the young middle class. But the 'new left' is bent on style, on rhetoric but not programme, and its meaningfulness is considerably reduced now that Canada has acquired a swinger as Prime Minister.

More interesting is the concern of some of these Toronto-based MPPs and their supporters to relate to local issues that affect the daily life of their constituents : the administration of the Ontario Housing Corporation, tenants' unions, human rights. What they have not been able to do, and probably do not wish to do, is to build people's organizations to achieve their objectives outside of, or parallel to the electoral system. It is also of more than passing interest, that this group, modest though its efforts have been to try to make the social democratic party relevant to people's lives, has aroused the suspicion and hostility of the party and especially the trade union hierarchy. It is no secret that it was the union bosses that assured Jim Renwick's defeat when he recently attempted to unseat Ontario NDP Leader Donald MacDonald.

The only school worth taking seriously from the point of view of ideas in the N.D.P. is that of Charles Taylor. It is noteworthy that his proposals are regularly being voted down or watered down by party coventions and meetings. Nonetheless, he does make an impressive attempt to define a program of reform for contemporary Canada, and is not obsessively hung up with greed for power—indeed, what his thinking notoriously lacks is a strategy for organising.

Despite the attractive consistency and intellectual rigor of Taylor's thinking, it is in the final analysis disappointing. It is at this level, the highest, that the failings of Canadian social democracy become most evident. Taylor's proposals for increased public involvement in the economy and a reallocation of resources in favour of collective goods is akin to the thinking expressed by Galbraith in "The Affluent Society". It shares with traditional, mainstream socialism the weakness of concentrating on the production and distribution processes, with total disregard for the problems of actual power. Taylor does not even follow the neo-marxists into the construction of a strategy for social change. His latest position paper to the party offers only regional decentralisation as an alternative to the present power structure. That leaves one with the unhappy suspicion that he proposes only to relocate the bureaucracies, not to upset them.

One can only conclude from this brief examination of the N.D.P. that not only is it not a viable channel for radical politics, but it does not even answer the requirements of contemporary reform-minded left liberals. Too bad it is still there cluttering up the left of the political spectrum.

NO MORE WAITING

by Dan Daniels

The more and more we probe into the CCF/NDP phenomena (and indirectly the CP) the more and more it seems apparent, at least to this frustrated human, that we must draw away from false images and illusions and come to grasp the reality.

The images and illusions subtly ingrained into most radicals by decades of shadow-boxing mistaken for the genuine, vomiting up hallucinations making far too many believe that the system could be changed while indulging in its plastic games of make-believe.

The reality being the need to bring into being the 'tomorrow' which we have so often postponed for the day after tomorrow. Far too long have we waited patiently and foolishly for Odet's Lefty or Becket's Godot. Far too long have we been governed by the euphoric day of judgement and held in romantic bondage by the 19th century barricades. The messiahs are dead and so is the time for waiting.

I have no desire or inclination to cast aside all that went into the birth of the CCF; on the contrary I want to embrace the hopes, dreams and desires that gave rise to this movement, indigenous to much of our soil (just as I cannot overlook or bypass those who believed the CP was the way). Because I relate to the feelings and aspirations which motivated the left to found the Commonwealth, I believe we should begin by becoming in effect the Commonwealth; a concept not entirely alien to the thinking of those who originally came together in Regina.

We start, not by continuing the masquerade and sham of electoral and reformist politics (an aspect rooted to most of the old left whether it was Communist or CCF), but by immediately giving birth and subtance to the alternative institutions and ways of life.

But before you consider and label me as completely Utopian or a cop-out let me instantly add the rider that we attempt to relate these counter-communities (whatever avenue and shape they take) not only to the Commonwealth of our needs as visualized by the hardy rebels of the Thirties but in every way possible to the immediate struggles and to those directly engaged in social confrontations; in essence a dual dialectical relationship.

At the same time as we steer away from electoral meaningless gyrations and come to place an emphasis on the 'here and now' of life styles mirroring the revolution we stride forward into the entire range of extra-parliamentary activities. Again, I'm not actually advocating anything radically unusual since the socialists who built the CCF (as well as those who were in the CP) were veterans of many direct actions including the Winnipeg General Strike, by far the most massive extra-parliamentary action ever launched in this country. In any event direct action (despite the camouflaged distortions thrown up by censorial historians) has been very much an integral part of our social fabric; not the least being the last ten years.

However, just as it isn't sufficient to construct alternative means without finding and establishing some genuine links with the ongoing campaigns neither is it adequate or meaningful to adopt or continue the concept of extra-parliamentary actions without at the same instance uniting them to counter-communities. This form of strategy to be real and long-lasting... to be effective... to be more than just reformist... must not only direct its strength and energy against the structures and conditions that must go but must mount those frames of reference that relate and spell out our 'tomorrow'. The future has to be brought onto the stage simultaneously while the past is attacked and demolished; in effect the same dual dialectical unity mentioned earlier.

Once more it is necessary to emphasize that this thinking is not exactly a departure since the unionists of the General Strike had in reality moved onto this area, more than a few having been molded by the Wobblies. Their central council although established essentially to look after the strike was at the same time a reflection of the administration and citizen's power that could have replaced the phony hypocritical government used against the majority of the people. (Also inherent in much of the libertarian writings as well as in such historical confront-ations as the Paris Commune and the Soviets of 1917.)

However, while the alternative was present in some rudimentary form during the Winnipeg situation, it was weakened considerably by the absence of genuine revolutionary perspective in the main ; an aspect also missing in the CCF albeit many were radical.

And while I might be politically naive I believe the time is now ripe for those radicals still in the NDP (as well as those in the CP) to come to comprehend that fundamental change is impossible while following the paths laid out by the masters. Ours is and must be a total revolution, an esthetic revolution and we start by openly declaring our vision. But if we stop there we'll be guilty of indulging in masturbat-ing rhetoric, a habit all too familiar in much of the left; we must live the revolution as well. We define ourselves not only by stating what we are but by becoming what we are.

The community essential if we wish to become what we are; im-possible to ripen fully as long as we continue to fashion and shape our ways in a society geared against the interests of man and insulated with habits and attitudes which make their way the norm. We return to the womb of the community so we can be reborn anew... in order to come into touch with ourselves.

But just as we have the past of the CCF to guide us and keep us from repeating the adolescent mistakes of yesterday we also have other examples helping us understand the direction of our decision. If not we could well end up as aborted foetuses instead. We therefore turn to the psychedelic milieu. (Quite a jump from the CCF of Regina to the drop-out scene but that's where it has been all this time; new man needing more than the normal nine months of biological birth.)

First and foremost the question of separation. Separation not guided by geographic space in the beginning but separation from *all* society including those involved in the movement for change.

Understandable that this should occur in the early days; most political activists still bowing their heads to the mores of the system. Their horizons hardly rising above the established values; the dropouts, hippies or what have you desireous of making a complete break—even if at first they didn't quite comprehend the totality of their rebellion. Natural therefore that they should turn *in* as well as on.

Also, another dimension to the question, one that is more directly political; namely the notion that if enough could separate this could have an effect on the straight society. Somewhat akin to the thinking of an old sea-mate of mine who began a one-man strike back in 1950. He maintained that if everybody should refuse to be exploited the system would by necessity have to collapse.

Not illogical, of course, but both overlook the role of the establishment. While a one-man strike will be tolerated (except when he's caught pan-handling) or a small percentage permitted to remove themselves the controllers can hardly be excepted to be docile as soon as the tactic begins to gather momentum or when it starts to affect too many of their sons and daughters.

The hippies not the first in North American history to opt for separation; from the very beginning of white man's colonization this concept has been present in one form or another. Not only prevalent basically amongst many of those who came voluntarily to those shores in order to escape oppression in their native lands but quite often breaking out after centralism began to take over and/or in an attempt to avoid bureaucratic regimes as in the case of the coureurs-de-bois during the French colonial regime or the Newlightism development in Nova Scotia during the American War for Independence.

Most social break-away movements were effectively crushed. Or when some were partially successful in evading total administrative control, turning so completely inwards that instead of advancing to a more dignified civilization, ending up as backward and retarded settlements impeding all or most progress as is still the situation today in many remote hills and valleys in the United States.

To a fair extent separation 'bastions' no different than 'fortresses' held by guerillas in a war of liberation; both, since they are isolated, prey and vulnerable to an all-out attack. Essentially (without going into great detail since a good deal of copy has appeared on this subject in the underground press) this is substantially what happened in Haight-Ashbury, to the Provos of Holland, to Toronto's Village as well as just about any area in which the alternative tried to create its own neighbourhood in the city.

The disruptions and distortions not only the result of authority harassment or due to the 'invaders' whose heads were not yet ready for what was happening, but largely because of the hangups, attitudes and habits of many who considered themselves to be liberated. And while today many undeniably are very much part of the struggle against the system their counter-communites no longer in existence beyond very minor surface facades.

Nor is it a simple matter of taking off and splitting from the city as is now the trend. Even if some were so fortunate as to find an island in the middle of the sea they'll still be subject to attack and eventual harassment. Also, since they will have withdrawn themselves even further from the ranks of those engaged in struggle they will be that more open to assault. No group by itself, without some support from allies, can hope to withstand the power and aggression of the state once it is unleashed. Even with allies and reserve forces it is difficult, but alone just about impossible.

But let us presume for a moment the impossible, or to be more realistic let us assume that being but an isolated incident that some will be left alone... in the beginning. Despite their realization that they should not follow the misleading roads paved by the dying society, despite their unwillingness to accept the roles decided for them by manipulative directors they will nonetheless become their own excutioners for a counter-community, regardless of the space that separates it from the rot, cannot avoid inheriting some (and at times a great deal) of the shit and muck they are trying desperately to avoid, particularly the aspect of personalism.

But even if the above should not occur they will still face obstacles that are fairly unsurmountable. In the first place, having turned inwards (even if the personalism should not rear its head) they will still become prey to the disease they are trying to fend off. For having established the community as a separate entity, the particular interests of the group will come to dominate even if these are in conflict and contradiction with the needs of the community of the people as a whole. Rather than collective tribal units representing the future they will become corporate bodies tied to the past and the decaying present.

We have but to look at the cooperative movement to understand the above. Originally organized as alternatives to the worst effects of capitalism (as we can see from the material furnished to us on the history of the CCF in the mid-west), concerned with the needs of the people involved instead of the profit motive they *all* eventually became corporate structures functioning as capitalist enterprises; in effect, though the numbers were collective and the rhetoric humanistic, basically no different than corporate institutions openly set up to chase the buck or those petty-bourgeois cooperatives aimed at protecting the small producers. (This happened regardless whether the leadership came from socialists or reformers in or near the CCF as well as those who followed the Communist Party.)

Martin Buber in his essays on Utopian Socialism stresses the need for a philosopical committment and consciousness in order to prevent or deter the Utopias from degenerating into capitalist appendages. While in total agreement with his thesis I must reemphasize the belief that even if such a profound understanding existed the communities would take on capitalist features as long as they stress and maintain a separ-

CREATIVE NONVIOLENCE

Many people feel that an organization that uses nonviolent methods to reach its objectives must continue winning victories one after another in order to remain nonviolent. If that be the case then a lot of efforts have been miserable failures. There is a great deal more involved than victories. My experience has been that the poor know violence more intimately than most people because it has been a part of their lives, whether the violence of the gun or the violence of want and need.

I don't subscribe to the belief that nonviolence is cowardice, as some militant groups are saying. In some instances nonviolence requires more militancy than violence. Nonviolence forces you to abandon the shortcut, in trying to make a change in the social order. Violence, the shortcut, is the trap people fall into when they begin to feel that it is the only way to attain their goal. When these people turn to violence it is of a very savage kind.

When people are involved in something constructive, trying to bring about change, they tend to be less violent than those who are not engaged in rebuilding or in anything creative. Nonviolence forces one to be creative; it forces any leader to go to the people and get them involved so that they can come forth with new ideas. I think that once people understand the strength of nonviolence — the force it generates, the love it creates, the response that it brings from the total community — they will not be willing to abandon it easily.

CESAR CHAVEZ
leader, United
Farm Workers,
"California Grape Boycott".

ation from the continuing battle for that in itself is a subtle bourgeois influence in tune with the horrendous notion of "I'm all right, Jack" or looking after number one. And should some even strive to avoid all contact, the danger of eventual retardation as in the case of those settlements that retreated inwardly and away from all strangers.

It would seem from the above that I've considerably undermined the premise for the community. Possibly but better to overstress the negative rather than plunge into waters without taking a sounding. Despite whatever arguments or gloomy Casandra-like omens I might have raised (and I've omitted many other disturbing factors that might be of equal importance) I'm still unquestionably in favour of any community of people who feel they can no longer stomach the alienation and must therefore remove themselves from the contaminating source of their agony... even if they should disagree entirely with my abrasive analysis.

After all is said and done it might well be that the very act of sowing a community signaling the future is by itself a total political fact surpassing its particular weaknesses, a catalyctic force enabling us to talk concretely and coherently about what we have in mind... the word strengthened by the visual. At least we will have a reality to point to... no matter how fragile or ephemeral... no longer a mere Utopian dream. And though emanating from another direction, or point of attack, very much a basis to the position projected regarding extra-parliamentary activities.

Although more than partial to direct action cannot *any longer* conceive of this measure without integrating it into the entire strategy of the counter-community. If this should not take place it is quite possible that extra-parliamentary struggles will be as fleeting and futile as communities separated from action. In essence without this dual and parallel relationship both movements are genuinely Utopian.

Also, despite proceeding from a different viewpoint, more than likely that direct actions by themselves will fall into the same sticky mire and swamp as electoral campaigns. To date the stress has been on smashing and overthrowing the present without at the same time consciously presenting the alternative aside from wordy proclamations or slogans which in the final analysis end up being verbal diarrhea. The constitutionalists look forward to a victory at the polls before ushering in the Commonwealth (which they keep on delaying and emasculating having become prisoners of the system through accepting their rules) while many extra-parliamentarianists freak out on myriad visions of the barricades. Both are still waiting, the polls or barricades having replaced the Christian-Judaic waiting for delivery, but all strung out on the same hangups.

Extra-parliamentarism by itself, instead of negating the negative, continues to embrace the negative. It is only after the affirmative takes place simultaneously with the offensive that the negation of the nagation occurs. We can screw as often as we want (depending on our stamina, of course) but until a woman gives birth no qualitative change has happened despite all the heavy breathing and energy expanded. Nor does a child wait for the old lady to die before making an entrance into the world. Like it's now or we're in the same old bag—their dirty old crummy bag—even if the orgasms are our own.

Emphasizing the alternative in relationship to struggle possesses two other inherent values as well; possibly more important than the question of whether the new structure survives permanently or not and fundamentally related to the notion of the community as a political fact in its own right. These values come under the heading of consciousness and apprenticeship.

The danger always exists that regardless of our revolutionary desires and objectives we will become so embroiled with the immediate situation that the goals and future will be lost as we grapple with the present, as happened to our predecessors in the old left. Desireous of immediate victories or changes (even partial) we will at times tend to overlook or push aside the future in order to make at least the present more tolerable and liveable. But not only that, the greater peril is that the mass of people, without whom we are helpless, will only see and relate to the given issue and never come to sense the alternative. (Anyone, with even a minor grasp of history, knows how often this has happened.)

In a sense our reaction on this question will clearly indicate the measure of our beliefs. For example, most dramatists of the theatre of the absurd believe that the best which can be accomplished in the affairs of man is in nullifying the cruelty since we are fundamentally helpless in a cosmos that is hostile, drafted for them many years ago by Shakespeare, "As flies to wanton boys, are we to the gods; they kill us for their sport". Their plays almost inevitably reflect this pessimism and impotency as with Estragon and Vladimir in "Waiting for Godot".

The radical theatre of today, on the other hand, believes everything is possible, especially the "Liberation of Man" as projected by Antonin Artaud. This theatre holding up a mirror not only to where it's at but where it could be. Had Becket's play been written by one of the new playwrights Vladimir and Estragon would have either gone after Godot and dragged him out of hiding or just completely ignored his absence and gone about doing what was necessary.

If we believe with the absurdists that the best we could hope for is in "nullifying the cruetly" then we are indeed reformers and we best stick to what is "realistic". But if we believe, along with Artaud, that the "Liberation of Man" is possible, we have no choice but to go as far as the theatre of revolt. The question is no more complicated than that.

This does not mean, of course, that we are so unfeeling as to sacrifice possible successes and general benefits in order to dogmatically safeguard our virtue (such as it might be) or that we don't work together with those who have no desire other than to alter the immediate condition. We would be idiots and irresponsible if we adopted such a stupid course. But it is essential that *we,* those who are interested in root causes and root effects, extend the struggle to take in the future—but beyond the rhetoric since that generally amounts to bullshit. Rhetoric must be replaced by example. People must feel... see... grasp... the future ; and what better way than bringing in units of the future ?

While there is a great deal of radical thinking today there is still very little consciousness of what we are seeking to build. Unfortunately the welfare and reformist regimes such as those in Saskatchewan or in England have done more harm than good in giving an inkling of the life we're working for ; especially since they're continuations of the ongoing setup. Nor have the Russians and their totalitarian centralism been much help to us. On the contrary, just as the social democrats are bastard offsprings of the establishment so are the Moscowites. Though the economic structure underwent some changes the social revolution still has to take place. Therefore we have no Utopias to indicate until we give rise to them ourselves.

Once we will have accomplished this task, no matter how primitive the example might be, we will have in some substance united the present and the future, gone beyond the rhetoric and brought into awareness that which is possible. And before a people will change they must first develop this consciousness... the imagination has to be present.

In addition, althought the structures could disappear since some might not have a permanent reason for existence or be crushed, a dialectical change will have occurred transforming the immediate since the consciousness will remain, the future having been embraced ; more potent and real than any trip triggered by hallucinogens.

At the same instance the counter-structures will enable greater numbers of people to come to grips with the question of self-government. For not only are they involved in destroying the obstacles that devour them but they are immersed in avenues of administrating and governing. And before a people can come to power, they must, as Marx emphasized, learn how to rule.

Quite likely too that we will be confronted by circumstances and problems about which we know little or nothing. Good. Preferable that we learn *now* rather than put of our education even if we should fail in this instances. We will in this manner, through facing and living with problems that will inevitably arise (even after a general revolution has taken place) come to know or at least have some clue about how to cope with the question tomorrow. This is our apprenticeship ; let's grab the opportunity and learn how to become journeymen.

The above tied up with the irksome question of elitism ; the communities developing thousands of experienced cadrés—cadrés educated not only by theoretical works but by the very raw experience of life— cadrés not only a small group of so-called vanguardists but cadrées being the mass of people themselves. And if there's one danger we must be constantly aware of, it's elitism ; a disease not only inevitable in the present culture but a disease that has penetrated much of the history of the left. [1]

And at the same time as we learn the art of self-government we continue to develop more communities—citizen's committees concerned with the fate of their neighbourhood—workers' councils concerned with all aspects of production and management—university student bodies determining the nature of their learning and the role of their universities —free press syndicates—theatre communes—free universities—farm communes—family experimental living communes—including in some cases local parish and municipal government that are vulnerable to control by the people (as in some areas of Quebec)—in just about every avenue of life until we are in fact a dual power existing and challenging the power of the few; in effect becoming that 'separated' neighbourhood which the hippies dreamed of, but instead of being isolated we will have moved in and alongside the whole of society.

It is at this point that we will be able to transform the society for we will have that parallel structure already in existence and will in fact be in control of much of our fate; probably culminating in a general strike finishing the job viewed by some in Winnipeg.

I realize, of course, that the above is a bit too neat and pat; many a rough road before we can reach this possibility. Nonetheless, regardless of the difficulties, the way possible. But we must start by becoming... we must start by waiting no longer. Some of the first steps have already been taken since the counter-community in many instances is no longer a mere term on paper. The act of birth requiring our willingness and readiness to penetrate. The rest will happen naturally just as it happens after a woman has been fertilized.

Published 1969

---

1. *See "Two Souls of Socialism" by Hal Draper, Our Generation, Vol. 6, No 3.*

NOTE ON ECONOMIC CONTINENTALISM :

Prof. George Grant stated in his book, LAMENT FOR A NATION (page 86) **"Canada has ceased to be a nation. .. Our social and economic blending into the empire will continue apace ... A branch-plant satellite, which has shown in the past that it will not insist on any difficulties in foreign and defense policy, is a pleasant arrangement for one's northern frontier."**

If we wish to understand what forces prevent Canada from making a more positive contribution to world peace and development, we must examine what external influences make this possible and how they go about their business. We must ourselves why does U.S. capital invest more in Canada than anywhere else (see map). For this reason we have published, J.M. Freeman's article "Economic Continentalism" as one illustration. This aspect of the quandary will be illustrated in future issues with examinations of what forces inside Canada contributed to this same process. This in turn will be followed by an examination of what it will take, and what coalition of new forces will be necessary to reverse this process of absorption into the USA.

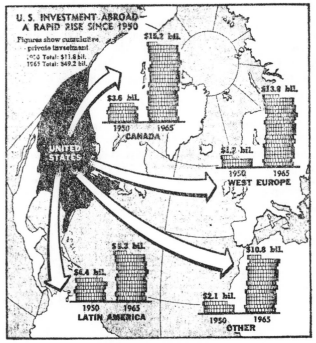

From New York Times

ECONOMIC CONTINENTALISM

by J. M. Freeman

Getting Away With The Big Lie

The facts of foreign ownership are well known within the oil industry itself, and to the readers of such publications as *The Financial Post,* the *Financial Post Survey of Oils, Nickle's Canadian Oil Register, Oilweek* and other industary magazines. But the general public is either in the dark or confused as to the goodness or badness of such ownership.

To be told by *Oilweek* that the Canadian oil industry is 80% foreign-owned is not too enlightening. The company you deal with may belong to the other 20%. It is more enlightening when we know who owns or controls what. This report is an attempt to provide such information. It may serve also as an introduction to the nature and importance of the oil industry, not just in Alberta, but also in Canada and the world.

Those Company Laws

If such sources as those mentioned above reveal the rape of the Canadian petroleum industry by "foreign hordes", one must admit that Canadian governments, past and present, federal and provincial, have

---

This article is an edited version of Mr. Freeman's pamphlet *Biggest Sellout in History : Foreign Ownership of Alberta's Oil and Gas Industry and the Oil Sands.* For the complete pamphlet write to Our Generation.

invited it. Unlike countries such as Sweden, Mexico and Japan, Canada has had no effective laws to protect companies from foreign control — with the exception of radio and TV stations, where no more than 25% may be owned by non-Canadians.

Historians may trace this lack to the gradual way in which Canada emerged from the status of a British colony, the concept that foreign money was necessary to develop our resources, and the desire on the part of the framers of the British North America Act to protect British investment.

If the original idea was to protect British investment in Canada, it has certainly backfired both in Canada and elsewhere. The land grants to the Hudson's Bay Company are now being used by the Continental Oil Co. (Delaware) which has its executive office in Houston, Texas. Canadian company laws enabled American oil interests to get an additional foothold in the Middle East, shortly after Standard Oil Co. (N.J.) and Sonoco Oil had forced their way, with the aid of the American State Department, into Iraq Petroleum. The U.K. Colonial Office had ruled that only British companies could operate in such a sphere of influence as Bahrain Island in the Persian Gulf. Canadian companies, however, enjoyed British status, and the company laws of Canada permitted complete stock ownership by foreign nationals. The Standard Oil Co. of California incorporated a wholly-owned subsidiary in Canada in 1929, the Bahrain Petroleum Company Ltd. This "British" company discovered oil in Bahrain in 1932. Like the nose of the camel, this has been followed by a rather pushy body in the Middle East, to the detriment of British Oil interests in that region of prolific production. Bahrain Petroleum's registered office, in 1964, was 48 Sparks St., Ottawa 4, Canada; but its head office was at 485 Lexington Ave., New York.

Alberta Dominates Oil and Gas Production

It is possible to talk about Alberta and Canada in the same breath, when discussing oil resources, simply because Alberta dominates the production of oil and natural gas in Canada. Also, when we consider the great reserves of oil in the Athabasca oil sands, Alberta has international importance in the future of world oil. Ownership of that oil becomes of vital interest to all Canadians.

In 1963, Alberta accounted for 69% of the crude oil produced in Canada, and for 85% of the natural gas. In processing the gas, Alberta produced 70% of Canada's sulphur.

In both 1962 and 1963, Alberta wells were producing at about half capacity. At full capacity, existing wells could supply all of Canada's oil requirements, without considering any potential production from the oil sands. Yet Canada remains a large net importer of oil, partly because of geography, but mainly because of the ownership of production in Venezuela and the Middle East by major oil companies operating in Canada, which can make a bigger profit importing from their subsidiaries in such areas. The National Oil Policy gives them everything east of the Ottawa valley for this purpose.

In 1963, oil and natural gas provided about 70% of all the energy consumed in Canada. The National Energy Board estimates that in 1966 they will provide 72.2%. The profits alone, not counting interest and fees of various kinds, that went to shareholders of this major source of energy in the United States, from the petroleum industry in Canada, amounted to U.S. $121 million in 1961, according to the annual report of the U.S. Commerce Department (*Financial Post*, Sept. 1/62, p. 13). That was just before the producers in Western Canada really started to make money. Such an outflow of capital hampers Canadians in the development of their own industry.

Social Credit Policy Favors Sellout

Premier Manning, whose government received a third of its revenue from the oil industry in 1963, and has received more in other years, told the Canadian Petroleum Association at its annual general meeting, in March 1962, that, although Alberta cannot offer low cost factors to the oil industry (a statement which is open to question), "We can offer, however, political stability — a very important factor and one becoming increasingly rare in many oil producing areas." In this context, "political stability" means that the government has no intention of questioning the extent of foreign ownership, let alone taking action to lessen it — except by luring the money of the deceived into an investment fund which will buy minority shares here and there, a complete waste of capital when it comes to ownership control.

On this occasion, Mr. Manning was persuading the big oil men that it was worthwhile to pay a slight increase in royalties on production and he spoke of the public owning 90% of the oil and gas in the province. He does this whenever the question of foreign owership comes up and what he is referring to is the provincial ownership of almost 90% of the mineral rights. This, unfortunately, and as a direct result of government policy, has nothing to do with the actual ownership of the oil and gas produced from leases granted by the province. The ownership of that production, except for the royalty, is held by the producing companies. Today the production is largely in the hands of big companies and they are overwhelmingly foreign-owned.

Foreign Control of Refining

Refining is the manufacturing end where value is added to the raw material. Crude oil producers must sell to a refinery to get paid for their production. The demand of refineries, in Alberta and elsewhere, for Alberta crude determines the total amount wells are allowed to produce, month to month, according to the prorationing regulations of the Alberta Oil and Gas Conservation Board.

In Alberta the refineries are all foreign-controlled.

Jersey Standard's Imperial Oil Limited (ESSO)

The major refiner in Alberta, as in Canada as a whole, is Imperial Oil Limited. At the beginning of 1965, Imperial owned 49.4% of Alberta's crude oil refining capacity (43,000 barrels per calendar day out of a provincial total of 87,100). This was an increase from 46% in 1962 because of the closing down of small refineries in the province — bought up and closed by foreign companies. Alberta capacity has declined, because of such takeovers, from 100,000 barrels a day in 1960 to the 87,100 total at the beginning of 1965, whereas other provinces have shown an increase for the same period.

Imperial Oil Limited is completely controlled by Standard Oil Company (New Jersey), 30 Rockefeller Plaza, New York, N.Y., which owns 70% of the voting stock.

It is hard to believe today that the original Imperial Oil Co. was owned by Canadians. Formed in 1880 by the merger of seven companies in Ontario, it was taken over by Standard Oil of the U.S. in 1898.

Concentrated Power in Private Hands

To understand Imperial, it is necessary to know something about Jersey Standard. The Standard Oil Co. (N.J.), whose Esso sign shows up in the strangest places around the world, is king of the "Rockefeller" Standard Oil group of companies. It is considered to be the largest and most widespread oil company in the world, just ahead of the Royal Dutch/Shell group. It is also ranked as the second largest private-investor-owned industrial enterprise in the world, just below General Motors.

It took nineteen years (1892-1911) for the government of the United States, under anti-trust legislation, to break up the original Standard Oil Co. of New Jersey into a number of parts. The action was taken because the company, by the most ruthless methods of competition, had achieved a virtual monopoly of refining and marketing. The government action was quite ineffective. The Rockefeller family, which had 25% of the original trust, is reported to have ended up with 25% of each of the companies created by the dissolution order. Several of these companies were soon as large as the original combination. While members of the Rockefeller family still have varying interests in the Standard companies, their participation tends to be remote. One is more apt to read of David Rockefeller as the president and chairman of executive committee of the $13 billion Chase Manhattan Bank, considered the top oil bank; and James S. Rockefeller as chairman of The First National City Bank of New York, another oil bank as big as Chase Manhattan, which now controls the Mercantile Bank of Canada, which opened a branch in Calgary in 1964; or of Nelson Rockefeller as Governor of the State of New York; or of W. A. Rockefeller of New York as a director of Home Oil Co. until he resigned in 1964.

The failure of the American government to curb the concentration of economic power in the hands of the directors of such companies as Standard of New Jersey has had a serious effect on economic policy in the United States and what may prove to be a disastrous effect on foreign policy.

In Latin America, because of United States interference in their affairs on behalf of Standard Oil and other big American oil companies, the U.S. State Department has been called "the fortress of Standard Oil". As Robert Engler, a professor of political science, pointed out in a series of articles on "Oil and Politics" in the *New Republic* in 1955, former U.S. Secretary of State John Foster Dulles was the senior partner of the law firm of Sullivan and Cromwell which represents Standard Oil Co. (N.J.) and so did the law firm of former Secretary of State Dean Acheson, Covington and Burling. To which we should add that Secretary of State Dean Rusk came to that office after eight years as president of the Rockefeller Foundation, worked closely with John Foster Dulles for years, and told the U.S. Senate Foreign Relations Committee that when he left the Rockefeller Foundation he expected to receive severance pay over a period of years by way of the Chase Manthattan Bank — the Standard Oil - Rockefeller family bank. (See *I. F. Stone's Weekly,* Sept. 20, 1965, pp. 3, 4).

Much has been written about the cartel agreement, again revealed by government investigation, between Standard Oil and I. G. Farben, the huge chemical combine of Hitler's Nazi Germany which was deeply involved in secret war preparations and espionage. This cartel resulted from I. G. Farben's development of the hydrogenation process by which gasoline and other light oil fractions can be made from heavy oil by adding hydrogen. The agreement, designed to outlast the war, hindered the United States in World War II, particularly in the production of synthetic rubber, which process Standard Oil would not release to others until 1942. The details of this unsavory situation are given by Wendell Berge, former Assistant Attorney General in charge of the Anti-trust Division of the U.S. Department of Justice, in his book *Cartels.* It is also to be found in Richard Sasuly's book *I. G. Farben,* based on U.S. examination of I. G. Farben's records following Hitler's defeat.

A congressional investigation in 1959 revealed that a subsidiary of Jersey Standard (shared at the time with Socony Mobil Oil Co.) was the largest American company in South Vietnam, that its oil imports were paid for by American aid, that it demanded stronger legal and military guarantees for its operations in that country. It obtained both.

Any way you look at it, Jersey Standard's subsidiary carries weight in Canada. Imperial topped all firms reporting sales figures in 1962, approaching total sales of a billion dollars. In 1963 Imperial's total income went over the billion dollar mark ($1,015.2 million) as it did its total assets ($1,002.3 million) — and 1964 was better still. The figure for total assets for 1963 was after a cumulative deduction for depreciation and amortization, on fixed assets, of $478.2 million. The net profit for 1963 was $71.1 million ($68.4 million in 1962) after putting $47.1 million of net earnings into the cash box for depreciation and amortization, and after allowing $40 million for income taxes. It also reported a deferred income tax of $52.1 million, and an earned surplus (accumulated, undistributed net profits not paid out in dividends to share-holders) of $439.2 million. Such an earned surplus is usually reinvested for expansion of the company.

Imperial is an integrated oil company, meaning that it is engaged in exploration, drilling, producing, transporting, refining, petro-chemicals and marketing.

Imperial owns two exploration companies. At the beginning of 1964 it had about 21 million gross acres under reservation and lease; it had 3,763 net oil wells and 198 net gas wells (net means that its interests in a greater number of wells were equal to complete ownership of that many wells); its net production of crude oil and natural gas liquids averaged 109,000 barrels a day and of natural gas averaged 160 million cubic feet daily in 1963. Such figures indicate its dominant position in production. Its oil wells in Alberta are concentrated in high potential fields with big reserves. In 1962, according to the *Financial Post,* it supplied 23% of all the gas sold to Trans-Canada Pipe Lines. Its holdings of oil and gas reserves are greater than those of any other company, amounting to 20% of the total.

Imperial initiated and is considered to control Interprovincial Pipe Line Co. Ltd. through its one-third ownership. This line has a monopoly of the interprovincial transportation of oil, running 1,930 miles from Redwater, Alberta, to Port Credit, Ontario. It has an 8.6% interest in Trans Mountain Oil Pipe Line Co. which runs from Edmonton to Vancouver and down to the state of Washington, and substantial interests in four other pipelines. In addition, it wholly owns four oil and gas pipelines, has ocean and lake freighters and tank trucks.

At the beginning of 1965 Imperial owned 32.64% of the total crude oil refining capacity of Canada, having nine plants with a total capacity of 335,700 barrels per day out of a Canada total of 1,004,600 b/d. Most of the capacity was at Sarnia, Ontario, and Montreal, Québec. Its capacity was almost twice as large as the next biggest refiner in Canada, Shell Canada Ltd.

In 1964, Imperial operated eleven natural gas processing plants, and in the previous six years had invested some $46 million in petrochemical facilities at its Sarnia complex.

In marketing, Imperial is nationwide with its service stations and bulk stations. The August 1964 issue of *Imperial Oil Review* claimed that the company had 8,037 dealers in Canada.

Out for Canada's Greatest Asset

Looking to the future, not only of Standard Oil Co. (N.J.) but also of the energy supply of the United States, Imperial has acquired extensive interests in the Athabasca oil sands in northeastern Alberta. It has a 30% interest in the Cities Service group, the research and future production operations of which were placed in the hands of Syncrude Canada Ltd., in which Imperial also has 30%, in January 1965. Vernon Taylor, a vice-president of Imperial, is chairman. Vernon Taylor is one of the many government employees connected with oil and gas regulations who have made good in the industry being regulated. He supervised regulations in the Turner Valley field in the 1920's and '30's before he joined Imperial about 1938. Imperial is associated also with the oil sands proposals of Richfield Oil Corp. of the U.S.A., one of which is to use nuclear explosions to extract the oil. Through such associations, Imperial had a 1962 interest in some 954,000 acres of leases in the oil sands. Other members of the Standard Oil group of companies, Socony Mobil Oil of Canada and Pan American Petroleum, had 196,700 acres leased in the sands in 1962.

The British American Oil Company Limited
B-A, Royalite, Purity 99

In Alberta, the British American Oil Co. Ltd. (B-A) operates refineries at Calgary and Edmonton with a total crude oil capacity of 21,000 barrels a day, giving at 24.8% of Alberta's refining capacity at the beginning of 1965. This makes it the second largest refiner in the province. In Canada it is the third largest refiner, having 16.5% of the total, in nine plants with a total capacity of 169,700 barrels daily.

British American, the big B-A of the ads, is completely controlled by Gulf Oil Corporation, Gulf Bldg., Pittsburgh, Pennsylvania, U.S.A.

In 1964, Gulf Oil Corp. owned 64.8% of all the outstanding shares of British American.

Gulf Oil Corporation, as the third largest investor-owned oil company in the world, is considered to be a member of the present world oil cartel. It is part of what is called the Mellon financial group of Pittsburgh, which includes the Aluminum Company of

America, Aluminium Ltd. of Canada, Koppers Co. and other big companies. Gulf owns 50% of Kuwait Oil Co. Ltd., the other half being owned by British Petroleum. This interest in Kuwait oil on the Persian Gulf is a source of great profit, Kuwait oil being the cheapest in the world to produce, and, as one would expect, it finds its way to B-A's refinery and petrochemical complex in Montreal. Gulf's interest in Kuwait is said to give it the largest stake in Middle East oil of all American companies. Gulf has also a 7% interest in the Iranian Consortium in the Middle East. It has complete ownership of the Mene Grande Oil Co. in Venezuela. It has refining and marketing operations in many countries.

Like Imperial, British American is an integrated oil company. During 1964, B-A's production of crude oil and natural gas liquids averaged 61,600 barrels daily in western Canada, while natural gas sold in that area averaged 257 million cubic feet daily. B-A expected its Western Canada gas production to reach 276 million daily in 1965. These figures indicate its importance as a producer in Canada, giving it about half the crude oil production of Imperial Oil but about two-thirds greater natural gas.

In transportation, B-A owns numerous oil and gas pipelines in producing areas and has substantial investments in nineteen oil and gas lines, including such major trunk lines as: Interprovincial Pipe Line Company (7%), Trans-Mountain Oil Pipe Line Co. (8.6%), Peace River Oil Pipe Line Co. (11.2%), Producer's Pipelines Ltd. (19.6%), Trans-Canada Pipe Lines Ltd. (5.6%), Alberta Gas Trunk Line Co. (14.5% of voting shares), and a one-third interest in Trans-Northern Pipe Line Co. which transports refined products from Montreal to Toronto, Hamilton and Ottawa. B-A owns ocean, lake and coastal tankers and barges, tank trucks, and uses railway tank cars.

In petrochemicals, B-A has complete ownership of big Shawinigan Chemicals Ltd., Montreal, and three other petrochemical plants. It controls Canadian Helium Ltd. which made its first shipment of the rare gas from its plant in Saskatchewan in 1963. It controls Cansulex Limited, formed in 1962 with Petrogas Processing Ltd. of northeast Calgary, to export sulphur to markets outside Canada and the United States.

In natural gas processing, B-A owns plants at Pincher Creek, Nevis and Gilbey in Alberta, with a total capacity of 256.5 million cubic feet of gas daily. It is the operator of a number of jointly-owned plants. In 1963, B-A was biggest gas processing operator in Alberta, only to be topped when the Empress plant of Pacific Petroleums opened in 1964.

In marketing, B-A had over 9,300 service stations and other outlets in 1963, including those of Purity 99, Royalite, Anglo-Canadian and B-A. This was about 25% of all service stations in Canada that year. In the west, the number of brand names creates confusion on some street corners.

Although B-A is the second largest oil company in Canada, it is only about half as big as Imperial Oil in gross income and net profit. For 1963, B-A reported a gross income of $554.8 million, Imperial reported $1,015.2 million. At December 31, 1963, B-A reported total assets of $741.5 million, after cumulative depreciation and depletion of $406.3 million on fixed assets; a net profit of $34.2 million after deducting $41.9 million from net income for depreciation, depletion of $406.3 million on fixed assets; a net profit of $34.2 million after deducting 641.9 million from net income for depreciation, depletion and amortization; an accumulated surplus of profits not distributed to shareholders of $263.2 million.

B-A has been paying very low income taxes for several years, using the expenditures made in earlier years by Canadian Gulf to reduce the amount. In 1963, only $8.3 million was allowed for income tax $4.4 million in 1962. This is a long, long way from the 50% income some oil publicists in Alberta claim the oil companies pay.

When men on the way up in British American Oil finally make it to the head office of Gulf Oil in Pittsburgh, they enter an ultra-conservative atmosphere. The *New York Times,* September 12, 1964, reported that Gulf Oil had urged its employees to make campaign contributions to Goldwater for president of the U.S. Gulf was reported to have made large contributions to extremist right wing organizations who in turn supported Goldwater. Do Canadians really want such extremists in control of the nation's petroleum energy ?

Texaco Canada Limited (TEXACO)

The third largest refiner in Alberta is Texaco Canada Limited, with a 12,000 barrel a day refinery in Edmonton, giving it 13.8% of the provincial total. In Canada, Texaco had total refining capacity of 119,500 barrels daily, in four plants, giving it 11.62% of the country's total and fourth place in refining.

Texaco-Canada is completely controlled by Texaco Inc., 135 East 42nd St., New York, N.Y., U.S.A., which owns 68% of the voting shares.

Texaco Inc. (formerly known as Texas Company) is a major American company with large foreign interests, having a worldwide marketing system. It has forty major subsidiaries and affiliates, 19 of them wholly-owned, 9 of them 50% or more owned. Like the parent companies of Imperial and B-A, it is considered a part of the world oil cartel and is the fourth largest company in the cartel. It has a 7% interest in the Iranian Consortium operating the former monopoly of Anglo-Iranian Oil (now British Petroleum). Much of the profit of Texaco Inc. comes from its holdings in the Middle East. It has a 30% interest in ARAMCO (Arabian American Oil Co.) operating in Saudi Arabia — the rest of the company is shared with Standard Oil of California, Standard Oil of N.J. and Socony Mobil Oil. It has joint ownership of Bahrain Petroleum Co. (incorporated in Canada in 1929 to get into the Persian Gulf as a "British company") with Standard Oil of California, with whom it shares also the Caltex group of companies, operating in the Eastern Hemisphere, on a 50-50 basis. In 1962 its Aramco wells in Saudi Arabia averaged 6,280 barrels a day each, compared to about 40 barrels daily average for wells in Alberta.

Texaco owns Regent Refining (Canada) Ltd. at Port Credit, Ontario.

Texaco is engaged in exploration and production of oil and gas in Western Canada, both in participation with Texaco Exploration Co. (a wholly-owned subsidiary of Texaco Inc.) and on its own behalf. Its production of oil and natural gas liquids in 1963 averaged about 9,320 barrels daily (8,900 in 1962). It has not reported gas production.

In transportation, Texaco owns two lake tankers, has an interest in four pipelines, including 50% of Federated Pipe Lines Ltd., in which Home Oil Co. has the other 50%, and which carries crude oil from Swan Hills and nearby fields in Alberta to Edmonton.

Gas processing is handled by Texaco Exploration Co., which operates three plants in Alberta with a relatively small daily capacity of 53.5 million cubic feet.

Marketing is done through some 5,300 retail outlets across the country, about 1,400 of which were owned or leased by the company in 1963.

Net sales and service income of Texaco Canada Ltd. in 1963 came to $214.2 million. At the end of 1963, it reported total assets of $232.3 million after depreciation, depletion and amortization of $117.6 million; a net profit of $10.7 million after deducting $12.2 million from net income for depreciation, depletion and amortization and $4.3 million for income tax. It had an accumulated surplus of undistributed profits amounting to $91.1 million. Its parent company had an earned surplus of $1,585 million at the end of 1962.

Shell Canada Limited
Shell, White Rose, North Star

Although Shell became the smallest refiner in Alberta in 1964 with the closing of its North Star refinery at Grande Prairie, it is examined next because of its connections with the preceding companies in the world oil cartel.

Shell Canada Limited owns the former Canadian Oil Companies Ltd. refinery at Bowden, Alberta, with a crude oil capacity of 5,000 barrels daily, giving it 5.7% of the Alberta total at the beginning of 1965.

Shell may be the smallest in Alberta, but it is the second largest refiner in Canada, with six plants having a total capacity of 181,000 barrels daily, giving it 17.6% of the Canadian total at the beginning of 1965.

Shell Canada Limited is completely controlled by Royal Dutch/ Shell (60% Dutch, 40% British) which owned all the stock until

September 1962, by way of its subsidiaries Shell Investments Ltd. and Shell Oil Co. (U.S.). In 1962 and 1963, to permit the sale of some shares to the public, there was a complicated rearrangement of the capital stock which, as far as one can gather, left Royal Dutch/Shell with about 87% of Shell Canada, by way of direct ownership and indirect ownership through its subsidiary Shell Investments Ltd.

Royal Dutch/Shell entered Canada in 1912 by building storage facilities in Montreal for products brought by tanker from Borneo. It built its first refineries in Canada in 1932, at Montreal and near Vancouver.

From Competition to Cartel

It has been said that you need to be a specialist in the study of Royal Dutch/Shell to understand its organization, which includes a group of some 500 companies distributed around the world. The control of this private empire is exercised by two holding companies, Royal Dutch Petroleum Co. of the Hague, Netherlands, and "Shell" Transport & Trading Co. Ltd. of London, England. These two own jointly two operating companies, with Royal Dutch having 60% and "Shell" Transport 40% of the stock. The two operating companies are: N. V. De Bataafsche Petroleum Maatschappij of the Hague, and Shell Petroleum Co. Ltd., of London.

The Royal Dutch/Shell group is the second largest investor-owned oil enterprise in the world, being exceeded only by Standard Oil Co. (N.J.). The combine of Royal Dutch Petroleum and "Shell" Transport & Trading was formed in 1907 to defend Dutch and British oil interests in the Eastern Hemisphere against the Standard Oil Trust's drive for world domination. By 1913 Royal Dutch/Shell was a world-wide giant defying Standard's price-cutting methods of eliminating opposition. In 1928 the big companies called a truce for the benefit of all big oil companies. In that year, Royal Dutch/Shell, Standard Oil Co. (N.J.) and Anglo-Persian Oil Co. (now called British Petroleum) got together to maintain world prices at Texas Gulf rates, the world's highest, to control overproduction, and to keep their existing share of world markets. It is only in recent years that this control has been weakened.

Some idea of the size of the Royal Dutch/Shell group is given by the report that its refineries in the world processed 2,835,000 barrels daily; its wells produced (after payment of royalties and similar deductions) a net of 2,587,000 barrels daily; it had an interest in 27,350 miles of pipelines; and it was using 471 oil tankers in its fleet of vessels, in the year 1962.

The "Dutchy" of Canada

Shell Canada wholly owns Canadian Oil Company Ltd., the new name adopted in 1963 for the merger of Canadian Oil Companies Ltd. ("Your White Rose Dealer"), which Shell Investments Ltd. acquired in late 1962 and early 1963, and Hesper Oil Co. Ltd., a wholly-owned subsidiary of Shell. The major shareholder of Canadian Oil Companies had been the Power Corporation of Canada, and it was its decision to sell out which eliminated this integrated company from Canadian control. This may be taken as the climax in the sellout of Canada's conventional oil industry, leaving the co-operative oil enterprise of Western Canada as the only integrated group left in Canadian hands.

In addition, Shell Canada wholly owns : North Star Oil Ltd. (which it bought in 1960); Shell Canadian Tankers Ltd.; Shell Oil Co. of British Columbia; Shell Petroleum Co. of Canada; Prairie Cities Oil Ltd.; Shell Exploration Alberta Ltd.; Deep Sea Tankers Ltd.; Shell Chemical Corp. of Canada Ltd.; Peigan Oil of Canada Ltd.; Nipegon Petroleum Ltd.; and Cree Oil of Canada Ltd.

In the raw material end of the oil business, Shell Canada was producing crude oil and natural liquids at the rate of 48,600 gross barrels daily, in 1963, which after deducting royalties gave a net rate of about 41,000 barrels daily (during the first nine months of 1964, gross production averaged 52,400 daily); gross production of natural gas averaged 256 million cubic feet a day in 1963 (this had climbed to 298 million daily during the first nine months of 1964). It was also producing a large volume of sulphur. It held 56 million acres of Canada under leases, reservations and permits at the beginning of 1964, according to *Oil and Petroleum Year Book 1964*. This included large lease holdings in the Athabasca oil sands (reported as 213,000 acres in 1962) plus the interest held originally by Canadian Oil Companies Ltd. in Great Canadian Oil Sands Ltd. Shell also has its own 100,000 barrels daily project for oil sands production, denied a production permit for the time being, but with the right to renew its application until the end of 1968. Shell's multi-million-acre federal permits to explore for oil offshore from B.C. and Nova Scotia have stirred up controversy between the provinces and Ottawa as to who owns the offshore mineral rights.

In transportation, Shell Canada has its own ocean, coastal and lake oil tankers and tank trucks. It has a 45% interest in the Sun-Canadian Pipe Line Co. which transports refined products from Sarnia to Toronto. It has a one-third interest in Trans-Northern Pipe Line Co. which carries refined products, made from foreign crude oil, from Montreal to Toronto, Hamilton and Ottawa. It has minority interests in Montreal Pipe Line Co., Producers Pipelines Ltd., Peace River Oil Pipe Line Co., Alberta Gas Trunk Line Co. Ltd.; and Trans-Mountain Oil Pipe Line Co.

In gas processing, Shell Canada owned and operated three plants with a combined capacity of 262 million cubic feet daily of raw gas, and held interests in 15 other processing plants.

In petrochemicals, Shell Canada has plants in Montreal, Simcoe and Regina, plus packaging and blending plants connected with refineries, turning out a wide range of chemicals, including many for agriculture.

TABLE I

FOREIGN CONTROL OF OIL REFINING CAPACITY IN CANADA
Plants operating at the beginning of 1965

Company	Capacity, barrels per calendar day	% of total capacity
REFINERIES CONSIDERED TO BE CANADIAN		
Consumers' Co-operative Refineries Ltd.	22,500	2.19%
Regina, 1 plant; the only integrated Canadian-owned plant remaining; wholly owned by Federated Co-operatives Ltd.		
Northern Petroleum Limited	1,000	0.10%
1 plant; private co., Kamsack, Sask.; no report on ownership available.		
New Brunswick Oilfields Ltd. (1 plant)	300	0.03%
80% owned by Western Decalta Petroleum Ltd. so possibly should be listed as British.		
TOTAL CONSIDERED CANADIAN	23,800	2.32%
THE BIG FOUR FOREIGN		
STANDARD OIL, U.S.A., GROUP (11 plants)	403,700	39.25%
Imperial Oil Limited (9 plants) with 335,700 b/d capacity; 32.64% of Canada total; owned by Standard Oil Co. (N.J.)		
Standard Oil Company of British Columbia Ltd. 1 plant, 18,000 b/d; a wholly-owned subsidiary of Standard Oil Co. of California.		
Irving Refining Ltd. (1 plant) 50,000 b/d; jointly-owned by Standard of California.		
ROYAL DUTCH/SHELL GROUP (6 plants)	181,000	17.60%
This Dutch-British group controls the refineries of *Shell Canada Limited,* which include those of *Canadian Oil Co. Ltd.* and *North Star Oil Ltd.* (North Star refinery closed 1964).		
GULF OIL CORP., U.S.A., GROUP (9 plants)	169,700	16.50%
British American Oil Co. Ltd. (6 plants) *Anglo-Canadian Oils Ltd.* (1 plant) *Royalite Oil Co. Ltd.* (2 plants)		
TEXACO INC., U.S.A., GROUP (4 plants)	119,500	11.62%
Includes the refineries of *Texaco Canada Ltd.* and *Regent Refining (Canada) Ltd.*		
OTHER FOREIGN CONTROLLED COMPANIES (8 plants)	130,700	12.71%
BP Refinery Canada Ltd. (2 plants, 55,000 b/d) *Canadian Petrofina Ltd.* (1 plant, 30,000 b/d) *Sun Oil Co. Ltd. (Canada)* (1 plant, 25,000 b/d) *Husky Oil Canada Ltd.* (2 plants, 8,700 b/d) *Golden Eagle Refining Co. of Canada Ltd.* (1 plant, 8,500 b/d) *Pacific Petroleums Ltd.* (1 plant, 3,500 b/d)		
TOTAL FOREIGN CONTROLLED	1,004,600	97.68%

Source : Financial Post Survey of Oils 1964, corrected for plants closed 1964.

Marketing is done through some 7,000 retail outlets and over 600 bulk plants and terminals, as of 1964, spread across Canada. In 1963, Shell had about 16% of the Canadian market. With Handy Andy Co., in which it has an 18% interest, Shell is expanding into automotive accessory stores.

Shell Canada reported a total revenue of $451 million in 1963, placing it third among oil companies in Canada. Its total assets at the end of 1963 were given as $670.2 million, after depreciation, depletion and amortization deductions from fixed assets over the years of $171.7 million. It reported a net profit for 1963 of $18.7 million (compared to $5.1 million in 1962 and a net loss of $11.8 million in 1961) after deducting $33.8 million for depreciation, depletion and amortization from net earnings. Shell paid no income tax in 1963, nor in 1962, nor in 1961. Its improved earnings in 1963 were largely due to its takeover of Canadian Oil Companies Ltd.

The "Oil Republic" of Alberta

As well be seen from TABLE 1 "Foreign Control of Oil Refining Capacity in Canada", the five companies,* which handle all the refining done in Alberta, represent a third of the separate refining companies in Canada, some of which operate under various names. The 87,100 barrels daily capacity in Alberta, owned by the five, is only 8.5% of the total capacity in Canada, although Alberta produces two-thirds of the crude oil and natural gas liquids obtained from Canadian wells. These five companies alone account for about one quarter of the crude oil production of Canada, and there are many other major, foreign oil companies operating in the country. This leaves Alberta a raw material producer in the oil business, with the raw material largely foreign-owned. Alberta might be called an "oil republic" as compared to a "banana republic".

Don't Spoil the Natives

Automatic control of complicated equipment is so advanced in petroleum refining that labour costs are only a small fraction of the selling price of the refined products.

In Canada, in 1961, the wages of hourly-rated production workers in refining amounted to only 3.36% of the selling price received by the refineries. In that year, the average selling price of the refined product was $4.20 a barrel (12¢ a gallon); the labour cost was 14.1¢ a barrel (0.4¢ a gallon — only four tenths of a cent).

---

* Standard Oil, Royal Dutch/Shell Group, Gulf Oil Corp., Texaco Inc., and Husky Oil Co. The author's analysis of Husky which appeared in the original text has been deleted. — Ed.

One of the striking features of wages in Canadian refining is that they have been consistently 50¢ to 60¢ an hour less than in refineries in the United States, until a major gain in late 1965 narrowed the gap to 20 cents. On the other hand, wages in refining — and in the oil and gas industry as a whole — are generally higher than in other Canadian industries. The same is true of salaries.

In this disparity of wages we have the "don't spoil the natives" policy characteristic of foreign ownership in colonial regions. In their foreign operations, the big oil companies add something to the going rate in the country to make themselves welcome and to discourage strong unions.

As Canadians know very well, pay in the United States is higher than ours in practically all fields of endeavor. This is justified on the ground that Canadians do not produce as much per man — that our productivity is lower. Another argument for the inequality is that Canada, like many regions subject to foreign exploitation, is largely a producer of raw or semi-processed materials that are exported, largely to the United States, and then bought back at greatly increased value as manufactured goods.

But what of an industry in which productivity is equal to or even greater than that in the United States and in which the manufacturing is done here from raw materials that cost less to produce ?

On the basis of figures from the Dominion Bureau of Statistics and the United States Bureau of Labor Statistics, in 1961 the output per man-hour in Canadian refineries was 18.4 barrels, (with a value of $77.28 at $4.20 a barrel) while in U.S. refineries it was only 14.6 barrels. This is productivity on the basis of production and maintenance workers only, and is obtained by dividing the total refinery production for the year by the total of man-hours worked by the hourly-rated wage-earners in refining.

It is to be noted also that productivity on the basis of all employees in Canadian refining has increased more rapidly than in the economy as a whole. In the five-year period from 1958 to 1963, productivity in petroleum refining increased at an average rate of 6.7% a year compared to an average increase of 3.8% in the Canadian economy. There is a similar contrast between the annual average for refining and for the economy for the period 1949-1963.

The Oil Workers Union

The labour union most concerned with refining is the Oil, Chemical and Atomic Workers International Union (OCAW).

Some may feel that since the union is international, with its main strength in the United States, it should have been able to eliminate the disparity in wage rates before this. Or again, some may suspect that the international character of the union prevents the Canadian section from pressing for parity.

The facts demonstrate, however, that the international, U.S.-headquartered union has been a major factor in narrowing the wage gap between the two countries since the first Canadian affiliations with the Oil, Chemical and Atomic Workers were made late in 1948. Canadian refinery workers were paid 64 cents an hour less in 1949 than their U.S. couterparts. By 1964 this gap had narrowed to 40 cents, and in a dramatic campaign conducted in 1965 the disparity was narrowed to 20 cents an hour.

More importantly, perhaps, the Canadians surged ahead of the Americans in the agreements reached early in 1966 — they secured clauses in their contracts providing some protection against layoffs caused by technological change. These clauses provided for the establishment of joint labour-management committees to work out a system of protection against such layoffs, providing a moratorium against technological layoffs for the duration of the contracts pending agreements by the committees, and providing for severance pay in case of layoffs caused by technological change.

As for eliminating the differential before this, the union operates in an environment which is extremely hostile to wage parity with the U.S. The hostility was evident in the wrath expressed by editorial writers of the daily press when the auto workers asked for a 60¢ an hour raise to obtain parity with their brother workers just across the border. The publicists for big business want to retain lower wages in Canada to have an advantage in competition for exports. The innocent might ask : What automobile exports ? What gasoline and fuel oil exports ? The question is certainly pertinent in the refining industry, where products are imported not exported.

Mackenzie King and Company Unions

Back in 1914, the young William Lyon Mackenzie King, who had been Minister of Labour in the Laurier government that was defeated in 1911, was hired by the newly established Rockefeller Foundation in New York. The Foundation had an endowment of $242 million to begin with, and by 1964, without adding more endowment, had given away $776 million and still had $643 million on hand — which proves something. But to return to Mr. King and 1914, his first big job was to solve the labour strife at John D. Rockefeller, Jr's, Colorado Fuel and Iron Company, largest industry in Colorado at the time, where a virtual state of civil war had existed for almost two years. Mr. King devised a plan, worked out in conferences with John D. Rockefeller, Jr., and officers and employees of the company, which was adopted by the board of directors and the workers in 1915. King's plan provided for an industrial council with joint representation of employees and management. It provided machinery for handling grievances, the settlement of disputes, terms of employment, living and working conditions. Considering the economic power and the autocratic history of the Standard Oil Rockefeller up to that time, it is probable that this plan was the best that could be achieved under the circumstances. Nevertheless, it has to be noted that Mackenzie King's joint council plan provided the basis for company unions (where control of the organization is really in the hands of management) in oil refineries. One of the first of such company unions was established at the Bayonne, New Jersey, refinery of Standard Oil in 1918. By the early 1930's such company unions existed in many major refineries. They became independent unions only after 1937 when U.S. federal law prohibited them.

While it is contrary to U.S. law for an employer to participate in a union, if it can be proven, there are suspicions that varying degrees of company influence lingers on in some of the so-called "independent" unions. Meanwhile, the company councils designed by King remain in effect in some Canadian refineries, *including all but one of Imperial Oil's.*

It is interesting to speculate about the possible connection between Mackenzie King's long reign as prime minister of Canada and the big business connections he made during the First World War, especially those with Standard Oil of New Jersey. It might be worth some Canadian's time to dig into it.

Gas Processing Puzzle: Find the Canadian Operator

In contrast to the refining of Alberta's crude oil, most of which is done outside its borders, the processing of natural gas is done within the province. Alberta regulations require this. Some may consider it a promotion of local industry by the government, but technical requirements related to corrosion and condensation make it necessary to process the raw gas before it can be transported any long distance by pipeline. Therefore, gas processing plants are located in the fields.

Another regulation, supposed to assure a 30-year supply for Alberta, requires government permission before natural gas may be exported from the province. Some including the gas utilities, are of the opinion that this regulation has been stretched beyond recognition to favour the exporting companies. It is the great increase in the export of gas that has multiplied the gas processing plants.

In 1963, the Canadian Petroleum Association estimated that Alberta was producing an average of 2,319 million cubic feet of natural gas daily, equal to 89% of Canadian production. The figure for 1962 was 2,142 million daily.

Early in 1964 there were some seventy gas processing plants in Alberta out of a total of about eighty in the whole country.

An examination of the nationality of the control of the operating companies gives a reasonably accurate idea of the extent of foreign ownership of gas processing and of the production of natural gas. Although the number and capacity of plants keep changing, an analysis of a report on gas processing plants published in *Canadian Oil and Gas Industries (COGI)*, Nov. 20/62, which included plants planned for completion by the end of 1963 or nearly 1964, gives a good snapshot of the situation. The *COGI* report has been adjusted to include some plants opened in 1963 beyond those expected when it was written.

The top twelve operators, judged by the total capacity of the plants managed, and in order of descending capacity, are : Pacific Oil Company Ltd., Hudson's Bay Oil and Gas Co. Ltd., Shell Canada Limited, Canadian Superior Oil Ltd., Home Oil Company Ltd., Pan American Petroleum Corp., Provo Gas Producers Ltd., Imperial Oil Limited, Jefferson Lake Petro-chemicals of Canada Ltd., Chevron Standard Ltd., and Canadian Fina Oil Ltd.

Only one of these, Home Oil Company Ltd., is considered a Canadian-controlled company.

Rest of the Operators Mostly American

Of the remaining companies operating gas processing plants in Alberta; sixteen were American-controlled; one was British and American; and three were considered Canadian-controlled, but all three are now part of the holdings of the Power Corporation of Canada and should be considered as one. Among the American in this group were such big companies as Socony Mobil, Sun Oil and Tenneco Oil (a subsidiary of Tennessee Gas Transmission Co., Houston, Texas). The control of gas processing and, by implication, of gas production, is firmly in the hands of American companies.

Pipelines: Promoters' Paradise

Pipelines are the means of transportation for most oil and gas, and like raiways before them, have been the beneficiaries of massive government aid while promoters have made fortunes out of options on shares at prices far below market value. Trans-Canada Pipe Lines Limited, and the connected Northern Ontario Natural Gas Co. Ltd., are well-known recent examples of such subsidy and "legal loot", familiar to newspaper readers.

The market value of oil produced in Alberta is still about three times that of natural gas and its extracted products, which puts oil pipelines way out front in importance. Dominating the oil lines are those which transport crude to refineries outside the province. There are two,* one east and one west, and both are foreign-controlled through "resident of Canada" companies which are foreign-controlled.

---

* The two pipelines are Imperial's Interprovincial Pipe Line Co. and Trans Mountain Oil Pipe Line Company. Although the original text discusses both pipelines, only the latter is included here. — Ed.

Trans Mountain Oil Pipe Line Company

Trans Mountain Oil Pipe Line Co. transports crude from Edmonton, and other points in Alberta, 723 miles to Burnaby, B.C., on the east side of Vancouver, with a 63-mile extension to three refineries in the State of Washington. Its capacity is 250,000 barrels daily. In 1963 it carried an average of 191,821 barrels daily, 70 million for the year.

Trans Mountain was incorporated as a Dominion company in 1951. Its bonds were guaranteed by a group of foreign-controlled oil companies, and it was built in 1953, paying its first dividends in 1956.

The major shareholders of Trans Mountain includes Imperial Oil, 8.6%; British American Oil, 8.64%; Shell Canada Limited, Standard Oil of California and Bechtel Corp. of San Francisco. (Financial Post, May 4/63, p. 1) These are all foreign-controlled companies.

Of the nine directors in 1963, two were from the board of Imperial Oil, one was the president of Standard Oil Co. of B.C. (wholly-owned by Standard Oil of California), one was the transportation vice-president of Shell Canada, one was a director of Union Oil Co. of Canada (83% owned by Union Oil Co. of California), one was the president of British American Oil, one lived in San Francisco, one in Los Angeles, and one in Vancouver. In short, firm, foreign control of Trans Mountain.

Pipelines Within Alberta

Oil pipelines form an increasingly complex network under the soil of Alberta. The more important ones have main, or trunk, lines leading to Interprovincial and Trans Mountain, as well as gathering lines in the oil fields. They are nearly all foreign-controlled.

Trans-Canada Pipe Lines Limited: Who Rules Canada?

Since the promotion of Trans-Canada Pipe Lines gave birth to The Alberta Gas Trunk Line Co. it is considered here, although its line begins at the Saskatchewan border.

Trans-Canada, with a monopoly of the movement of natural gas eastward to Canadian and American gas utilities, is the largest purchaser of Alberta gas.

It is notorious as the American-conceived project that cut so much ground from under the Liberal government of Louis St. Laurent and C.D. Howe that the government fell in the election of 1957 and was squashed in 1958.

Trans-Canada has a certain awesome beauty as a masterpiece of American-style promotion of a public utility, complete with big capital gains on stock options for insiders. It defied the Canadian government and made Ottawa, notably the Hon. C.D. Howe, back down and pay out. It is just possible that its victory in the pipeline debate, outside and inside the House of Commons, sounded the death knell of Canada's political independence, or at least its entrance into a state of coma.*

Enter The Murchisons of Dallas, Texas

The original company, incorporated by a special Act of Parliament in 1951, was a subsidiary of Canadian Delhi Oil Ltd., which in turn was a subsidiary of Delhi-Taylor Oil Corp. of Dallas, Texas, owned, until it was liquidated in 1964, by Clint W. Murchison, Sr., C. W. Murchison Jr., and J.D. Murchison of Dallas, often referred to as the wheeler-dealer Murchisons (Clint was reported as a backer of Sen. Joseph MacCarthy). F.A. Schultz, of Dallas, the president of Canadian Delhi Oil, was a director of Trans-Canada Pipe Lines in 1963, as was Smiley Raborn, Jr. the executive vice-president and managing director of Canadian Delhi Oil Ltd. In January 1965, Canadian Delhi was taken over by Sohio Petroleum Co., a wholly-owned subsidiary of Standard Oil Company (an Ohio Corporation) of Cleveland, Ohio, but Canadian Delhi's big holding of Trans-Canada Pipe Lines shares had been distributed to Canadian Delhi shareholders and did not go to Sohio. This holding was 843,327 shares, equal to about 8% of Trans-Canada at the time. (See *The Albertan*, Calgary, Jan. 6/65, p. 15)

The March to Monopoly

The bare chronology of the development of Trans-Canada Pipe Lines reveals the American oil power play at work on Canadian governments.

In January 1954, the Murchison's Trans-Canada Pipe Lines Co. and Western Pipe Lines, which had been formed by a group of Canadian business men, were amalgamated into a continuing Trans-Canada Pipe Lines Co.

In April 1954, the Act to incorporate the Alberta Gas Trunk Line Co. was passed by the Alberta government, thus providing a monopoly to gather natural gas for Trans-Canada and deliver it to the company at the Saskatchewan border. Trans-Canada was represented on the original board of directors of Alberta Gas Trunk Line that was formed in August 1954.

In May 1954, the Alberta government granted Trans-Canada an export permit to take out 4,350 billion cubic feet of natural gas, over

---

* This appears to be confirmed by the success of the oil industry in getting the federal cabinet to reverse its decision on Trans Canada's proposed pipeline through the United States, from thumbs down to approval, late in 1966. — J. M. F.

a 25-year period, at the rate of 183 billion a year, 620 million cubic 12,080 billion (12.08 trillion) cubic feet over a period to 1989, as of Dec. 1964, at a much bigger annual rate.

In July 1954, the Dominion Board of Transport Commissioners granted Trans-Canada its initial permit to construct a pipeline across Canada, with construction supposed to begin in 1955.

Then came the crucial battle between foreign-controlled oil and gas interests and the government of Canada, supposedly representing the public interest. This conflict delayed the start of construction for a year.

The company was guided in this period by its president, Nathan E. Tanner, former Minister of Mines and Minerals in the Social Credit government of Alberta, who had left the government in 1952.

The fight was over government aid. Trans-Canada Pipe Lines was seeking large financial assistance from the government of Canada. The government wanted its loans to Trans-Canada to be convertible later into common shares of the company, thus giving Ottawa a voting, ownership interest in Trans-Canada, if the government desired it at the time of redemption of the loans. American owners of gas fields in Alberta, reported to be led by the president of Gulf Oil Corp. of Pittsburgh, stated flatly that they would not sell their gas to Trans-Canada if the government of Canada was in a position to obtain voting shares in the company.

The Canadian government backed down.

This justifies the question: Who rules Canada, American Oil companies or the elected government?

In September 1955, Prime Minister Louis St. Laurent and Premier Frost of Ontario agreed to form a Crown company to build a 675-mile section of the Trans-Canada pipeline from the Manitoba border to Kapuskasing, Ontario. This was the most difficult section of the route. The agreement gave Trans-Canada an option to purchase the Crown company and credited part of the rent to be paid by Trans-Canada towards the purchase payment. The company was called the Northern Ontario Pipe Line Crown Corporation. Canada was to put up two-thirds and Ontario one-third of the estimated $120 million needed to build the section. It actually had a final capital cost of $129,866,242. In May 1963, Trans-Canada exercised its option and bought this Crown company from the government of Prime Minister Lester B. Pearson for $109.5 million, with funds borrowed mainly in the United States. But to return to our chronology:

In October 1955, Gulf Oil, which within a few months was to obtain control of the British American Oil Co., signed a long-term sales contract to supply Trans-Canada with about one quarter of its 25-year export permit — 1.3 trillion cubic feet of natural gas out of its total export permit of 4.35 trillion.

In November 1955, Tennessee Gas Transmission Co. of Houston, Texas, the largest pipeline company in the United States, obtained 50% of Trans-Canada by getting an option to buy Trans-Canada shares equal in number to those held by the original principals, in return for financing a difinite order for 34-inch diameter pipe to be used in the western section of the line. The order was given to the United States Steel Corporation in November 1955. Tennessee Gas Transmission Co. exercised its option to purchase shares in Trans-Canada in February 1956. Earlier, in August 1955, Tennessee Gas Transmission had signed a contract to buy gas from Trans-Canada at Emerson, Manitoba, and to sell gas to Trans-Canada at Niagara, Ontario; also to buy surplus gas. Deliveries to a subsidiary of Tennessee, at Emerson, began in December 1960.

In February 1965, Gulf Oil's subsidiary in Canada (soon to be B-A Oil) and Hudson's Bay Oil and Gas Co. (subsidiary of Continental Oil of the U.S.) became partners in Trans-Canada, at the same time as Tennessee Gas Transmission.

By this time Trans-Canada was very much American-owned.

The government in Ottawa wanted construction to begin early in 1956, but Trans-Canada still did not have enough money. The company asked Ottawa for an additional bundle of aid. It wanted a $72 million loan from the Crown corporation towards building the line from Alberta's border to Winnipeg, Manitoba. The loan was to be repaid in nine months at 5% interest.

In June 1956, the government bill approving the Crown corporation and enabling a loan of $80 million to Trans-Canada was passed in the House of Commons over great opposition from the other political parties.

Twelve days later, the first pipe arrived at Burstall, Sask., the western end of the pipeline.

On July 10, 1956, construction began on the western section.

On January 31, 1957, the federal government authorized the start of construction of the northern Ontario leg of the line by the Northern Ontario Pipe Line Crown Corporation.

On February 26, 1957, Trans-Canada Pipe Lines repaid the government loan.

In October 1957, gas began to flow into the western section, and on October 10, 1958, the whole 2,340-mile line to Montreal was completed.

In May, 1963, Trans-Canada bought the Crown corporation section.

The overall cost of this original line was about $378 million. Governments put up $210 million of this, at the start, to make it a success. That is, the people of Canada financed almost two-thirds of a project comparable in importance to the first trans-Canada railway, without obtaining a single ownership share in a vital energy transportation system. All this public aid went to American corporations, with some Canadian camp followers, so that they could make money out of our energy needs. It went to them because they already owned the natural gas, and they owned it because of Premier Ernest C. Manning's oil and gas policy in Alberta.

Is Trans-Canada Canadian-Owned Today?

In 1958, his mission accomplished, the prominent Alberta Social Credit politician, Nathan E. Tanner, packed whatever capital gains he had made on his share options at low prices, and departed from the presidency of Trans-Canada Pipe Lines. He moved on to the sanctity of the upper circles of the Mormon Church in Salt Lake City, Utah, where, in 1962, he was named to the Council of Twelve Apostles.

It is difficult to believe that the American oil and gas interests, who forced Ottawa to back down on ownership shares, were content to take capital gains from the $1 par shares that went to over $38 in 1958, and sell control to Canadians. The potential profits of such a line are too great. There are reasons to believe they have not given up controls, although Home Oil Co. was claimed to be the largest single owner of shares, holding about 21% at the beginning of 1964. One reason is the make-up of the board of directors, another is the existence of a large number of convertible bonds. The American corporations were not against convertible bonds as such, only against the government of Canada obtaining any.

In 1963, Trans-Canada had eighteen directors. Two were from Canadian Delhi Oil, representing the original promoter, Delhi-Taylor Oil Corp. of Dallas, Texas. Two were from B-A Oil, representing Gulf Oil Corp. of Pittsburgh. One was from Hudson's Bay Oil & Gas Co., representing its boss Continental Oil Co. (Delware). One resided in New York City. The three American companies mentioned were represented from subsidiaries that are "residents of Canada".

Home Oil Co. had two directors, but this does not mean that the ten others represented Canadian holdings.

As for the convertible securities, at the beginning of 1964, Trans-Canada had 2,400,000 common shares reserved for issuance against debentures and notes convertible into common shares. There were 5,861,183 common shares outstanding at the beginning of 1963, of the 10,000,000 authorized. How many of the convertible securities are held by "resident of Canada" subsidiaries of foreign firms, how many by non- residents of Canada ? We have not been told. But in the case of Home Oil Co. we do know this. During 1963 Home Oil Co. has built up its holding of Trans-Canada shares, and half the issue had been offered in the United States. These debentures were redeemed in December 1963, and Home Oil paid out 662,521 Trans-Canada shares leaving it with 1,231,255 shares, 21% of those outstanding at the time. This Home Oil transaction certainly increased the non-resident holding of Trans-Canada.

It Is Profitable

After setting aside millions in cash for depreciation account each year, Trans-Canada has been showing a net profit beginning in 1961. In 1963, this net profit had risen to $10.5 million on total sales of $102.5 million, but one analyst hopes to see this net profit rise to about $25 million in a few years. Says the shares are a good buy . . . Too bad the government of Canada doesn't own any.

Athabaska Oil Sands: The Biggest Sellout in History

A conservative estimate of the recoverable oil in the Athabasca sands, based on extensive survey work, is 300 billion barrels. Just how conservative this is may be indicated by a 1963 estimate which claimed the recoverable crude oil to total 626 billion barrels. These oil sands cover an area of approximately 13,000 square miles (some 8,320,000 acres) and, according to Frank K. Spragins of Imperial Oil, average about 100,000 barrels per acre, with the better sands going as high as 250,000 barrels an acre. It is mostly the better areas that are leased.

This conservative estimate is so vast that it is difficult to grasp its significance. It is almost equal to all the existing conventional oil well reserves of the whole world, about two-thirds of which are in the Middle-East. It is almost sixty times the conventional oil well reserves of Canada, estimated at the beginning of 1963 to be 5.2 billion barrels of crude oil and natural gas liquids, with 4.5 billion of the total in Alberta.

The Big Lease Holders

By October 1, 1962, over 2,600,000 acres of the Athabasca oil sands had been leased by the government of Alberta to oil companies at 25¢ an acre (one quarter of the conventional oil lease rental), in solid, not checkerboard, leases, ranging from 1,400 to 50,000 acres per lease, and with some companies holding lease after lease. At that time the vast majority of these companies were foreign-controlled, mostly American, and the largest holdings were in the hands of U.S. companies. Since that date, the Canadian holdings in the sands have decreased, because of the takeover of such companies as Bailey Selburn Oil & Gas by Pacific Petroleums and of Consolidated Mic Mac Oils by Hudson's Bay Oil & Gas.

The top eight lease owners at October 1, 1962, of the thirty then holding leases, with the nationality of control in parenthesis, and the number of acres held were:

Richfield Oil Corp. (U.S.)	689,000
Texaco (Exploration & Regent) (U.S.)	393,500
Cities Service Group (U.S.)	265,000
Shell Canada (Dutch & British)	213,000
Hudson's Bay Oil & Gas (U.S.)	120,000
Pan American Petroleum (U.S.)	100,000
Socony Mobil Oil (U.S.)	96,700
Sinclair Canada Oil (U.S.)	84,000

THESE EIGHT HELD 1,961,600
acres of 2,600,000

These names and figures, taken from Oilweek, Oct. 1/62,, p. 17, are misleading in some respects.

For one thing, the name of Imperial Oil Limited is missing, but Imperial is very much present in the oil sands. It has a 30% interest in the Cities Service Group with its 265,000 acres, and the president and general manager of the research and future production arm of the group, Syncrude Canada Ltd., is Frank K. Spragins, Imperial's oil sands expert. The chairman of Syncrude is Vernon Taylor, vice-president of Imperial, and there are two other Imperial men on the board of eleven directors. Again, Imperial is associated in Richfield Oil Corporation's project for removing oil from the sands, which gives it an interest in Richfield's big holdings.

Secondly, Oilweek's list does not indicate the real extent of Richfield's holdings. Richfield owns 30% of the Cities Service Group, and so does Cities Service. But Richfield itself is controlled by Cities Service Company, Inc., 60 Wall Street, New York, and Sinclair Oil Corp., 600 Fifth Ave., New York. Since 1937, Cities Service has owned 31% of Richfield and Sinclair Oil has held 30.1% of the stock. Therefore, to Richfield's own holdings should be added 60% of the Cities Service Group holdings and the leases of Sinclair Canada Oil Co., which is a subsidiary of a wholly-owned subsidiary of Sinclair Oil Corp., in order to get a true picture of Richfield's interest in the oil sands. This gives the Richfield - Cities Service - Sinclair combine 932,400 acres. One may ask why Richfield has such a big interest. An investigation of the shareowners of Richfield might turn up a name or two to ponder about.

Also, the name of British American Oil does not appear in the Oilweek list but B-A is present through its ownership of Royalite which has a 10% interest in the Cities Service Group.

Foreign Control of Production Projects

The first production permit for the oil sands was given to Great Canadian Oil Sands Ltd. It is foreign-controlled. So are the companies that have applied for such permits and others which have indicated their intention to apply for production.

Great Canadian Oil Sands Limited

Incorporated as a Dominion company in 1953, Great Canadian owns the license to a process for recovering oil from the sands. The process is owned by Oil Sands Ltd., 427 St. James St. W., Montreal, and was acquired from International Bitumen Co. Ltd. under rather peculiar circumstances dealt with in the next chapter. In 1958, Great Canadian made an agreement with Sun Oil and Abasand Oil Co. (at one time operated by the federal government) to sublease half of Lease No. 4 in the oil sands, in which Abasand Oil has an interest, and to produce and deliver to Edmonton synthetic crude for sale to Sun Oil and Canadian Oil Companies (now owned by Shell Canada Ltd.). Agreement with the purchasing companies were extended in 1962. It is on Lease No. 4 that Great Canadian's extraction plant is being built, with the Bechtel Corp. of San Francisco as the general contractor in charge of the work, through its subsidiary Canadian Bechtel Ltd.

Great Canadian Oil Sands Ltd. is completely controlled by Sun Oil Company, 1608 Walnut Street, Philadelphia, Pa., which in turn is controlled by the Pew family of Philadelphia, well-known for their ultra-conservative Republicanism and financial support of extreme rightist, even lunatic fringe groups. J. Howard Pew, chairman of Sun Oil, was reported as a fund raiser for Barry Goldwater during the 1964 U.S. presidential campaign. There are four Pews on the board of Sun Oil Sands Ltd. Shell Canada Limited is the other major share owner.

Originally, when Great Canadian made its application for a production permit, it had granted options to buy up to 51% of the shares to the CPR's Canadian Pacific Oil and Gas Ltd., Sun Oil Co. Ltd. (Sun Oil's Canadian subsidiary) and Canadian Oil Companies Ltd. (bought by Shell Canada Ltd. after October 12, 1962). The orignal group was granted a permit October 2, 1962, to proceed with a project to produce 31,500 barrels daily, production to start in the autumn of 1966, with delivery of oil by pipelines to Sarnia, Ontario, to be used by associated refineries, and expected to cost them 20¢ less a barrel than conventional crude. The permit depended upon the company arranging financing by Sept. 30/63. The royalty to the government was set at 8% of production up to 900,000 barrels a month, 20% of barrels over 900,000 a month. Since 8% was only about half the royalty rate of similar conventional oil well production, protests were made that the Alberta government was subsidizing oil sands production at the expense of conventional oil.

Prior to the deadline for financing, in response to pressure from Sun Oil, the company asked for a new hearing before the Alberta Oil and Gas Conservation Board in which it applied for an extension of time and an expansion of production to 45,000 barrels daily from a $191 million project. If such an expansion were granted, Sun Oil Co. was prepared to buy $67.5 million of ownership shares and to assist in raising $123.5 million in loans to make the project possible. Sun would also take 75% of the production for its refineries at Sarnia Ontario, and Toledo, Ohio, with capacities of 25,000 and 95,000 barrels daily respectively. Sun also wanted a majority of directors on the board.

A hearing was granted late in November, 1963. Sun was supported by the big guns of Chase Manhattan Bank of New York and First National City Bank of New York (now operating in Canada as the Mercantile Bank). Sun was represented at the hearing by its president, Robert G. Dunlop of Philadelphia.

Sun Oil's proposals were accepted by both the Conservation Board and Premier Manning's cabinet, with a bit of window dressing for the populace about the government demanding that Sun meet certain conditions, one of which was that residents of Alberta be permitted to buy $12.5 million of 6% convertible debentures of Great Canadian Oil Sands Ltd. in $100 units, the debentures to be guaranteed by Sun Oil Company of Philadelphia. Applicants were to apply for any number of units they wanted, depositing $100 to cover one unit. Each applicant would receive one unit, and any balance of units left over would be distributed according to the number of units applied for. After the third year of the ten-year debentures, holders were to be allowed to convert $32 of the debenture into Great Canadian shares. These crumbs from the oil sands cake were to go on sale in September of 1964, but dispute over the method of distribution delayed things. Another demand on Sun Oil, sort of a footnote, was that Alberta labour and technicians be used where possible.

The cabinet granted the permit on April 10, 1964, and early in July, Premier Ernest C. Manning went down the Athabaska River to Lease No. 4 where he placed a marker at the datum point of the processing plant, in the presence of Mines and Minerals Minister A.R. Patrick, and representatives of Great Canadian, Canadian Bechtel Ltd. and Sun Oil. The rape of the oil sands was under way, with production expected to begin by September 30, 1967. What a way to celebrate Canada's Centennial Year, with the treasure of the oil sands flowing into the coffers of Sun and Shell and certain Canadian accomplices.

The granting of the permit stretched Premier Manning's avowed policy of restricting production from the sands to 5% of the total demand for Alberta oil (demand was about 536,000 barrels a day in 1963, 5% of which is about 26,800, so demand will have to nearly double by 1967 to make 45,000 barrels daily equal that 5%) but, after all, one "free enterpriser" should help another. Sun Oil Company's offices, everywhere, are decorated with a framed "Creed We Work By" inculcating all the virtues in its employees and extolling "free enterprise" for profit. As for the latter, it declared a net profit for 1963 of $61.2 million (U.S.), after setting aside from net income the nice sum of $62.2 million for depletion, depreciation and retirements. It had $103.7 million earned surplus carried forward. Total revenue for the year was $885.2 million. It can afford the paternalistic internal policy which has excluded the oil workers' union.

Ignoring the woe pronounced upon those who add field to field, Sun had added 100,000 acres of prospecting permits in the oil sands by November 1963 to the 65,000 leased acres it held in October 1962. It also picked up a piece of paper from Eric Harvie late in 1963 for 11,000 acres of leases. All this was in addition to its rather extensive holdings in the conventional oil production of Western Canada. Then, in 1964, it moved into the Saskatchewan section of the oil sands, as did Imperial Oil, and also took up 3,500,000 acres of oil shale prospecting permits straddling the Saskatchewan-Manitoba border. It had the aid of new regulations passed by both governments, and was guided in its staking by the shale survey work done by the Geological Survey of Canada.

While hunting the raw material in the west, Sun Oil owns 55% of the Sun-Canadian Pipe Line Co. Ltd., which pumps refined products from Sarnia to Toronto (Shell owns the rest), and markets its products through some 900 service stations, under the Sunoco sign, where you can get gas blended to suit your car, in Ontario and Quebec.

Cities Service Group — Syncrude Canada Ltd.

The Cities Service Group is composed of Imperial Oil, Richfield Oil Corp. and Cities Service, each with 30% and B-A's Royalite Oil with 10%. These are all American companies.

In January 1965, Syncrude Canada Ltd., incorporated in Alberta, took over the research, and future operating and production functions, that had been carried on previously for the group by Cities Service Athabaska Inc., a wholly-owned subsidiary of Cities Service Company, 60 Wall Street, New York.

Syncrude Canada Ltd. is owned 30% each by Imperial, Cities Service, Richfield, and 10% by B-A's Royalite. Its president and general manager is Frank K. Spragins, former manager of Imperial Oil's oil sands department. The board includes representatives from all the companies involved.

The proposed production project of this group has been attacked by independents as a device for obtaining priority of claim on the exploitation of the oil sands by the major outfits involved. The group's application for a production permit, made in January 1963, calls for the production of 100,000 barrels daily from a $356 million project on a 49,788 acre block, which is Lease No. 17, right next to and running northwest from Great Canadian Oil Sands Ltd.'s Lease No. 4 on which the first production plant is being built. At the time of its application, the group was said to hold an additional 279,796 acres under lease, an increase from the holdings of October 1962.

In October 1963, after long cogitation, the Board deferred the group's application, but allowed it to reapply up to December 31 1968, *with priority during that period over any new applicants,* with the exception of Great Canadian and Shell. The Alberta government approved the deferral in December 1963.

It is possibly a high note in the comic opera of Canadian sovereignty that the American-owned Cities Service Co. Ltd. was working on a six-acre floral garden near its Bronte refinery, 20 miles west of Toronto, to be known as the Cities Service Centennial Garden, to be completed in time for Canada's centennial celebration in 1967. This was taken over by British Petroleum of the U.K. in 1964, when it bought Cities Service's refinery and its service stations in Ontario and Quebec. The garden to include plants from all the provinces and the two northern territories, was believed to be "the first garden of its kind in the country." Oh well, if you can't build your own garden, let international oil do it for you.

Shell Canada Limited

Following the Cities Service Group, Shell Canada Limited applied for a production permit. It proposed to produce about 100,000 barrels daily from a $260 million project, which would use an underground "in situ" method of extraction reaching the deeper sands not suited to open pit mining.

The application was heard in February 1963, and deferred at same time as that of the Cities Service Group. Shell Canada, controlled by Royal Dutch/Shell (60% Dutch, 40% British), *was given the same priority terms* as Cities Service up to December 31, 1968. In both cases, the deferral was based on the ground of protecting the $4 billion investment in the conventional oil industry, which has been producing as high as 40% of the total provincial public revenue.

With these large foreign companies having established priority, others were left considering their proposed applications. Among them were: Pan American Petroleum Corp., Socony Mobil Oil Company Inc. (name changed to Mobil Oil Corp. in 1966), Richfield Oil Corporation*, and Can-Amera Export Refining Company Ltd.

---

* In 1966 merged with Atlantic Refining Company of Philadelphia, Pa., to become Atlantic Richfield.

What Now?

With what is considered to be the best part of the Athabasca oil sands leased by foreign companies, the beginning of production in the hands of an ultra-conservative American family and company, and the other proposed production projects foreign-owned, have the people of Alberta, and of Canada, lost an ocean of oil to private empire builders?

The province has had control of petroleum resources since 1930, the Social Credit party has been in power since 1935, and Ernest C. Manning has been at the helm since 1943. There can be no doubt who is responsible for the present situation and about what the people of Alberta have to do, if they want a change in policy that will restore this treasure to Canadian hands.

The present concern of the Social Credit government is not with the alienation of this truly fabulous store of energy, but with how to prevent it upsetting the conventional oil industry in the province, and thus protect the government's stake in the revenues it has been obtaining from that conventional oil industry. That is the purpose of Premier Manning's avowed policy of limiting the production of synthetic crude from the oil sands to five per cent of the demand for Alberta oil. This could protect the industry for a long time. The demand for Alberta crude oil and natural gas liquids was estimated to average 576,500 barrels daily in 1964. Five per cent of this is only 28,825 barrels daily, far below the 45,000 b/d allotted to Great Canadian Oil Sands. It would take a tremendous growth in demand for Alberta oil to launch another project in the oil sands under Manning's restrictive policy.

There is, however, a factor in the situation which could change Manning's policy on oil sands production because of the pressure it would create from the major oil companies, and his policy has been their policy in the past. That factor is the cost of production of oil sands crude.

There are reasons to believe that crude from the sands, at least from those areas subject to surface mining, will be low cost oil. Russel J. Cameron, head of a firm of consulting engineers in Denver, who has been active in oil shale research, expressed the opinion that within twenty years oil from Athabasca sands and Colorado shales will be the cheapest source in North America. (*Oilweek,* May 4/64, p. 13) Dr. A. R. Plotnick, of the University of Alberta, Calgary, who has written articles on oil pricing in Canada, expressed the opinion Jan. 8/64 that Athabasca oil would become cheap enough by 1975 to be laid down in western Europe at $2.50 a barrel. This of course would enable it to penetrate markets not served at present by Alberta oil. Part of Mr. Manning's oil sands production policy is that there will be no restrictions if the oil is marketed in areas not served by conventional Alberta crude. When he announced this policy in October 1962, Mr. Manning envisioned oil sands production of about 200,000 barrels daily by 1975. (*Oilweek*, Oct. 29/62).

You will notice that Mr. Manning's policy of restricting oil sands production to some 5% of the demand for conventional crude, and, at the same time, placing no restriction on production to markets not served by conventional crude, is designed to preserve the existing price structure of oil in Canada, if oil sands crude is low cost. To be blunt, it is designed to prevent the Canadian consumer benefitting from low cost energy from the sands, and to provide extra profits to those who obtain a permit to produce.

Regardless of the cost of production, the people of Alberta would serve their own and the national interest if they changed the government in power for one with a policy of restoring the Athabasca oil sands to Canadian hands. Since it is a waste of capital to buy a minority interest in existing foreign firms, and it would cost too much to buy a majority or total interest in the parents of the companies in the oil sands now, it would appear that restoration of the sands to Canadian hands requires the taking over all production in them by a crown corporation, or by a joint state and co-operative and private investor company, empowered to engage in all aspects of the oil industry.

If the people of Alberta are unable or unwilling to do this, then the government of Canada has the power, if it wants to use it, to take over the sands in the national interest.

Published 1967

" The *Kitchener - Waterloo Record* of November 9 reported that in the last seven years Washington has spend $ 1 . 6 billion in Canada for defence jobs. This defence sharing pact is not a classifield secret but it is regarded as a sensitive area and consequently played down as much as possible. Three hundred and eighty-one Canadian firms, over this period, have participated in the production of defence equipment for the American armed forces."

THE MULTI-NATIONAL
CORPORATION AND CANADA

by Melville Watkins

It is only very recently that Canadians have learned to talk about multi-national corporations rather than simply foreign investment. The term is already obsolete; the American business schools now call them multi-national enterprises. Apparently even the word "corporation" is now too strong.

The issue with which I am concerned is: where does the power lie in the technological society of the West?

While there are a very large number of possible answers, four seem relevant for my purposes:

1. power lies with the corporations, domestic and multi-national, that is, western societies in general and North American societies in particular are characterized by the dominance of corporate capitalism.
2. power lies with governments and, vis-à-vis the multi-national corporations, with the nation-states or governments of the host countries.
3. power lies with the technocrats, who really run both corporations and governments.
4. power lies with nobody; technology is simply out of control, or what Ellul calls the autonomy of technique.

A fifth possibility which has no relevance to present-day reality is that power lies with the people.

Few would doubt that corporations have power at home, notably in the United States, and that multi-national corporations have power abroad. But there are differences of opinion as to how great that power is in each case.

Within the United States, there are power centres other than the corporate boardrooms, notably Washington. John Kenneth Galbraith, who is a sensitive though not profound observer of his times, maintains that the New Industrial State of Nature capitalism is characterized by an intermingling of the private and public sectors, or a technostructure, and that there is no private sector, at least so far as big business is concerned. The technostructure—which others, including Dwight David Eisenhower, have called the military-industrial complex—is run by technocrats. Real power lies with them. From this point of view, the hope of the future lies in completing the victory of the techoncrats and then democratizing the technostructure and humanizing the technocrats.

While Galbraith is more realistic than most liberal economists, he is a liberal economist, and it seems a reasonable presumption that he under-estimates the power of the corporations. Since the 1930's, there has been much talk about a managerial revolution. It is not clear that the technostructure is anything more than a new label for this—and with the serious drawback that the reality of the military-industrial complex which is masked is much more ominous now. Also, this way of looking at things fits well—too well—into the end-ofideology thesis so popular among American liberal intellectuals. What is increasingly evident, however, is that the end-of-ideology is simply the liberal ideology in its highest form.

Corporation as Institution

The corporation as an institutional form absorbs technocrats without changing its own imperatives : to grow, to innovate, to control and to manipulate people—all largely mindless of the consequences for the human environment. Technocrats within the corporation improve its internal efficiency and increase its social costs. Technocrats within governments link the corporation and the government more closely together, both directly by pushing programmes which increase corporate sales and indirectly by assuming responsibility for attempting to tidy up after the corporations.

Academics, by being technocrats rather than intellectuals, contribute not only by also helping to tidy up but, more importantly, by providing a rationale for this system of corporate capitalism. I.F. Stone has recently pointed out that even that greatest of technocrats, Robert McNamara, was unable to contain corporate greed for arms escalation. On two critical issues, the missile gap and the anti-ballistic missile, the technocrats were overridden by the necessities of the military-industrial complex. Noam Chomsky has shown how American political scientists aided and abetted the Pentagon in the War in Vietnam. Indeed, to read Chomsky is to wonder whether the world would not be safer if the corporations had more power and the technocrats less.

It is true that we live in a technological society. But the technology is invented and applied within the structure of corporate capitalism—its mode of production and its goals. At best, we have a technology biased towards instruments of violence and toward a range of harmful effects on the air we breathe, the water we drink, and so on. At worst, we have a technology that under the name of progress is out of control and may yet get us all.

The United States is presently characterized by a number of serious problems —not only its contribution to the balance of nuclear terror but imperialism and aggression abroad and poverty and black ghettoes at home. It may seem unfair to blame all this on the corporations but who else so clearly runs America ?

What has this to do with the multi-national corporation ? The multi-national corporation is simply the extension of the corporation into other countries. Most of the multi-national corporations are, in fact, American-based with Americans as shareholders and top managers, so their foreign activities can be regarded as the global extensions of American corporate capitalism. In terms of rhetoric, perhaps even of intentions, these corporations see themselves as having evolved into a new form as they have become multi-national. In terms of their internal structure, particularly their communications systems and to some extent their decision-making structure, many have. But in terms both of the basic corporate imperatives and the hierarchical, authoritarian structure, little if anything has changed.

The Nation State and Power

What about the nation-states ? Do they have power ? By going abroad, the American corporation comes into more direct contact with foreign governments than in the old days when trade mattered rather than direct investment. Now the American corporation at home, as it went national in the late nineteenth century, had to cope with sub-federal governments. Abroad, it must now cope with other national governments. On the whole, the latter are more troublesome than the former, but the corporations control many things others want—technology, brand names, tied markets—and can play off governments against each other.

The economist Dudley Seers wrote an article with the pregnant title : "Big Companies and Small Countries". In terms of income generated, General Motors is larger than many countries in the world. [1] American investment abroad considered as an economy is presently exceeded in size by only two national economies, the U.S. and the U.S.S.R. Not surprisingly, and appearances to the contrary notwithstanding, few countries have been able to develop anything like an effective national policy for dealing with foreign ownership. While Canada is at the extreme end of the policy spectrum with a do-nothing policy, other countries with positive policy have had to make important concessions to the real power of the multi-national corporation. De Gaulle found that a hard-line policy in France only caused American firms to set up in Belgium and export to France, a process made possible by the cutting of tariffs consequent on the American-backed E.E.C. Japan, a large industrialized country, had to yield to I.B.M.

Is there any room for maneouvre? What ought the policy of host countries to be? In the parlance of economics, foreign direct investment creates both benefits and costs for the host country. So the economists advice, which pervades the Watkins Report, is to maximize net benefits. This is easier said than done. The benefits and the costs inhere in the very process of direct investment; it is impossible to eliminate the costs and retain the benefits. Both are complex mixtures of the economic, political, social and cultural. Since they do not lend themselves to being reducted to a common denominaor, the notion that a net benefit, or net cost, can be calculated, or quantified in money terms, is an illusion.

Political economy having died, it is conventional to see the benefits as economic and the costs as political. This is useful for policy-makers, who can then try to increase specific benefits and decrase specific costs in specific ways; hence the Watkins Report.

New Perspective

From a different, perhaps more fundamental perspective, the distinction between economic benefits and political costs breaks down. Foreign ownership creates a branch plant economy. The result is economic growth, as incomes tend to rise in pace with the larger economy to which the branch plant economy is tied—that is, rising per capital income within an existing institutional shell absorbing foreign technology but not generating its own—but not economic developement in the sense of continuing transformation of the economy as a prerequisite for autonomous and sustained growth. Hence the customary dichotomy between political independence and economic benefits—namely, that independence would create costs in terms of lowering the standard of living—may be false, at least in the long-run.

To focus more directly on the political, it can also be argued that a branch plant economy tends to become a concessionary economy dominated by elites who see their job primarily as minimizing tension within the imperial system. We could debate whether the long-standing Canadian practice of quiet diplomacy is or is not in Canada's interest, but we would be certain that it is in the American interest.

In fact, strong advocates of foreign ownership and the multinational corporation always say that there are both economic benefits and political benefits. Strong critics should say that there are both economic costs and political costs.

Another way of generating insights is to see the problem of foreign ownership as resulting from the interface between the multinational corporation and the nation-state. There is a tendency in some quarters to see this as an unequal struggle, with the multi-national corporation being hailed as the wave of the future and the nation-state as the dead hand of the past. The future is uncertain, but the multi-national corporation is, in any event, the wave of the present. As previously noted, there are a number of serious problems today—to which at the world level we should add the poverty of most of the world and the apparent failure of most countries to develop in spite of the multi-national corporation—suggesting that corporate capitalism is dysfunctional, even dangerous. The nation-state may have its limitations, but what other political and social entity is there to cope with reality? And, of course, one should be suspicious of the extent to which it is Americans like George Ball who praise the multi-national corporation and deplore other countries' nationalism. After all, they have most of the multi-national corporations and see them as a way of spreading the American Great Society around the world. If nationalism is to be deplored, American nationalism must head the list. Other countries need to be nationalistic to protect themselves from American fall-out.

While nationalism is therefore a virtue, that is not to say that some varieties are not more virtuous than others. I do not have in mind here the prevalent Canadian view that nationalism is good, but anti-Americanism is bad. Indeed, it should require only a moment's reflection to realize that anti-Americanism is a much more viable position than pro-Canadianism—since I had to invent the latter term. Rather, what I have in mind is the limitations of sentimental nationalism, which for Canada includes bourgeois nationalism. The business class of this country has always been emasculated and cannot provide a base for a viable nationalism. I am increasingly of the view that nationalism for Canada must mean, and can only mean, a nationalism of the left.

If we damn both the multi-national corporation and the nationalism we have known, it is only to place a very heavy burden on those who would give us an alternative future. A tolerable future—if there is to be one at all—can mean only the humanizing and democratizing of a technological society presently dominated by corporate capitalism. Difficult though it may be to translate such a statement into practical political terms, we should at least know what the name of the game is.

Canadian Guidelines

And difficult though it is, we should at least try. Let me attempt to lay down some guidelines—if you will forgive me such a banal term:
—to the extent that rising standards of living remain a legitimate and necessary goal, Canada should attempt to create a more self-sustained economy more capable of autonomous growth, that is, an economy more under Canadian ownership and control. Given Canada's comparative advantage in resource exports, resource policy should favour Canadian ownership as breeding grounds for Canadian entrepreneurship, private and public. The Trudeau government is concerned about Canadian ownership within the Arctic Circle; the rest of Canada remains for us to worry about. Given the inefficiency of Canada's secondary manufacturing industry, rationalization programmes are needed which are, in fact, economic planning to increase Canadian control, private and public. A first step is the Canada Development Corporation.
—to the extent that Canada as a nation-state must be created to fight American intrusions, institutions and policies should be created to countervail American extraterritoriality via the parent-subsidiary re-

lationship. The Watkins Report makes specific and useful proposals in this regard. The proposed government export trade agency to attempt to counter American restrictions on trade with communist countries should be extended to engage in state-trading.

—the mercantilist, or neo-colonial, strategy of seeking special status within the American Empire and smoothing over issues by quiet diplomacy must cease. While this would not be easy, it is a necessary part of the strategy of bringing the Canadian economy more under Canadian control.

—the politics of the future must transcend the impersonality, bureaucracy and mindless pursuit of technological "progress" of corporate capitalism if it is to really matter. Old conceptions of national planning—which have been kept alive by organizations such as The Ontario Woodsworth Memorial Foundation and for which we should all be grateful—are seriously in need of being rethought and supplemented. The nation-state is needed as a holding-operation against the multi-national corporation—and hence the case for much stronger Canadian policy. But the greater need is for communal action, probably largely at the sub-national level, to plan environments rather than to live in those imposed by the present system. A community worthy of the name must at least be able to deal with the social costs of technology, and at best begin to establish different priorities.

If these things are to happen, people must be politicized. The solution does not lie in giving power to the technocrats. Nor does it lie in electoral politics alone. For electoral politics needs to be supplemented by confrontation politics focussed less on national issues and more on day-to-day felt concerns.

University students protesting Dow Chemical's recruiting on campus contribute more to Canadian understanding of American imperialism than could any national debate on foreign ownership. When workers complain about inflation, they should be informed that in the Canadian branch plant economy, no effective means exists to control prices. When middle-class workers get uptight because they are priced out of the housing market and middle-class students cannot find remunerative jobs, they should be told that they are experiencing a fate common to one-third of the population of this country that lives in genuine poverty. When the N.D.P. finds an easy target in the lethargy and inefficiency of Canadian capitalism, we should ask that the possibility be considered that the real enemy is American capitalism.

To lengthen this list would be a useful exercise for all of us.

Published 1969

THE DYNAMICS OF POWER IN CANADA

by Philip Resnick

I T IS now three years since *The Vertical Mosaic* appeared, representing a major contribution to the analysis of class and power in Canada. A full decade after C. Wright Mills' *The Power Elite,* with pluralist ideologues such as Dawson and Corry still in the ascendant in Canadian Political Science, elitist theory found in Porter its first important proponent.

The climate was ripe, overripe. The smug managerial credo of the Liberal *ancien regime* had given way to a more questioning politics in the early 1960's, symbolized by the emergence of a dynamic Québec, and the nuclear weapons controversy. In the social sciences, the study of institutions and social forces had enjoyed spectacular growth, and a whole literature analysing advanced industrial society had developed.

As a result, Canadian politics welcomed with open arms Porter's critical reassessment of Canadian society. His empirical documentation, drawn from DBS and census tracts, corporate annual reports, and newspapers, filled important lacunae which traditional scholarship had left untouched. His anti-elitism appealed to the more egalitarian temper of the period. His findings regarding power directly contradicted the conventional wisdom, introducing into Canadian social science excitement and controversy, which had been largely lacking.

But if Canadian sociology appeared to come of age with *The Vertical Mosaic,* we may question the accuracy and the completeness of the picture it offers. While acknowledging the merits of much of Porter's analysis, we are also more conscious in 1968 of crucial themes that have been left out.

Most importantly, radicals in search of an analysis linking Canadian society to developments in the US and Western Europe these last years, and laying the basis for a radical politics in this country, will find Porter inadequate. For as I shall argue, *The Vertical Mosaic,* despite its impressive data, fails to locate and name the underlying force in Canadian politics — *liberalism.*

PORTER'S MODEL

Though Porter's analysis is now common knowledge to the attentive Canadian public, I propose in this section to recapitulate his main points, before proceeding to a critical appraisal.

Essentially, Porter is concerned with restoring a measure of reality to the distorted middle class image of Canada as an egalitarian society. To this end, he is prepared to revive class categories as cogent operating tools, all the more since the functionalism of American sociology masks social rank and inequality, and yields a conservative picture of society.

At the same time, however, he rejects Marx's theory of class, arguing that neither its strong emphasis on consciousness, nor its positing of conflict, find application in post-industrial, bureaucratized societies. Although economic power in the private sector is concentrated in a few hands (unlike what the managerial school argues), there is an institutionalization and separation of labour which prevents outright capitalist mastery in modern society.

Porter is led, therefore, to an empirical definition of class — statistical categories, draw from economic processes, not in themselves forces for social change. And it is a taxonomy of Canadian society, rather than a theory, that he sets forth in the book.

Class and Ethnicity

If class is Porter's main theme, however, it merges with another preoccupation, ethnicity, to constitute the twin criteria for ranking social structures. Central to Porter's analysis is the theme of the charter groups, and in particular the disproportionate share of power that has accrued in the hands of the British element.

Making use of census data, he shows the overrepresentation of the British in the professional and higher financial brackets, and delineates a society in which ethnicity reinforces low class status, to hold down both the immigrant and the poor. (see statistical table No. 1)

The Canada of the 1960's is one in which 50% of the dividend income is concentrated among the corporate elite of Toronto and Montreal, in which rural decline and the rise of tertiary industries have created conditions of downward social mobility and regional depression for unskilled and manual workers.

TABLE I

Occupational Levels of French and British in Québec, 1951 and 1961

1951

	Percentage of total Québec labour force	Percentage of over or under-representation	
		British	French
Professional, financial	6.0	6.1	—1.2
Clerical	6.4	6.3	—1.1
Personal Service	3.4	—0.2	—0.2
Primary and unskilled	13.4	—6.1	1.1
Agricultural	16.6	—7.9	2.5
All Others	54.2	1.8	—1.1

1961

	Percentage of total Québec labour force	Percentage of over or under-representation	
		British	French
Professional, financial	7.8	7.1	—1.5
Clerical	7.8	5.2	—0.7
Personal Service	4.5	—1.4	—0.4
Primary and unskilled	10.4	—6.0	1.1
Agricultural	9.1	—4.4	1.6
All Others	60.4	—0.5	—0.1

Sources : Census of Canada, 1951, vol 4, Table 12
Census of Canada, 1961, vol 4, 3.1-15, Table 12

(Porter, *The Vertical Mosaic*, p. 94)

TABLE II

Percentage Distribution of University Students' Parents, by Occupational Level, 1956

Occupational Level	Student's Parents	Total Labour Force
Proprietors and Managers	25.7	8.3
Professionals	24.9	7.1
Clerical and Sales	12.3	16.5
Skilled and semi-skilled	21.1	30.6
Agriculture	10.9	15.7
Labour	5.1	20.5

Source : DBS University Expenditure and Income in Canada, 1956-7, cited in Porter, *The Vertical Mosaic,* p. 184.

It is a society in which educational opportunities continue to be unevenly distributed. Thus while British Columbia in 1961 had 22% of its population with only grade school education, Newfoundland had a full 58% of its population in that category. Where 65.9% of males age 15-19 were at school in urban areas in 1961, the figure drops to 52.4% in rural areas. With education recognized as the instrument of social mobility, the educational system continues to discriminate against lower class families, both economically and psychologically. Where 25.7% of university students in 1957 came from families classified as proprietors and management, only 5.1% of students were from families classified as labour (20.5% of the labour force). (See statistical table No. 2)[1]

Statistics of this kind form the backdrop to Porter's study proper, namely his analysis of the corporate, political, labour, and intellectual elites of Canada.

Function of Elitism

Before embarking on it, however, Porter first presents us with a construct of elitism, in which his model of power structures is delineated. "Power arises because of the general need for social order,"[2] he tells us. In modern society, where great differentiation of power roles exists, it is possible to identify a number of sub-systems. Besides the political and economic, they include the military, governmental bureaucracy, and intellectual institutions, i.e. mass media, universities and churches.

In Western type society, boundaries exist even while coordination occurs on certain fundamental levels. The small size of elite groups facilitates communication between their members. There is "general agreement on the ground rules to govern the conflicts of power and to ensure a minimizing of violence."[3]

Although the unifying ideology of communism is absent in Western society, Christianity, capitalism, and nationalism unify Western elites, especially capitalism, whose very rationality ensures its victory over the other two. Nonetheless, the exercise of power is limited through barriers to encroachment by one elite upon another, and it is the extent of this balancing off which determines the pluralist content of the society.

Porter places great emphasis on the recruitment of elites, and particularly the cross-membership among them, in determining the "openness" of the system. Where a particular kind of social background is considered necessary for entrance into an elite, an agglutination of elites will take place.

Following Weber, Porter emphasizes the bureaucratic nature of institutional power, and the key role which knowledge plays in maintaining it. Legitimizing this power is law, interwoven with charismatic and traditional elements.

This is the general character of the beast. The particular traits of Canadian elites are derived through individual studies, beginning with the most important, the economic.

Though figures regarding the degree of concentration in the Canadian economy vary, all agree that at least half of Canadian manufacturing is controlled by under 150 corporations. "Rosenbluth found that in 1956 twenty-eight of the $100 million corporations in manufacturing had about 29 per cent of the real assets of all manufacturing firms both incorporated and unincorporated. When corporations between $25 million and $100 million were added to the giants the concentration pattern in manufacturing was 143 corporations controlling 53% of the real assets."[4] Unlike the US, Porter argues, the relationships between investors, directors, and managers is a very close one in Canadian corporations. The boards of directors are real corporate governing bodies in Canada, and their interlocking ties, exemplified in such holding companies as Argus, bring a unity of interest and outlook.

The problem of foreign ownership of course complicates the task of defining the economic elite. Should the external elite that directs the dominant US subsidiaries in this country be included within its terms of reference ? Porter decided against it, arguing that since foreign directors have not belonged to the Canadian social structure, their relationship to it is irrelevant. On the other hand, the directors of such subsidiaries who reside in Canada are very much a part of it.

Economic elite

The economic elite tends to be university trained, (with engineering and law heavily represented), and overwhelmingly British in composition. Private school backgrounds are common, and at least 67% are of upper or upper middle class backgrounds. Their ties with both Liberal and Conservative parties are close, and their representation on government boards, Royal Commissions, university boards of governors, and organized philanthropies, out of all proportion to their numbers. Moreover, they are united in outlook, sharing the same clubs, free enterprise ideology, and power.

Labour elite

The labour elite, with which Porter next deals, is on the fringes of power by comparison. Of far lower status and educational origin than any of the other elites, its place in the Canadian pecking order is recognized only because of its undoubted power.

Yet the British charter group is overrepresented in its ranks as well, and its members drawn from the higher levels of manual work. Bureaucratic and professional full-time officialdom has grown by leaps and bounds, and though many of these support the NPD, as

Porter himself acknowledges "their radicalism is a muted one... It does not call for such radical measures as changes in the institution of property and corporate capitalism."[5]

Federalism as Political System

Porter waxes most eloquent on the subject of the Canadian political system. The right-left polarity to be found in the US or Britain is muted here, national unity is our obsession, at the price of "creative politics" that might mobilize human resources and challenge entrenched power, as in the economic elite.

He blames the opportunism of the two major parties for the conservative tone of Canadian politics, and their failure to harness its potential for dynamic politics. Compromise and brokerage have been their credos, with "political ends achieved, not by mobilizing the body politic, but rather by making appeals to institutional elites."[6]

Federalism, in particular, has served as an instrument for the entrenchment of economic power, and for the maintenance of economically inefficient and socially outdated activities. The confusion in jurisdictions between federal and provincial levels hopelessly confuses the electorate, and has meaning only for politicians and civil servants. Provincial powers in labour relations provides federal politicians with an excuse for not acting against the interests of the corporate economy. Cultural particularism has too often had conservative overtones, especially in Québec, and though federalism cannot be abandoned, Porter is clearly a centralizer.

Political elite

As regards the political elite, the overrepresentation of lawyers (64%) at the higher levels of the political systems comes as no surprise. They are the power brokers par excellence, the stratum whose career advancement is perfectly compatible with political activity.

The striking feature of the Canadian political elite is the amount of co-option that has taken place from outside, the relative absence of professional political careers. If MacKenzie King's tenure provides the most numerous examples of co-option, the avocational nature of political careers has generally weakened the political system as an independent source of power. The overwhelmingly middle class origins of the elite has further meant that "conservative and progressive social forces have never worked themelves out within the political system."[7]

Bureaucratic elite

The bureaucratic elite merits a separate chapter, not only because of the rise of the expert in all Western countries, but because of the avocational, administrative character of Canadian politics. If anything, the rationalized federal bureaucracy is too highly developed for Porter's liking, sucking up technical and expert advice which might more profitable find expression in the political system.

The educational requirements for the senior bureaucracy tend to be uniformly high, and though this elite allows for somewhat greater upward mobility than does the corporation, its British component also dominates. Its members through constant interaction come to share common intellectual values, as evidenced in the "Old Boys" ties in the post-war Departments of Finance or External Affairs.

The bureaucracy's influence on policy is far greater than the textbooks normally prescribe, and frequent co-optation from business, politics, and the universities gives it a far more political character than its British counterpart.

Socializing Institutions

The role of the mass media, universities, and churches, in articulating social values and justifying the social and political order is central in Western society. Even as the mass media make sense of a myriad of national and international events, so the universities supply the expertise and conventional wisdom for what is to be done.

Newspaper ownership in Canada is highly limited, with control resting in the hands of well-established families. Their class ties are clearly upper, all are members of the British charter group, their politics, whether Conservative or Liberal, favours the ongoing social order. They move among the businessmen of the community, and play important roles in the political system, as illustrated by the friendship between Joseph Atkinson and MacKenzie King.

Thus the Southam Co., with interests in many Canadian newspapers and 3 television stations is still controlled by the Southam family. "Its directors held three bank directorships, three in insurance companies, and four in other dominant corporations. Most of the directors came from prominent upper class families and attended private schools such as Trinity College School or Ridley College."[8]

At the same time, publishing has become increasingly intertwined with broadcasting, and important corporate entities control the private television stations, which their own intensive lobbying helped create.

Finally, in neither Canadian universities nor churches does one find social critics for whom Canadian society cries out. Instead of the tension between avant-garde and clerisy found in American intellectual life, Canadian thought is wholly lacking in dynamism.

The Royal Society of Canada, with its exclusively university membership, overwhelmingly British in origin, self-perpetuating, publishing only in restricted academic circles, is archtypical of the problem. The depoliticization of Canadian higher learning is a manifestation of the sclerosis from which Canadian politics suffers.

Power elite

In his final chapter, Porter sketches the relationship among these elites. He does not regard these as necessarily conspiratorial, or forming a single, unified elite as in C. Wright Mills' study. Instead, he holds some unity among elites to be necessary for the structure of the society to have any stability. A confraternity of power, in which various institutional leaders share attitudes and values, is frequent.

Both the kinship and friendship ties at the top are strong, among that small segment of the population than can lead what Porter calls a "middle class style of life." To old university friendships and added frequent cross-memberships of members of the elite on government advisory boards, university boards of governors, the Senate, etc., career interchanging is also frequent, symbolized by Mitchell Sharp, or J.J. Deutsch, or C.M. Drury.

Throughout the present century, Porter shows, using examples from the MacKenzie King era, there has been a close coalition between political leadership, the mass media, and the corporate elite. At the same time, there have been important conflicts as well, as between the B.C. government and B.C. Electric, or between the Diefenbaker government and A.V. Roe.

The oligarchical principle à la Michels underlies Canadian life, Porter concludes. Class, ethnic, and religious affiliations continue to determine the chances of an individual. Democracy is absent, and the elites are not open to recruitment. The lack of upward mobility, fragmented political structure, and the absence of clearly articulated values, explain the retardation of Canadian democracy.

A CRITIQUE OF PORTER'S MODEL

In approaching Porter's analysis, we must consider not only the relevance of his data, but also the context in which he frames it. It is well and good for Porter to stress the empirical nature of his study, but the questions he asks are no more divorced from ideological biases, than the pluralist or Marxist theories which he criticizes.

Porter's central theme revolves around the inequality of power and influence in modern Canadian society. He has been greatly influenced by the early elitists, and at times (as in his discussion of the political system) appears in the guise of a radical democrat, indignant at the blights of liberal society.

At other times, his stance borrows from the cultural pessimism of Weber and Freud, and he resigns himself to recognizing the flaws of human nature. He accepts bureaucratization as inevitable, or the interlocking of elites as definitional.

At still others, he is a straight liberal, accepting Aron's distinction between Western, other and Soviet-type societies, and arguing for clearer boundaries between the political and economic systems, or greater openness in the recruiting of elite members.

Confusion as process

As a result, there is a confusion of purpose, which makes the argument of *The Vertical Mosaic* far less clear-cut than it ought to be. Yet it is a confusion flowing from Porter's methodology, and from the absence of a global vision.

The problem can be traced back to his opening chapter, where he deals with the problem of class. He rejects the fundamentalist argument, as we have seen, as an end-of-ideology statagem. Yet in the next breath, he argues against Marxism as too ideological a theory.

In divorcing class from its historical context, he robs his own use of the term of *praxis,* in effect, situating class in a statistical, as opposed to the real world. His argument that class consciousness is absent in North America is naive, insofar as any analysis of social class in Canada worth its salt must also touch on the reasons and extent that class is accepted or rejected by the classes objectively defined.

Instead of seeking a theory of Canadian society in which subjective and objective definitions of class would be correlated, and deductions derived from ideology and interest, Porter plunges ahead with his statistical method. Expecting a theory about elites and power to somehow turn up on the way, he ignores the warning of Lukacs that "The monographic method is the best way to close one's horizons before a problem."[9]

It is not Porter's documentation that is under attack here, for this is the strongest element in his study. Rather, it is the way documentation becomes a substitute for theory.

While a whole literature on class conflict and neo-Marxist theory has been appearing in Europe in recent years, from Gorz's analysis of the new working class to the Italian writings on workers' control, while the works of Bloch, Lukacs, and Gramsci have been reappearing after a generation of eclipse, Porter persists in viewing Marxism through a glass darkly. He ignores the subtlety of contemporary Marxist analysis, the dialectical use of terms such as exploitation and dominant class, above all the concept of totality without which social analysis becomes one-dimensional.

Important omission — liberalism

Thus, when Porter does turn to consider values, as in his discussion of elitism in the West, the weakness of this analysis is all too patent. The description of power as determined by the general social need for order is abstract. The acceptance of boundaries between what he defines as the sub-systems of industrial society is preceeded by no debate, despite the opposite argument from such writers as Marcuse and Ellul. His discussion of ideological forces in the West includes Christianity, capitalism, and nationalism, yet leaves out *liberalism,* as important as any of the others in Canadian society.

Porter's belief in the boundaries between elites leads to a decision to examine them separately. Through he later argues affinities among elites, this fragmentation in treatment reinforces the fragmentation of this view of Canadian society.

To be sure, such a focus on Canadian institutions is admirable, all the more in the light of the legitimacy which appertains to them in this legal-rational society. The greater the pity that no conclusions are drawn regarding the deference and gentility paid to the elites who run them, the relationship between this attitude and the conservative character of Canadian political values.

Where Porter is content to argue that Canada has classes, as evidenced by income and ethnicity ranking of elites, a radical analysis would go much further, showing how the particular class structure of Canada infuses its control on the whole society.

Porter is little concerned with social values (except in his treatment of the political elite), a reflection of his partial vision, and his lack of historical perspective.

The inspired sociologist would begin by delineating the totality of Canadian society, the values that dominate therein, and the relationship between these and dominant social forces.

Canada as colony

We find nowhere in *The Vertical Mosaic* a discussion of Canadian liberalism in politics and universities. No mention is made of the counter-revolutionary values that underlie Canada's foundation. Our colonial relationship to the US is touched upon only marginally, in this query regarding the place of subsidiary directors in the corporate elite.

Yet as any thinking Canadian is aware, there is a good case for including an external elite in the analysis of Canadian political and intellectual life, as well as economic. The question as to whether Canada is truly an independent society, whose social structure has evolved autonomously, must also be integral to any analysis of class and power in Canada.

The exclusive focus on the Canadian elite tends therefore to obscure a fundamental truth about that elite, namely the extensive network of shared values and interests linking it to outside elites. It is not just that Canada shares with the United States and Britain certain political-legal concepts, or the generalized structure of advanced industrial society (as defined by Weber or Aron).

Rather, the historical dependence of the Canadian elite on outside capital and outside leads, constitutes a junior partner relationship, with great influence on the conservative character of Canadian political life.

Liberalism in Canada

Similarly, the question of Canadian liberalism requires more than a lament or denunciation of the brokerage character of Canadian politics, and the pusillanimity of our intellectuals.

To be sure, Porter sees Canada's unpolarized party system as having worked historically to obscure class and economic issues, and this in the interest of the dominant elites. But because there is a rejection of Marxist analysis of class, he does not see Canadian liberalism *per se,* as the ideology of the advanced capitalist society, taking a somewhat conservative form in Canada, because of the colonial structure of our economy.

To posit the absence of conflict and underlying harmony of post-industrial society is not a conservative ideology, but a porfoundly liberal one. Keynesians and the industrial relations ideologues, senior civil servants and university administrators are intelligent liberals after all, yet their belief in the fundamental stability and good sense of the existing order is second to none.

He notes the absence of radicalism in the Canadian Labour movement, particularly with regard to ownership and control. He admits the hopeless liberalism of the NPD yet never seems to ask why this is so.

Weber should be read carefully in order to recognize the spirit of liberalism suffusing Canadian capitalism, even as Protestantism was the ideological force of an earlier day. Sorel must not be forgotten in his discription of the role of the social myth in bourgeois society. Is Porter's rejection of Marxism so complete that he can no longer recognize a dominant ideology (even if he refuses to link it with a dominant class) ?

We must ponder the relative absence of mass movements in this society, indulging in the types of direct action we have seen in the US or Western Europe in recent years. And drawn conclusions regarding the consensus-making pressures, arising from a hang-up with parliamentary procedures and responsible demands.

We must emphasize the stability of Canadian society, flowing from a hundred years of conservative conditioning. We must realise that Canada has a founding myth, insofar as the rejection of the American revolution served as our original raison d'etre. If liberalism has in the twentieth century taken over from hierarchical conservatism as our dominant ideology, enough of the old value remains to account for the gradualism of social change in Canada.

How else explain the absence of outrage in Canadian public life at the close links that exist among the elites, be it between insurance companies and provincial governments, or university boards of governors and the corporate elite ?

Deference is far more a part of the Canadian social fabric than the American, while the dominant liberal ideology militates against any global vision of how power is aggregated and used.

Porter does, to give him due credit, give us important insights into the interplay among the elites. He traces the kinship, class, and institutional ties that bind them, and the commitment to common elitist values that results.

He shows how the intellectuals are mobilized into government service, how the newspaper magnates are spokesmen for the market values of the society. His analysis of the class bias in higher education is cogent, as is his account of the greater power of the directors in Canadian corporate entities, thus debunking the myth of separation between management and ownership, at least as regards Canada.

Liberalism of the Old Left

Thus, in dealing with the intellectuals, he is properly critical of their placid, propagandizing role for the established order. Yet if he chose to examine even those who are formally at war with that order, e.g. the League for Socialist Reform of the 1930's, or the economic nationalists of today, he would be forced to recognized the element of liberal co-option in their actions.

The LSR, though demanding the replacement of the capitalist by a socialist system, was itself so wedded to a moralistic, liberal framework, it never conceived of any other forms of success than the strictly parliamentary. It failed to produce a generation of young socialists in the universities, spurned for itself the direct tactics being developed in the labour movement, and fell to pieces in the 1940's, with such prominent alumni as Frank Underhill singing the praises of Mackenzie King.

Similarly, the economic nationalists so prominent at the U. of T. and in other universities today, seem more concerned with preaching a virtuous doctrine than in organizing Canadian society around this theme. They have tried working with institutional forces, e.g. the Walter Gordon task force, propagandizing through the *Toronto Star,* yet they have failed to mobilize the younger college generation around their goal. Nor has the doctrine at the level of dissent come close to articulating counter-values for the society, even compared to the LSR. And now Trudeau threatens to make dangerous inroads in their ranks.

This flimsiness of Canadian intellectuals is more than a failure of nerve. It represents the *trahison des clercs par rapport* with radical values, the co-option of intellectuals by a liberal society, whose very liberalism appears as a measure of good sense.

Yet behind this liberalism lies the pluralism Porter himself accepts, in his discussion of elitism. True, he demands a democratization of the elites, with somewhat greater power to the political over the economic than in the present set-up.

But in the end, his vision of the good society is not all that different from Galbraith's, whose theory of countervailing power he earlier criticizes. For the essence of democracy à la Porter remains balance between contending elites, not structural changes in the nature of ownership or of bureaucratic institutions.

TOWARDS RADICALISM

To read Porter radically, *it is necessary to focus on the liberal institutions in Canadian society,* and on the liberal ideology which dampens radical consciousness.

Porter, as we have seen, has gone far in presenting us with empirical data on the concentration of power or the interlocking of the elites. Where he has failed however, is to show how these elites use liberal values, e.g. pluralism, electoralism, legalism, to subsume social conflict, and how Canadian institutions reflect the biases and conservative values of the market society.

Thus, in his chapter on the political system, Porter waxes eloquent on the brokerage character of Canadian politics, yet significantly offers no critique of the parliamentary system itself. Yet this sacred cow has probably been as responsible as anything in discrediting radical thought in this country, and in making direct action appear illegitimate. (See Civil Disobedience and Democracy by Christian Bay, Vol. 5, No. 4 — OUR GENERATION).

From the public school system to the university, the emphasis on representative government and parliamentary procedure inculcates Canadians with a conservative view of society, and robs them of any insight into the role of conflict in bringing about social change.

Lacking even the liberal premises of the American Constitution, which in its more radical interpretation serves to justify the rebellion of an oppressed citizenry, Canadians must make do with counter-revolutionary values (which emerged in opposition to the American revolution). They accept reform as desirable, but only in the context of respect for law and order. They may pressure government, but seldom go over the head of government and take to the streets to create change.

Parliamentarism

The parliamentary system emphasizes compromise and brokerage as ends in themselves, at the expense of principle. It militates against a global vision of society, or the university, or the industrial plant as characterized by power relationships and conflict, positing instead harmony and cohesion as social reality.

Yet parliamentarism is rooted in a society profoundly non-egalitarian, as Porter has shown. And its domination is at the expense of direct democracy and perpetuates the market society.

Legalism and civil liberties

To denounce parliamentarism is to attack in the same breath the place of legality in the Canadian mosaic. Porter spends some time discussing law in rational-bureaucratic society, and underlines the crucial role played by lawyers as intermediaries between the Canadian elites, and within the political elite. Yet he draws no conclusions regarding the use of law as a conservative social tool, except, perhaps, in his discussion of federalism and its frustrations.

No radical, aware of the historical role of the courts in this country in smashing labour movements (e.g. at the time of the Winnipeg General Strike), aware of the fear of arrests which frustrates sit-ins and other confrontations, can regard the legalism in Canadian society as anything but an opponent.

Law performs not only the functions of legitimizing property relations, as in the classic Marxist schema, but in bureaucratic market society has become the very agency of fragmentation and alienation.

Legalism takes the place of human interaction, bars direct participation and control, transforms conflict and politicization into shadow-boxing and indifference. The spirit of the law is co-option, and from Royal Commissions to Labour Relations Boards, from Macpherson Reports to Seminars on Poverty, Canadian social history is strewn with the skeletons of co-opted radicalism.

Legality vs. Justice

Above all, law serves to prevent raising any fundamental questions about the rightness and wrongness of Canadian society, or the character of Canadian institutions. Where law dominates, the legitimacy of the manager, or civil servant, or university administrator, is assured. Not for nothing did the Sorbonne revolutionaries place *"Il est interdit d'interdire"* on the forefront of their banners.

If legalism and parliamentarianism are the modes by which

power is exercised in Canada, class and the market-place define the reality of the society.

Not only is there inequality in the distribution of wealth or in accessibility to education, but the corporate elite imposes its values at all levels of society.

The educational system

At the universities, boards of governors transmit the prejudices of Bay Street into the educational plant. The end of education is service, not to some abstract human end, as liberal rhetoric implies, but to the specific purposes of market society. From the engineer to the economist, the skills acquired are those of management and social control, within the context of the ongoing order. Even the independence of the scientist or humanist serves to legitimize and enhance the power of their indirect patron, the corporate elite.

Universities, in their relations with the outside community, reflect the capitalist ethic. Their university funds are shrewdly invested in stock and real estate with little public divulgence. Their relation to the slums that surround them is that of a slum landlord, with expropriation a common procedure.

In the mass media, the temper of market liberalism is disguised behind a veil of impartiality. The CBC is bedridden by an obligation to equanimity in its presentation which all too often results in a castrated journalism. The political hand is never far away, and controversial broadcasting, like *This Hour has Seven Days,* brings the axe down upon itself, once it begins to challenge the institutional elites for power.

Control of newspapers and private radio and television stations rests with a few established families or holding corporations, as Porter has shown. Extensive links with the corporate or political elites ensure that the prejudices of editorial boards reflect closely those of the market society.

Not by accident is the labour reporting in most Canadian newspapers unsympathetic or uninformed. Nor does one find much sympathy for the hippie, or the political activist, or the militant poor.

Canada may lack a Springer press, but its newspapers are no less suffocating with their smugness and repressive liberal biases. Between the *Globe and Mail's* tirades against Yorkville and the Dow sit-in last November, and Springer's pathological anti-Communism and student-baiting, the difference is one of degree, not of kind.

Labour and the Old Left

The Canadian Labour movement and the NPD are also impregnated with the market philosophy. Porter has, therefore, rightly included the trade union movement among the Canadian elites, albeit at the periphery, because its goals are broadly integrative.

To be sure Canadian unionism is less marked by the Gompers style of capitalist unionism than its American counterpart. To be sure, its demands go beyond wages to embrace structural problems such as automation or job security, or broader questions of social and economic policy.

Still, by no stretch of the imagination can one claim that the Canadian labour movement is at present seeking a radical alteration in the relations of production in industry or in the character of economic ownership. The unions have failed to radicalize young workers, concepts of workers' control or public ownership find little echo in their ranks, and though demands for reform are voiced, the legitimacy of the market society goes unchallenged.

The pragmatism of the labour movement is more evident in the case of the NPD. It has long ceased to define itself as a socialist party, preferring the more liberal term left-of-centre. Its acceptance of parliamentarism is total, and its competition with the "old-line" parties is on the very issues of brokerage politics, inflation, taxes, or housing, which Porter roundly condemns in his discussion of the political system.

Admittedly, the social content of its programme is moderately progressive. Admittedly, at the constituency level, there are NPD militants pushing for a more radical kind of politics.

But not unlike the Socialist and Communist leadership in France, the NPD brass is more interested in power from the top than in power from below. And not unlike the German SPD or the British Labour Party, it will compromise its principle for the taste (or smell) of power.

Points of departure

A radical critique of Canadian society must therefore, cut through the liberal rhetoric in Canadian political life, before it can hope to challenge the corporate elite. Yet the experience of radical movements in Germany, France, and the United States, supplies would-be Canadian radicals with much food for throught.

In Germany, the grand coalition allowed the SDS to challenge a society even more bourgeois than Canada, and expose the "economic miracle" and liberal ideology (à la Springer and Willy Brandt) as sham.

In France, the authoritarianism of the Gaullist regime amongts other reasons provoked a rebellion and demand for radical change, which caught all the French elites off guard. This, in a society which but three months before had been touted as the most stable in the world, by *Le Monde.*

In the US, the war and the ghetto uprising made possible the situation at Columbia, where the legitimacy of the liberal power structure was destroyed, and the university's repressive role in Harlem and in Pentagon research, exposed.

Although there is nothing automatic about similar events occurring in Canada, the conditions for revolt exist, as even the university establishment has recognized, commissioning the Ford-Foundation-backed enquiry into student radicalism.

The Achilles heel of the Canadian elites may prove to be their colonialism, even as in the US, the instrument for radicalism was the existence of the military-industrial complex *per se.*

Though Porter downplays the colonial theme in his analysis of the Canadian corporate elite, and reveals little sympathy for nationalism in his discussion of federalism, one can argue that the only creative politics in this country in the last few years has been nationalist.

Specifically, the development of separatism in Québec, and the challenge this has posed for the Canadian elites, political, economic and intellectual, has affected national politics more dramatically, and potentially more positively, than any other event.

Similarly, the colonialism of our elites vis-a-vis the United States could be used more effectively by Canadian radicals, arguing not just for economic nationalism or an independent foreign policy (good liberal demands) but for a revolutionary change in the structures of Canadian society.

Arguing against the counter-revolutionary principles upon which Canada *was founded,* and the conservative-colonial values that underlie our national life, the demand for an end to colonialism becomes a critique of the Canadian vertical mosaic itself.

The Canadian student in his university is a colonial, even as the Canadian worker is within his enterprise, whether branchplant or not; and the Canadian economy, within the American Empire.

To attack Canadian liberalism, becomes therefore an attack on the colonialism of the Canadian market society, not only the external colonialism, but even more importantly, the internal.

For the corporate elite dominates Canadian society as completely as a colonial elite its colony. And the role of Canadian radicalism becomes to demystify and explose this reality.

FOOTNOTES:

1. DBS, University Student Expenditure and Income in Canada, 1956-7, cited in John Porter, The Vertical Mosaic, Toronto, 1965, p. 184
2. Porter, ibid., p. 202
3. Porter, ibid., p. 211
4. ibid. p. 238.
5. ibid. p. 353
6. ibid. p. 411
7. ibid. p. 412
8. ibid. p. 473
9. George Lukacs, Histoire et Conscience de Classe, Les Edition de Minuit, 1960, p. 50

Published 1968

THE NATIONAL QUESTION IN CANADA

Part I
The Social Democrats and the National Question in Canada

H. Milner
with B.R. Lemoine

The most recent surge of Canadian nationalism has its primary roots in intellectual events of the sixties. Symbolically it begins perhaps with the publication in 1965 of George Grant's *Lament for a Nation* — a bitter denunciation of the continentalism of the political and economic rulers of Canada. Walter Gordon became the second victim of the Liberal contientalists (according to Grant, Dief was the first) who found even his mild mid-sixties economic nationalism intolerable. (Eric Kierans is the third).

It was just at the end of Walter Gordon's political career that the Watkins Report on foreign ownership, which Gordon had commissioned, was released. While it could not save Gordon, the report became the first major public portrayal of the effects of American economic domination on Canada. In fact the economic analysis on this issue since 1968 when the report came out, serves mainly to update and to add detail and weight to the work of the report itself. It is little wonder that Watkins remains the chief economic spokesman of nationalist groups, though of course, he has changed his political colours in the interim.

Politically at least, Grant's tone of lament for a nation he saw dying appeared justified. Intellectually, Canada became, beginning with the centennial perhaps, an "in thing" : There were study groups to explore Canada's real history Registration in courses in Canadian politics, history sociology, economics, whatever, soared at the universities. Creighton was quoted left and right ; Innis was ressurrected. But politically, apart of course from the Bobby Gimby CA-NA-DA sort of centennial chauvinism, the national question was not posed. The Tories, Grant and Creighton's ertswmile heroes had pretty much rejected the accidental anti-continentalism of John Diefenbaker replacing it with the Wasp metooism of Stanfield. But it was metooism vis-à-vis the Liberals — continentalists par excellence. In other words there was no political outlet for nationalists on the Center and Right. The Creightons were stifled. On the other hand, there was the Left ...

The left side of the Canadian parliament is occupied by the NDP. The NDP, like its predecessor the CCF, has not been unconcerned about the national question, nor, however, has it let its concern translate itself into clear policy commitments. For one thing, the founding achievement of the NPD had been its successful winning over of the labour bureaucracy, and the national question has not been dear to the hearts of this group. Apart, however, from leaders and supporters, the NDP has, like all liberal democratic parties of the left, a great many intellectual sympathizers and spokesmen. It is this group of people, expressing the growing intellectual ferment, who constituted the nationalist as well as far left group within the NDP soon to be known as the Waffle.

Just how was socialism or social democracy to be related to the national question ? Gad Horowitz, among, if not the, most articulate writers on this question, laid the ground-work for the answer in a seminal essay published in 1966, entitled "Conservatism, Liberalism, and Socialism in Canada."

> "Canadian socialism is ... unamerican in the sense that it is a significant and legitimate political force in Canada, insignificant and alien in the United States ... When Socialism was brought into the United States, it found itself in an ideological environment in which individualism had long since achieved the status of a national religion ; the political culture had already congealed, and socialism did not fit. American socialism was alien not only in this ideological sense, but in the ethnic sense as well ; it was borne by foreigners from Germany and other continental European countries. These foreigners sloughed off their socialist ideas not simply because such ideas did not "fit" ideologically, but because as foreigners they were going through a general process of Americanization ; socialism was only one of many ethnically alien characteristics which had to be abandoned.
> A British socialist immigrant to Canada had a far different experience. The British immigrant was not an "alien" in British North America. The English-Canadian culture not only granted legitimacy to his political ideas and absorbed them into its wholeness ; it absorbed him as a person into the English-Canadian community, with relatively little strain, without demanding that he change his entire way of life before being granted full citizenship. [1] "

For Horowitz the relationship between nationalism and socialism is not intrinsic, it is tactical : within the national culture of Canadians lies a potential class consciousness foreign to the American — and hence continental — political culture. The results have taken form in the present reality of the two countries ; as Horowitz put it more recently.

> "If the United States were socialist, at this moment, we would be continentalists at this moment. If the possibilities of building a socialist society were brighter in the United States than in Canada, or as bright, we would not be terrified by the prospect of absorption. We are nationalists because, as socialists, we do not want our country to be utterly absorbed by the citadel of world capitalism. [2] "

It was the presentation of the "Waffle Manifesto" to the NDP national convention of 1969 and the resulting national publicity which made it a cause celebre, that changed what had been an essentially intellectual endeavour into a potentially political one. The manifesto was signed by many of the leading party intelligentsia ; it had been the work of Mel Watkins, Jim Laxer and others — the same Watkins of the Watkins report who had moved left — in fact to the left wing of the NDP. As an academic rather than a representative of Bay Street, Watkins drew the final conclusion that Gordon could and woud not. The reason the old parties ignored the national question was because continentalism was in the interest of the class they represented. The Canadian Bourgeoisie profited from continentalism. As E.P. Taylor put it : "Canadian nationalism : how old fashioned can you get !" (We will investigate this question per se below.)

This took Watkins to the NDP and to socialism, but it didn't quite bring the NDP to Watkins and economic nationalism. The youth and intellectual wing of the party was quite attuned to a description of the status quo as follows from the manifesto :

> "American corporate capitalism is the dominant factor shaping Canadian society. In Canada, American economic control operates through the formidable medium of the multi-national corporation. The Canadian corporate elite has opted for a junior partnership with these American enterprises. Canada has been reduced to a resource base and consumer market within the American empire.
> The Amrican empire is the central reality for Canadians. It is an empire characterized by militarism abroad and racism at home [3]."

It did not, however, go over big with the leadership and vocal rank and file. The Waffle Manifesto, which was really a sort of latter day political conclusion to the Watkins report, became the basis for a party (or Movement) within a party — the Waffle. The Waffle has played an important role in educating the Canadian people on the national question, but it has failed in general, to turn this education into the creation of a political force outside the intellectual community and the NDP.

The last 5 years have seen increasing investigation of American domination of Canada. Kari Levitt's important work which was published in book form as "Silent Surrender", the work of Gonick, Taylor and others in DIMENSION, articles by Wafflers such as Watkins and Laxer, and anthologies especially that of Lumsden in 1969 added completeness to the analysis. The most-up-to-date figures were provided by the "leaked" Gray report to the federal cabinet published by Rotstein in CANADIAN FORUM. Furthermore occasional case studies began to be attempted of the auto pact for instance. Another area was non-renewable resources, especially those producing energy, and it grew to be the most important locus of the nationalist thrust. Cultural imperialism was not omitted either : Matthews and Steele documented the "Americanization" of the universities, and were part of a group who took upon themselves the cultivation of Canadian literature and culture. In much of this work there is little distinction to be found between the center Liberal position and that of the social democratic left ; many share the same criticisms based on data provided by the same analysis. However a short description of the positions of the relatively few but influential Liberal nationalists is warranted.

It is thus rather difficult to distinguish the spectral differences between the liberal and social democratic positions on the national question. We could add some reasons for this. To begin with, we have the transient nature of the metropole in the Canadian situation ; Canada has served as hinterland area for France, Britain and the U.S.A. in that order — obviously a rather unusual situation if one compares the situation with the various third world countries.

A second major source of difficulty in defining the Canadian liberal position is the singular absence of an acceptable historical definition of the Canadian power structure. It would certainly be easier to interpret the philosophical position of the various ruling strata in Canada if these were scientifically delineated as to their economic and political role and power.

The lack of a clear distinction between the liberal nationalists and their social democratic counterparts on the national question is very evident in a special issue of THE CANADIAN FORUM where a representative group of liberal and social democratic economists and other intellectuals were asked to present their respective concepts of an industrial strategy for Canada in answer to the problem defined by the Gray report. In general, the authors offer a collection of technocratic solutions which attempt to answer the limitations of the Gray report. Most of these technocratic models for a new industrial strategy involve the innovative use of federal fiscal and monetary policies, high priority, is given to industrial reorganization and manpower policies to go with it. Unfortunately none of these models for change is presented within an original perspective ; everything is oriented towards greater productivity and more consumption. There is no "vision" in the liberal strategy for ensuing Canadian economic independence ; and the "just Society" is not clearly perceived. Even the preoccupation with natural resources. which they share with both the social democratic and socialist Canadian left, is seen simply as a weapon in bargaining with the U.S. ; the ecological dimension is absent. The limitations of the liberal path to national independence is most clearly seen in the proposal for an industrial strategy put forward by Abe Rotstein and Viv Nelles, both editors of the Canadian Forum.

> "Our modest proposal is to begin the decentralization of economic planning and the fortification of business in it, through the creation of Industry Councils for each sector of the economy. Businessmen themselves would be brought together to state their own long-range goals for their particular industries, including the survival of a Canadian business sector, and to consider strategies of improving productivity, employment and export performance. In our minds such councils would initiate the process of business thinking in national terms once again, and at that stage the co-ordination of public and private planning would at least be theoretically possible". [4]

"Modest proposal" is clearly an understatement ; business is given the central role in economic planning ; there is no mention of cooperatives, trade unions, or citizens committees. Should we have expected anything more, radical or innovative from the editors of a magazine which is so closely identified with the Committee for an Independant Canada which itself recently proposed a plan for the Canadianization of International unions as its first major contribution to the struggle for Canadian independence ? It is significant that the C.I.C. proposed a program for the nationalization of unions before presenting detailed proposals for the socialization of Canadian industry : one more reason to question the desirability of a national liberation strategy in concentration with the liberal nationalists.

Only Eric Kierans among the better known liberal nationalists seems to be capable of an opening to the left. Perhaps this is due to the variety of experience Kierans has been exposed to — academic, business and political, and to the activist approach he has favoured in all three. There is an obvious link between Kierans' direct protest to the American government against certain imperialist economic policies while he was a member of the Quebec government, in contravention of acceptable diplomatic protocol, his open opposition to the Trudeau government's economic policies, and finally his role as an active advisor and consultant to the NDP governments in Western Canada.

On the question of natural resources Kierans certainly shares the concerns of Canadian socialists and social democrats.

> "A nation's natural resources are not past production. They are the wealth

of its soil and waterways. As such, they cannot be viewed in the same light as current production, to be disposed of at will by the factors that created the new goods and services. They are a trust received from the past, to be husbanded by the present and to be passed on to future generations. A generation that deliberately squanders a nation's natural wealth to enhance its own standard of living, to live high off the hog, will have much to answer for. A government that deliberately pursues a policy of selling off the natural wealth of its people to achieve short run gains in GNP breaks forth with its own future. It reveals, by the forced sale of its assets, its inability to devise the set of objectives and policies that will increase output and distribute it more equitably on an annual basis". [5]

And on the limitations of the Gray report and liberal economics generally :

> "It is only in the context of an overall mix of economic policies and a declaration of basic economic objectives, that one can draft an economic policy. Such a policy comes after a society has defined its major purposes and priorities. It cannot come before. Once a society's ends are stated, the trust of its industrial policy can be determined ; those aims dictate the emphasis, whether it be civil or military efforts, a rising standard of living, concentration of wealth and industrial might, technologies that improve the environment or conquer space."

> "An industrial policy will be meaningless unless there is a definition of what Canada is, what are its aims, where it is going and how it proposes to get there. An industrial policy, a screening board and a Canada Development Corporation are, no doubt, useful — but they are only the fringes on top." [6]

The above quotes clearly indicate the philosophical and ideological framework in which Eric Kierans drafted the recommendations to government to nationalize the three large mining companies functioning in that province. These proposals are not too different from the program being carried out in Chile in the area of non renewable resources.

In essence, then, the case of Kierans shows the close relationship between the nationalists of the center and the social democratic left.

On the whole, the major work of the left-nationalists has been the documentation and analysis of the Americanization of the economy of Canada. The Gray report cleared up any remaining doubts about the facts. The Canadian economy is roughly half American owned. Furthermore, in the manufacturing and heavy industry sector, where there are high profits and a particularly important impact on the very shape of the Canadian economy, the proportion goes up almost to two thirds. And even further, within manufacturing and heavy industry, it is the highly profitable, highly technological, capital intensive sectors where American ownership is most pronounced, in several cases at or near 100%. Add to that the fact that this relationship is one that is growing and has been growing ; add as well that opposition to it, nay even recognition of this problem, is stimied by cultural domination on the part of American media and intellectual frameworks, and the domination of organized labour by American oriented bureaucrats (see below), and the situation becomes more than critical, it becomes desperate.

Without going at all deeply into the economics involved, we can sum up the major consequences for Canada of the present economic condition as outlined in the different works of the social democratic observers.

1) Our economy is based and dependent on primary industry : non-renewable resources are mined, cut down, or whatever and then sent to the U.S. for processing. This results in the fact that we export mainly raw materials and import mainly processed ones — the classical pattern of economic underdevelopment. It means that we fail to

develop the economic infrastructure in manufacturing leaving ourselves open to depression when the resources are depleted. Finally, primary industry of this sort provides few jobs per dollar investment, hence causing unemployment.

2) Our economy became inefficient because it is generally structured to serve the needs of continent-wide industrial concerns. This results, in many cases, in the production of items not directly suited to the Canadian market, in over-production, in higher costs. A documented occurence is one where the multinational overcharges its Canadian subsidiary for the materials or components of production it purchases there-hence artificially decreasing profits in Canada, raising prices, and withholding taxes from the different levels of Canadian government. These kinds of practices make branch plants in Canada almost impossible to regulate according to Canadian law.

3) Because branch plants import technology, the economic domination of Canada, has, as the science Council has shown, the effect of discouraging R and D of any kind in Canada, resulting in unemployment among scientists and engineers, the brain drain, and a lack of sufficient resarch into Canadian needs.

4) Canadians are more and more excluded from any influence over the major corporate concerns that shape its future. It is, for example, impossible to buy shaves in many of the major Canadian branches of large American corporations ; they are 100 per cent owned by the parent and only shares for the parent are sold. This also has the effect of directing much of Canadian investment outside of Canada.

5) Politically our governments exercise little control over the multinationals whose political sensitivites must be primarily tuned to Washington. Hence political pressure from D.C. will result

in the loss of Canadian jobs — e.g. through D.I.S.C. Furthermore branch plants fall under American law and this has led in some cases to Canadian foreign trade policy effectively vetoed by American owned corporations that dominate the relevant sector of the economy.

In sum the facts are clear. Economically Canada is effectively a colony — a prosperous one to be sure — but still a colony. The economy of no other comparable country is as completely dominated from outside its borders. Unfortunately, the weaknesses of the work of social democratic nationalists are also apparent. First, is its inability to find sufficient popular roots outside of intellectual circles* . The second is its essential economism, i.e. it has made economics the central issue, so that the consequence of American control is only economic — dollars and cents. Even where the cultural aspect of imperialism has been raised by Matthews and Steele, it has tended to be in **numbers** and jobs, i.e. 80% U.S. professors here. 60% there, — quota demands. In this way it has neglected the sociopsychological level of cultural nationalism ; there has been no English Canadian Parti Pris to spell out the reality of the Colonisé as it applies to Canada.

The conclusions drawn from their economic analysis by the social-democratic nationalists bear close examination. These, we should add, are never spelled out anywhere nearly as clearly as are the effects of economic domination. These conclusions are :

1) Canadian nationalism is not in the interests of the bourgeoisie ; hence it must come from below.

2) There is a visceral, though not articulated, national anti-continentalism that can be found among ordinary Ca-

* For further thoughts on this, see Walter Johnsons piece in the Discussion Section of this issue.

nadians and this nationalism can be tapped to achieve 3 and 4 below.

3) The political instrument of this drive and the political education that must go with it is to be an NDP party reformed from without and within (or some other national left wing party if the NDP ultimately proves unamenable).

4) The administrative instrument of the reassertion of Canadian national sovereignity is the Canadian state through nationalization. (On this point they are often vague ; typical is Mel Watkins : "We will advocate that the only sensible alternative to foreign private ownership of the Canadian economy is Canadian public ownership, a Canadian economy owned and controlled by Canadians for Canadians." [7])

It is our position that the argument stated in points one and two is essentially correct : the bourgeoisie as we shall argue below, is continentalist, and there is a visceral nationalism among Canadians which expresses itself particularly on issues of non-renewable resources, water, fuels. The question is whether one can accept points 3 and 4 based on these facts.

We might put this question in this way :

1) Can Canadians be mobilized NATIONALLY, i.e. 'ad mare usquam ad mare', on the national question ?

2) Is the Canadian national state an instrument which will lend itself to the creation of "an independent socialist . . ." If not, then how else ?

Any response to these questions must begin with the question of Quebec — though this is one that Canadian nationalists would too often rather avoid seriously considering.

On the Quebec issue, it appears, there is some dissagreement among English Canadian nationalists. The official Waffle position calls for self-determination for Quebec but takes no position on the desirability of an "independent

socialist" Quebec. This permits Waffle types to be divided among those who support the liberation struggle and those who keep alive a pan-Canadian vision with Quebec adding appropriate colours to the national rainbow. With this second view we have no sympathy whatever, for not only is it contradictory to the principles of left nationalism, and unrealistic in view of Quebec's reality, it is essentially condescending. As long however as "self-determination" remains the official line this kind of position will remain legitimate.

Let us, however, attribute to the left-wing Canadian nationalist a view of Quebec like the first one posed. He accepts that Quebec too must develop its own struggle for national independence through socialism and hopes that some kind of alliance can be worked out between left nationalists of each nation. Then the next step is a rather demanding and treacherous one, yet the Canadian nationalist on the left must take it. We have not as yet, however, seen much evidence that this step has been seriously undertaken anywhere. What is required is that if Quebec is to be taken seriously, and not merely rhetorically, as a sovereign nation, then the existing nation of Canada, in its political institutions, in almost every aspect of its reality, must be negated and transcended : the federal system of 10 provinces including Quebec, the bilingual nature of Canada, the geographically-based myths ; and most important of all, the institutions of the central government, parliament, bureaucracy and judiciary in Ottawa.

All of these as well as other political institutions have been structured to perform certain functions and a major one among them has been preserving Canada, as it was set up, that is keeping French Canada down and in. As long as one sets one's sights on capturing these institutions one is likely also to confirm the status quo. Parliament is not merely an instrument, it has a certain reality based on its real functions ; the same is true of the federal bureaucracy. Anyone wishing to take over these institutions is likely to continue to perform these same functions.

This process has shaped our central institutions not only in relation to Quebec but to other regions as well. Class voting has generally been weaker federally than provincially because quite often regional rather than class representatives are sent to Ottawa ; this was the case in 1972 (In Quebec this has become a clear cut rule). Other factors have added to this process of regionalization.

1) The constitution has placed in the hands of the provinces jurisdiction over two important areas.
   a) Social welfare widely defined : as this area becomes more and more basic, the provinces come closer to the people and Ottawa, though it has attempted to preempt this field, more distant.
   b) Resources : as American domination of the economy increases it will be on the question of resources that this issue will be fought out, and resources are under provincial jurisdiction.

2) The increasing American influence has had its basic impact on the federal level of government especially the bureaucracy. What we see is a greater degree of coordination of the U.S. and Canadian federal bureaucracies, especially in the areas of finance, trade, technology, foreign policy, and defense. The predominance of the American political-economic structure leads to the creation of a continentalist ethos and culture at this level, making it unamenable to national considerations.

3) Opinion polls have shown that there is popular attachment to the central government slightly greater than to the provincial governments everywhere except in Quebec. Nevertheless these same polls show that the attachment to the federal government is more symbolic than practical and that most Canadians look to the provinces for pragmatic purposes in the forms of concrete actions. One might conclude that it is the provinces that are seen more and more as the scene of real action and the central apparatus as an interesting but essentially irrelevant and externally dominated United Nations. With the trend toward regional integration in the Maritimes and the West, such sentiments appear likely to increase. This tendency goes hand in hand with what might be the most lasting contribution of the New Leftism of the sixties — a fundamental distrust of large, impersonal and distant organizations whether they be private or state-run and a willingness to place trust in the people in their own communities and regions to know what's best for themselves.

M.I.S.C. (the Movement for an Independent Socialist Canada) recently changed its name back to the Ontario Waffle. The implications of this change-based on the admission that M.I.S.C. was a "non-starter" — should be seen in light of the points made above. Perhaps Quebec is not alone ; perhaps the nationalist mood and thrust should be a regional one, that the preservation of the Canadian *nation* lying paradoxically, not with its national institutions but with its regions. Perhaps the new slogan of the Left in Canada should be "Two, Three, many Quebecs".

We might hypothesize all this as follows : supposing that a government were to come into power in Ottawa and prepared to use the federal state to preserve our economic sovereignity ; could this come about. Perhaps nationalization would still allow further continental integration, given the closeness of the Canadian federal apparatus to the continental structures of power. The previous question, that of the instrument of mobilizing Canadians, poses itself here. Canadian social democrats will contend that the assumption of power by left nationalists will only come after the success of a major campaign of political education on the socialist alternative to foreign domination ; hence the national institutions could be thus transformed. We suspect that even here the national ARENA will not do for this kind of campaign — especially given the contemporary role of Quebec. Consider this contradiction :

As long as Quebec remains capitalist, it will fight, through its provincial and federal political hierarchy, any attempt on the part of Ottawa to acquire greater powers even if these are in the realm of Canadian economic self-determination. Furthermore, the representatives of the dominant classes in Quebec will always direct nationalist feeling toward Ottawa while taking a disgustingly-cap-in-hand attitude before the bankers of Wall Street. This was true of the rural oriented conservatism of Duplessis and is equally true of the urban, technocratic, slightly progressive, Bourassa. This does not mean that Quebecers are Yankeephiles. What it means is that as long as socialists are not in power in Quebec, anti-continentalism will not enter the political fray. And in Quebec the socialists are, practically to a man, indépendistes. Hence, within Canada, Quebec will continue to have a powerful continentalist influence ; on the other hand, were Quebec independent, there is potential for an anti-imperialist alliance. This same pattern may be seen in the total lack of support from Quebecers of Canadian nationalist-left parties and the resultant impact of Quebec on the political party constellation of Canada.

Could we not say the same for other regions of Canada ? Could we not suggest that Canadians are class conscious and potentially open to the implications of outside domination of their economy and society, but that such class considerations are not expressed, at least not primarily, on the level of federal politics ? Could we not add that even to the extent that they are expressed they do not have any effect on the content of federal politics due to the continental orientation as well as the circumscribed role of the political institutions of the national government ? If this is so, then what strategy for the left in Canada ? At this stage any definite answer on our part would be exceedingly presumptuous.

We might suggest at the very least, that among the required tasks of social democratic nationalists in Canada are now : 1) to come to terms with the fact that Quebec is a different nation ; 2) to begin a thorough critique of the role and function of the *political* institutions of Canada. Kari Levitt, for example, has recently raised just this call :

"Ultimately the 'foreign investment' issue raises for reappraisal the function and character of the whole Ottawa establishment. By this I mean not only the federal bureaucracy or public service, but the whole show, including the so-called national political parties. Since Canada left the orbit of the British Empire and trading system, and moved into that of the United States, federal authority has waned, and provincial authority has grown. Yet, it seems that Ottawa continues to be modelled on the better traditions of British Colonial Administration. It is an honest, competent bureaucratic, centralizing administration, containing an old boys network in the best English tradition, putting up a valiant fight to pretend that nothing has really changed ; that the mandarins and submandarins are in control of the economic life of this country. [8]

and 3) to redirect cultural nationalism from quotas in universities and government grants to Canadian publishers to the more profound lack of discovering Canadian working class culture.

Finally, we cannot obscure the *regional* realities of Canada as a whole and what this reality contributes to a strategy on the national question. But before consideration of this strategy as such, it would indeed be valuable to clarify the most recent and important theoretical statements of this question and the strategic implications that follow. The nationalism of the center and social democratic left has been surveyed. It is worthwhile to move a bit further left to examine this question.

Part II

Canadian Independence and the Marxist Left

D. Roussopoulos

"When the revolution is far off, the difficult task of the revolutionary organisation is the practice of theory. When the revolution begins, its difficult task is more and more the theory of practice."

Anonymous

The relationship between US imperialism and Canada raises the question of the relationship between the development of Canada since its founding as a national-state and its socio-economic system. These two aspects are part of the same process. A complete analysis of colonialism and imperialism north of the 49th parallel cannot in turn be separated from the question of the relationship of Canada to Québec on the one hand, and the relationship of these two principle cultures within their territories to other racial and ethnic minorities. In other words, the pattern of exploitation and domination has many overlaping features. All are interdependent, one feeding on the other. This system of relationships cannot be abolished without a wholesale sweep from the bottom to the top.

What has the Canadian Marxist Left to say about all this ?

We will not deal here with the multitude of Marxist-Leninist sects whether they be the Stalinists, Trotskyists or Maoists. With the exception of an issue of PROGRESSIVE WORKER produced in Vancouver devoted to "Independence and Socialism in Canada — A Marxist-Leninist View" which represents a sophisticated view of this position, our efforts in getting the positions of the other vanguard parties of the workers bore little fruit. We can only come to the conclusion that they do not have a developed position on imperialism and the national question in Canada. We do not deal either with the "arrivistes" or "nouveau-marxistes" in Ian Lumsden's confusing book, *Close the 49th Parallel — The Americanization of Canada.* Instead we choose to deal exclusively with the best of the independent Marxists.

In an edited collection of important writings, *Capitalism and the National Question,* by Gary Teeple,[9] a number of essayists assert some basic positions with which the editors of this journal can only agree. The book has the natural weaknesses of any collection of essays and it is noted by the editor that not all the contributors necessarily will agree with either the entire contents of the book, or some of the basic positions taken by himself or his colleague Tom Naylor with whom Teeple shares a great deal. But the book in the sum total of its parts does clearly put forward that : Canada is not now and has never been an independent country ; Canada does not now and has never had an independent ruling class ; Canada has no independent trade union movement ; the country's social problems are the basis upon which any independence movement must be built. These social problems must be set in their cultural setting which entails an understanding of the specific cast of these problems in Canada.

In his contributions to the book Teeple maintains that Canada "has the political trappings of independence but not the reality because politics under capitalism are ultimately subordinate to the amassing of capital by individuals and corporations, the most powerful of which in this country are American". Teeple further maintains that there is no Canadian ruling class as such, distinct from American capital. The capitalist group here is basically an extension of US multi-national corporations and has no collectively expressed desire of its own to establish anything different.

> "Most of the large concentrations of capital today," he writes, "perform complementary (or at least non-contradictory) roles in relation to US capital — the form of which is more powerful because it dominates the sphere of production, while Canadian capital prevails largely in circulation, that is, in transportation, communication, retailing and finance. The Canadian capitalists who accumulate the capital in the area of "circulation" invest it in turn in sub-imperialist activities, e.g. the Caribbean, Brazil. This is a privilege they are accorded by metropolitan US imperialism.
> "The central fact of the Canadian ruling class before and after Confederation was, and is, its foundation in mercantile capital. (A thesis attributed to Naylor — the editor.) This form of capital is accumulated in the process of circulation of goods ; that is money is made by buying and selling articles (raw materials or manufactured goods) — not by producing the article, this latter process being the basis of industrial capital. It is this central characteristic of the Canadian ruling class which explains why, even to the present time, Canada has not become the industrial nation with a large population that it might have been. The point is, as Marx argued, that 'wherever merchant's capital still predominates we find backward conditions'."

This thesis is supported with an impressive argument found in Tom Naylor's "The Rise and Fall of the Third Commercial Empire of the St. Lawrence".

In it he contends that,

> "... conventional liberal studies have failed to give explicit consideration to the peculiarities of the Canadian capitalist class and Marxist studies have misinterpreted its character. By comprehending this class as a mercantile one, accumulating wealth through circulation rather than production, one realizes that the dominance of a few staple trades leads not to independent capitalist development, but to the perpetuation of colonialism and underdevelopment. Canadian Confederation results not from the inability of the Canadian bourgeoisie to find a new dependency. The National Policy was one of mercantilism, of consolidation and expansion within a strong state structure.

Naylor's Harold Innis-inspired thesis which is offered as a neo-Marxist perspective clashes with the traditional Marxist thesis *Unequal Union,* by Stanley Ryerson. Ryerson suggests that Confederation was the result of a drive by growing industrial capitalism to harmonize tariffs among the various British North American colonies : in other words that there was a direct lineage between the old mercantile and the new industrial ruling class. Naylor, on the other hand, writes, "Finance capital emerges, not from industrial capital, as usually supposed, but from merchant capital, through the pooling of merchants' resources and their development of a banking structure, and through the earnings of the entrepôt trade. Corporation capital in its American form thus merged industrial capital and finance capital never became a potent force on its own."

Teeple sees the 'new national consciousness' as a product of certain sections of the middle class professionals. He asserts that without fundamentally challenging the established order, "compromise and accomodation will be used to mitigate the nationalist complaints of professors, teachers, artists, lawyers, engineers, government functionaries, and other technocrats . . . But what has not been so subject to appeasement is the struggle between labour and capital — in the main, American capital."

What is important to underline here is that both Teeple and Naylor make clear repeatedly that there is no independent capitalist group either English-or-French speaking which has national interests as a class that are in contradiction with those of the US power elite and ruling class, or with their multi-national corporations. Although in the last few years since the Canadian centennial celebrations many people have been caught up with "a feeling of being Canadian", the process of integration into the American empire is so far advanced that nothing short of a social revolution can reverse the tide. The previously mentioned middle-class professionals do not have the stomach for initiating such a struggle as a group nor do the Canadian capitalists feel their interests clashing enough with those of the Americans to justify allying themselves however cautiously with any radical departure from the status quo.

Unlike Québec where the awakening and active resistance of a small group of cultural workmen had an enormous impact in a society which was isolated by its language, the problem in Canada is quite different. In the broad cultural world we find a tremendous tension between regions in Canada. The small beach-heads established in Toronto and elsewhere among publishers, artists, writers, playwrights are in continual competition for the "too little, too late" handouts that some provincial governments and the federal state offers. And on the whole cultural workmen in Canada are so deeply colonialized that they simply grumble a bit, and accept. In Québec on the other hand we had

a period of tremendous social conflict during the early 1960's ; when large sections of the student population were mobilized, a full blown terrorist campaign was underway, and militant minorities were pressing in the streets with all sorts of direct action. The climate into which the small minority of English Canadian middle-class professionals, and the Quebec cultural workmen cried out was dramatically different. *

Teeple goes on to say, "Any profound challenge to the domination of capital, domestic and foreign, must begin, as it has in Québec, in the organised sector of the working class, because this sector has the means — at present poorly used — to organise and raise consciousness of the class which creates wealth but does not benefit from it." "That struggle in the context of the 'national' boundaries of Québec gave rise to a 'common front' of unions and articulated class consciousness in the face of American capital and its administrators in Québec." This needless to say is facile substitutionalism. The forced inter-action between the CNTU and QFL in Québec, not to mention the CEQ, plus the absence of a long-established social democratic party like the New Democrats converges into a particular set of factors underlining the origins of the Common Front. In Canada the powerless strata of the wage-earning population cannot wait for some similar change at the top of the trade union pyramid to say and do the things that its counter-part is doing in Québec. We shall return to this later.

Nevertheless, the primacy placed by Teeple and Naylor on mass actions in the context as they analyze it, places the "social question" well ahead in importance to the national question in

---

* see Patrick Coleman's review of *The Shouting Signpainters* by Malcolm Reid, in *OUR GENERATION*, Vol. 8, No. 4.

Canada. By the social question we mean that people's desire for social justice is much stronger than any national consciousness which concerns itself with mere symbolism or problems estranged from people's daily lives. Only when the solutions to social problems are impeded by the presence of imperialism, is it logical and necessary to add the national context. This happens to be the case with reference to almost all social problems in Canada today. But this approach to imperialist domination is far wiser and less likely to degenerate into jingoistic chauvinism or to national liberationism which postpones the abolition of a class society and capitalist relations of production for the distant future.

One implication of this primary emphasis on people's social problems and the condition of their daily lives is that there can be no 'first stage' coalition with the few nationally-conscious capitalists. This latter view is usually propounded by Marxists, and is supposed to encourage more individual capitalists to seek their fortunes with the nationalists, and at the same time show still other industrialists or businessmen an alternative to US domination. This is the 'national liberation front' idea. It is a strategy used in "third-world" colonies. Thus national liberationists here appeal to 'all Canadians' and are convinced that once the dynamic of nationalism spreads we can begin the break of US control. It is, then, contended that another "stage" emerges after victory when the working-class settles its accounts with Canadian capitalists.

We are leary of abstract 'stages' of development for coalition movements. If the analysis presented by Teeple/Naylor for instance is a correct one, namely that there is no independent Canadian group of capitalists that have fundamental differences with the American way of doing things, then the social

struggle of ordinary people is the most important hope we have. This class of people must start its own liberation from the bottom of society (and in some instances have begun to do so), without formal alliances with privileged individuals and elites at the top of the power pyramid. The powerless class in Canada has no one to rely on but itself, and its weapons are creative social conflict, class struggle, and mass mobilisation, along the lines of an extra-parliamentary opposition. This is a clear rejection of the national front strategy, whose core idea is collaborationist no matter how 'temporary', consisting of a coalition of various national interest groups and a multi-class approach that puts the growth of nationalism first, and "national independence" before social revolution.

What has been the background to popular struggle for social justice in Canada ? Volumes can be written but unfortunately Canadian historiography is blinded by the recording of what various elite or amorphous social forces did and did not do, rather than accounting for popular struggles. "The People's History of Cape Breton" or Jack Scott's forthcoming "Class Struggles in Canada, 1789-1899" represent the kind of approach to history which is most meaningful. In another fine essay in Capitalism and the National Question, Roger Howard and Jack Scott in "International Unions and the Ideology of Class Collaboration" add more evidence to the perspective of placing the social question first, and how from this position it relates to the national question. The authors deal with the fight for socialism, and the struggle between classes within the concrete setting of the all-pervasive influence of the reactionary American trade union organisation, the AFL-CIO's presence in Canada. The relationship between the form and the content of the social struggle has two aspects and is squarely stated. (1) There is a need to break organisationally from the American unions, and this must be done because a full social mobilisation of the working people of Canada must be based, and can only succeed, in the context of the historical experience and capacity of this class set in the particular cultural topography in which it has developed and functions. (2) Howard and Scott, whose essay is superior to that of Lipton's in the same book, state,

"It is clear that a total break, organisationally *and* ideologically, with the internationals is a necessary first step towards the building of a movement that will serve the real interests of Canadian workers. If the organisational change is not accompanied, or preceded, by ideological change, there will be no possibility of permanent transformation ; for it is in the field of ideology — the policy of class collaboration — that labour and especially its 'left' section, suffers the greatest defeat.... American unions fight furiously for control of Canadian locals and, in recent years, have spent millions to defeat efforts to establish an independent Canadian movement. John L. Lewis once claimed for instance that the United Mine Workers of America poured $1,124,000 into Nova Scotia up to 1920 to prevent the creation of a Canadian union."

With the rise of industrial unions

"... the leaders of the AFL, in fact, co-operated with the government and employers in destroying industrial organisations, such as the Knights of Labor, IWW and One Big Union. This situation was to continue until grass-roots pressure led to the organisation of the Congress of Industrial Organisations."

"The AFL started out as an organisation based on principles of exclusion, and was bitterly opposed to industrial unionism, especially as it was represented by the Knights of Labor".

"Antagonism developed and the AFL appointed John Flett as their paid organizer in Canada, charging him with responsibility for quenching the flames of revolt. At the TLC (Trades Labour Council) convention of 1901, President Ralph Smith dealt with the growing crisis, saying : 'I think it is of vast importance that this Congress should adopt some method of increasing its own usefulness. There ought to be a Canadian Federation, for, while I believe that unionism ought to be international in its methods to meet the necessity of combatting common foes, this usefulness is only assured by the strength of national unions. A federation of American unions represented by national unions, each working with the other in special cases, would be a great advantage over having local unions in Canada connected with the national unions of America.'

"The pro-internationals element was at a disadvantage at the 1901 covention. To avoid defeat on the issue, they adopted the tactic of tabling Smith's recommendations for an independent Canadian federation until the Berlin (Kitchener), Ontario, convention scheduled for 1902. This gave the AFL organizer Fleet and his colleagues another year to mobilize support.

"Following his report on anti-AFL sentiment in Canada, P.M. Draper, general secretary of the TLC, appealed to the 1901 AFL convention for additional funds to be assigned to Flett, and warned that 'a very strong feeling' in favour of national unions was growing in Canada. The convention delegates responded by voting $300 to finance Fleet's activities, and a convention committee commented, 'It is to be regretted that ... there seems to be a tendency toward severance among our Canadian brothers.' Flett and others busily whipped delegates into line for the 1902 convention, while international executives put pressure on Canadian branches. J.H. Watson, BC vice-president of the Trades and Labor Congress, complained : 'what do we find ? Canadian organizers paid by the American Federation of Labor organizing members of local unions and drawing their charter from a foreign country. But Flett's (and the AFL's) concerted and well-financed campaign proved unbeatable. Even Smith failed to get delegate nomination from Nanaimo, BC. branch of the United Mine Workers, whose district he represented as a member of Parliament. Instead, he was delegated by a Vancouver local union.

"A study of the 1902 convention proceedings suggests that the Canadian in-

197

dependent group realized that defeat awaited them. Only a token fight was offered ; and, after a one-day debate, the delegates passed a constitutional amendment which shaped the destiny of the Canadian Labour Congress from then until present. The amendment read : 'in no case shall any body of working-men belonging to any trade or calling at present having an international or national union be granted a charter. In the event of an international or national union of the trade or calling of the unions so charted being formed, it shall be the duty of the proper officer of the Congress to see that the said union becomes a member of said international or national union. Provided that no national union shall be recognized where an international union exists'.

"That 'international' meant 'American' was made very clear in 1912, when British-affiliated unions were expelled. The congress elected the AFL organizer, John Flett, as president, and he went begging to the American masters in a resolution : 'Resolved that as the Trades and Labor Congress of Canada has placed itself squarely in accord with the principles of international unions, and as such action will reveal the loss of revenues ... it is the opinion of the Congress ... all federal labor unions and central trades and labor councils should be instructed to take immediate steps to make such arrangements with the American Federation of Labor'.

"The question of charters was referred to the Executive Council, which met with Flett and Draper in Toronto on 25 April 1903. Council minutes show how these two colonials represented Canadian interests : 'President Flett and Secretary Draper said they were willing to concede the issuance of charters to the AFL.' The request for the right to issue charters was withdrawn without even a reference to the Congress which had passed the resolution. The line of capitulation was clearly drawn, and from this point on a long list of American-supported functionaries would attack independent unions as dual organizations.

"The evidence points to a deliberate plan of conquest plotted by the American unionists, and the record of the AFL in Latin America tends to support this thesis ..."

Quoting at length from the Howard/Scott essay is justified because of the little known origins of the domination of American unionism in Canada. But we also want to quote at length to outline the resourcefulness and tremendous capacity of the working people of Canada. During the period when American unionism sought to control the labour movement here the One Big Union emerged. It is important to note that the OBU arose during a period of social conflict.

"The most significant attempt to create an independent Canadian trade union movement was the organization of the One Big Union. It was called into existence during the upsurge of labour radicalism by 1921-22. But during this short period of activity, the One Big Union raised some of the central issues involved in the development of an independent movement.

The impetus for the organization of the OBU arose from the dissatisfaction of the more radical union leaders (almost entirely Westerners) with the prevailing policies of the international labour movement. These dissatisfactions centred around two interrelated themes : class collaboration and trade union organization.

The issue of class collaboration came to a head when the conscription bill was introduced into the House of Commons on 1 June 1917, the day the US Congress adopted a draft conscription law. Prior to the war, the TLC had denounced the impending conflict as a struggle between the capitalist classes of various nations in which the working class had no stake. Even after the declaration of hostilities and the shock of the disintegration of international labour solidarity, the TLC opposed conscription either completely or within the context of the demand for 'conscription of wealth' (i.e., nationalization of industry) if conscription of manpower were legislated. But with the passage of the conscription bill and the wholehearted support given to the war by the AFL, the leadership of the Canadian movement wavered.

At the TLC convention of 1917, the radicals proposed a national general strike to block conscription. But the

TLC executive rejected this proposal on two grounds. . . ."

The first objection was because it would break the law, and the executive did not want to oppose the Federal government.

And the second objection was this :

"It is just as well, at this time, that I should point out that the organized workers of Canada stand in a position that has no parallel in any other country of the world. This Congress can only exert its moral influence in the enforcement of decisions, and the economic power to support legislative demands is not vested in our movement, but is under the control of international officers of our representative unions. When the executive council of the American Federation of Labor reaches a decision, members of that council, being heads of powerful international trade unions, can use their influence effectively. The same applies to the parliamentary committee of the British Trade Union Congress, but in Canada we cannot use our economic power without the sanction of the heads of our international unions . . . In cases where our decisions are at variance with decisions taken by the American Federation of Labor regarding important national issues, it is difficult to secure that sympathy, that support in the exercise of our economic powers, as we otherwise would receive if the executive of the Congress were composed of powerful economic organizations. As a delegate put it : 'President Gompers had committed the workers of the United States to conscription ; therefore, a general strike was not feasible.' "

This issue, and the question of labour leaders participating in government bodies, plus the issue of industrial versus craft unionism moved the radicals to organize the Western Labour Conference in Calgary during March 1919. One of the most important debates centred around political activity.

"Although it did not go as far as the IWW stand of rejecting all political activity, the conference did reject the narrow parliamentarian view of politics. In the words of one delegate : 'Power in politics is not found in Parliament but in the country prior to the election. Politics only exists where there are classes, and any action taken by a class in defense of its interest is political action. Hence you cannot define any particular action as political, but any action . . . used to control political power in order to use it for the benefit of that class — that is political action, and it matters not what method it takes.' The founders of the OBU considered ongoing education in class consciousness to be more significant than occasional election campaigns and allocated one-third of its monthly dues to the general executive board for that purpose."

Howard and Scott then proceed to discuss the defeat of the Winnipeg General Strike by the combined forces of the Canadian ruling class and its government on the one hand, and the American Federation of Labor on the other. The authors also criticize the policies of the Moscow Communists in undermining the internal solidarity of the OBU by adopting the policy of the US Communist leader William Z. Foster which was one of working within the AFL and not founding separate trade unions. These people still maintain this permeationist "boring from within" position today in Canada, as do the Trotskyists and the New Democratic Party. We do not support this position. On the contrary, libertarian socialists have never shied away from the task of building new institutions or new organizations from the bottom up as the occasion determines, especially when bureaucratic degeneration has set into the established ones. There we join those who would urge the creation of new independent associations of producers in Canada. This is not simply a call for independent national or nationalist unions, but rather for new unions within a framework of revolutionary syndicalism.

We wish to use the same criteria consistently. To urge the creation of nationalist trade unions in and of itself is to urge a dangerous half measure. It's the previously mentioned 'first stage of development' approach again. The working people, both unionized and non-unionized, when they are prepared to move, will see through this 'intermediate' objective. Again as in all other questions the social content of the conflict must come first, and not the form.

Howard and Scott sum up by saying :

> "But necessary as it is as a preliminary step in the direction of more important developments, the switch from international to independent Canadian unions will not, of itself, result in any fundamental transformation of the unions from organs of class compromise to weapons of revolutionary class struggle."

They go on to add,

> "The roots of the crisis in the unions are internal, not external, and are embedded in the class-collaborationist policy which is built securely into what has become the main activity and proud achievement of the labour movement — the union contract, the signing of which is a fundamental act of compromise with the class enemy."

Finally the authors do well to warn us that,

> "It would be a serious mistake to equate the union movement with the working class. The bulk of the working population is not in the organized union movement."

Ending the book, Teeple has an essay called "Liberals in a Hurry : Socialism and the CCF-NDP", and Naylor, adds an appendix on the same question called, "The ideological foundations of Social Democracy and Social Credit." These essays contain many important insights, including some dealing with the origins of the CCF. When we hear certain nationalists in Canada rally various 'American ideological influences on the Left' while at the same time upholding the NDP as a genuine Canadian invention, they should be reminded if they are at all aware of it, about the disastrous influence of British fabianism on the CCF and later NDP.

Teeple ends his essay by challenging the stream of socialist orthodoxy on the question of State-ownership of the means of production. He rightly takes on this powerful myth, not only to demonstrate the vacuous nature of CCF/NDP socialism but also to bring in the more generous vision of Marx. We shall deal with this later.

With reference to Waffle, Teeple again rightly suggests :

> "The Waffle, however, is due some credit for helping to develop a consciousness of the colonial nature of Canadian society. Although, this left wing has attempted to link the struggle for independence from the United States with socialism, these two struggles are linked only in name because the Waffle has not moved beyond democratic liberalism."

To summarize this collection of essays : Canada is not now and has never been an independent country ; it does not have now and has never had an independent ruling class; it has no independent trade union movement, and the few efforts attempted in this direction were crushed, with the collusion of certain sections of the so-called Left. Finally any independence movement has to be based on a radical analysis of the day to day problems of the working people : namely the primacy of the social question is the only genuine basis for struggle against foreign domination, and for collective self-determination. Further solutions to these social problems must not be sought in vague abstractions but within the cultural backdrop out of which they arise which entails an understanding of the specific cast these problems in Canada assume. The impossibility of finding solutions for some of our social (economic, political, cultural) problems in a thoroughly colonized society under the domination of US imperialism will make the relationship between the social and national question clear. All this is implicit in *Capitalism and the National*

Question and a logical extension of its arguments.

Well and good. Much beyond this point, the book arouses all the disappointments that most collections of essays generate. The book brings together the work of some of Canada's outstanding independent Marxists, a relatively rare event on the Canadian Left. For instance, there is a very competent treatment of the class structure in Canada by Leo Johnson which is recommended although its relationship to the national question is unclear.

Nevertheless, the book collectively demonstrates the limitations of Marxism in Canada, and even more the abject poverty of the socialist project. It is stunning to us for instance, that although the book is called *Capitalism and the National Question in Canada*, there is in fact no thorough discussion of contemporary capitalism. In other words capitalism in Canada is in no way situated in the general development of international capitalism, and the array of contradictions in which its contemporary form is emersed. There is no discussion of the nature of the productive process in Canada, and the relations of production. There is no thorough discussion of the nature and present crisis in the meaning of socialism today, or what a socialist programme should include in Canada. There is no discussion of the Canadian Left, outside of the NDP. And finally there is no discussion of a revolutionary strategy or alternative, namely how and with what new principles can we get from here to there.

Even a bare outline of some of the missing discussions is imperative for our part if we are going to take seriously the present discussion of the social revolutionary project. To begin with, we may be reminded that in an earlier section of this critical review essay, we stated that it is incorrect to pay attention to Canada's ossified "federal" political super-

structures. In effect the different principal regions of Canada, and in some cases the provinces are more genuine geopolitical units than the federal one, and that any revolutionary movement must first and foremost be rooted in this regionalism. This means that movement building will have the quality of regional authenticity. Different regions having different urban/rural relationships will mold a different shape on the movement there than elsewhere. The political economy of the regions and the level of its development will contribute in particular ways to the strengths or weaknesses of the movement.

This means that when we speak of putting social problems in their cultural cast, we mean placing them in their localist setting, taking into account the particularity and history of the popular struggles, popular aspirations, and quests for social justice of the region in question. What we are admitting here is reality : namely that the west coast ; the prairies ; northern Ontario ; southern Ontario ; the Maritimes ; and the North have much more of a cultural reality to them, than the vague abstraction called Canada held together by a powerful centralizing state with its mystified but socially impotent political institutions. Indeed there are probably cultural sub-regions within these larger land masses we just mentioned, as Acadia, or Cape Breton in the Maritimes. Any movement solidly rooted in such organic areas becomes virtually impregnable against outside assault, especially if it is also based on a popular revolutionary consciousness which is itself inter-laced with the daily lives of the people of the area. Any federation based on these genuine units, co-ordinated over the years from the bottom up is more likely to be organic and meaningful.

But in order for this rich diversity not to degenerate into balkanism or fragmentation, the decentralised and localized social struggle envisaged here must be of a libertarian nature. Not only would it otherwise be reactionary and bankrupt, it would also not work, and this would allow for the complete triumph of U.S. imperialism. The kind of social struggle which is seen here as necessary is identical to a libertarian socialist revolution, for this is the only way it can survive and flourish. Such a mass movement based on small autonomous units blended into local and regional cultures, eco-systems in fact, will not only be self-reliant but will implement large-scale coordination on a more egalitarian and effective way. Such a revolutionary movement would be more of a reflection of the future liberated society, than any vanguard political party ruled by 'democratic centralism' and its consequent military discipline which inevitably leads to Stalinism. What in effect is foreseen here is the exact opposite of the traditional 'revolutionary' group's view of social struggle.

The only realistic defence for areas north of the 49th parallel, is by a people with a high consciousness of solidarity and mutual aid, capable of struggling city by city, community by community, street by street. The actual means of defence are several, and need not be discussed here. All potential enemies would know that any attempt at conquest would meet with total resistance.

But what are the conditions in our society which are laying the basis for the emergence of such a movement ? What is meant more precisely by the social question in the light of this perspective ? At this point we wish to offer a number of theses.

(1) THE CHANGES UNDERGONE BY CAPITALISM DURING THE LAST FIFTY YEARS SHOW THEMSELVES PRIMARILY IN THE INCREASING CONCEN-TRATION OF BOTH CAPITAL AND BUREAUCRACY.

Monoplies, trusts, cartels, multi-national corporations abound in countries of "private capitalism". During this same period of development the State has become the main economic factor and coordinator in these countries. *

This process of concentration has led to certain changes in the economy. The failure to recognize these changes accounts for the shallowness of much that passes as 'marxist analysis ? today.

The increase in the mass consumption of commodities has become an essential feature in the smooth functioning of capitalism. "Commodity fetishism" has become an irreversible aspect of this kind of society. The old forms of capitalism as characterized by economic depressions, massive unemployment, and general stagnation must be put aside (see analysis in editorial of OUR GENERATION, Vol. 6, No. 4, "Towards an Extra-Parliamentary Opposition"). Neo-capitalism generates expansion of both production and consumption for the sake of consumption, interrupted by minor fluctuations. This 'ideology of growth' is obtained at the cost of an increased scope of exploitation and alienation of the producers in the course of their work. Labour discipline is bought especially in key industries, at the workplace in exchange for certain wage concessions. Increases in wages on the whole now approximate increases in productivity of labour. This means that the proportion of the total social product going to the workers and to capitalists remains constant.

* See OUR GENERATION, Vol. 8, No. 4, for an analysis of the economic role of the State in Canada and Québec, and THE POLITICAL ECONOMY OF THE STATE published by BLACK ROSE BOOKS for additional information including an analysis of the role of the State in the U.S. economy.

(2) THE SOCIAL STRUCTURE HAS CHANGED WITH THE GROWTH OF BUREAUCRACY

The modernizing of capitalism has meant the 'rationalization' of human activities. The bureaucratisation of all spheres of social life becomes a dominant feature of our type of society. In the process, inherited individual wealth is not the only criterion whereby influence can be gained either in the economy or the State.

The "traditional" ruling class based on the ownership of heavy industry, manufacturing, bank, insurance, is forced to share, on an increasing scale, the functions of administration and management both of the economy and of society at large, with a growing bureaucratic stratum. This has already happened in Canada during the last fifteen years and has brought persons into the power structure whose ideology is part and parcel of Canadian liberalism grounded in the "Pearson Years". In Québec the situation is somewhat different as this stratum developed much later on. *

This stratum, in Canada or in other advanced capitalist societies, has become an indispensable part of the smooth functioning and 'efficient' operation of the economy and shows deep, irreversible changes in its structure.

The bureaucracy has some of its roots in the workplace. The concentration of capital and the 'rationalization' of production from outside create the necessity for a bureaucratic apparatus in the factory, office, or institution. The function of this apparatus is to 'manage' the labour process and the labour force and to coordinate the relations of the enterprise with the rest of the economy.

The bureaucracy also finds roots in the increasing number of persons involved in the higher reaches of State activity such as public corporations and state economic agencies. This is a result of the profound changes that have taken place in the economic role of the State.

The bureaucracy finally finds its roots in the political process of parliamentarianism and in the trade union organisations. In order to channel people, and to better integrate them into the existing social order, a special political apparatus is necessary. This apparatus participates to an increasing degree in the day-to-day management of society, by muffling conflicts, and seeking modifications of this or that demand from below.

The growth of this bureaucratic and technocratic stratum has profoundly altered the internal structure of the ruling class. New elements have had to be incorporated into this minority, and privileges have had to be extended. In a word, hierarchical relationships have been realigned. This stratum is not a homogenous social formation in Canada. It has developed to varying degrees in various regions of the country. It is important to note that this managerial bureaucracy is not based on any fundamentally new mode of production or new pattern of the circulation of commodities. It is based rather on changes in the economic basis of capitalism's need for survival. Historically such developments usually appear at the end of an era.

(3) CAPITALIST SOCIETY IS BASED ON CLASS DIVISIONS

The social relations at the workplace, in an economy of artificially enforced scarcity based on a centralizing technology remains the basis of class society. In

---

* See "Classes Sociales et idéologies nationalistes au Québec, 1760-1970" by Gilles Bourque and Nicole Laurin-Frenette, where they deal with the split between the 'technocratic faction' and the 'neo-capitalist faction', reviewed in OUR GENERATION, Vol. 8, No. 2.

all societies the world over these social relations are capitalist relations ; that is, they are based on wage labour. Human beings are obliged to sell their labour like a commodity for money. This makes working persons into objects by selling their labour to someone else in order to survive. Their labour, bought and sold at will by a small minority is the only thing valued by capital, because it alone can produce more capital. The rest of the human is incidental. Those who buy and sell labour power own most of the wealth that it produces and thus control in one way or another society as a whole. Those who are forced to sell their labour power to the highest bidder available, are powerless as individuals.

Working people in factory or office constitute less than half of the total exploited population of Canada. Nevertheless, should they stop working the economy would grind to a halt. Therefore the tension at the workplace, the point of production, dominates directly the whole organisation of the economy and indirectly the whole of society. The organization of work is becoming more and more bureaucratized and is taking the form of an increasing division of labour, of time and motion studies, and a tendency to speed-up the work process. The conditions of the workplace which are not unlike a military operation are subjected to the ruthless will of capital, personified in the bureaucratic managerial apparatus. As a consequence of new forms of both exploitation and domination, this class of working people are becoming more de-humanized, de-personalized ; they are being proletarianized in the sense of *1984* and *Brave New World*. *

The fate of this proletariat in political and social life has not changed over the years. It is as powerless vis a vis established power as ever ; it has no substantial power to affect changes in the quality of its day to day life. The whole pattern of neo-capitalist society, of its

economy, of its State, of its housing, or of its education, of the objects it will consume and of the news it will receive, of the questions of war and peace themselves, remain decided by a self-perpetuating minority. The mass of the population has no control or power over this minority, be the society one of 'private capitalism' and a 'liberal democracy' or 'state capitalist' and a 'dictatorship of the **proletariat'**.

The development and bureaucratization of capitalism today has not lessened its irrationality. Both at the level of the factory and office and at the level of society as a whole, the bureaucratic technocracy is a mixture of despotism and confusion which produces a fantastic human and material wastage.

This then, we suggest, is what preoccupies working people far more than anything else. Unless we speak to these concerns we speak to nothing fundamental. These are the problems of neo-capitalism in Canada. This is the social question. But because Canada is a colony, the social question cannot be dealt with outside the fact that Canadian capitalism is an extension of American capitalism. And that in the end our economy and its social, political and cultural institutions serve the ideology and objective needs of the American empire. Thus the social question must be taken on in relationship to U.S. imperialism. In other words, people in this country can go just so far in their social liberation before they have to deal with the question of outside con-

---

* With reference to blue collar workers alone, a rash of studies have recently been published documenting this trend : *Where Have All the Robots Gone ? Worker Dissatisfaction in the 70's,* by H.L. Sheppard, *The Hidden Injuries of Class,* by Richard Sennet and J. Cobb, *The Company and the Union — The 'Civilized Relationship' of General Motors and the United Auto Workers,* by W. Serrin, *Bitter Wages,* by J.A. Page, *Work in America,* a HEW study, *Worker's Control,* edited by Hunnius, Garson and Cage.

trol. However, we cannot proceed with the question of outside control first (the national question) and work down to the social question, for this path especially in an advanced industrial society like Canada is dangerous as well as historically blocked.

(4) THE DEGENERATION OF THE LEFT IN CANADA

The roots of the impotent situation in which the Left in Canada finds itself is to be found in two intimately interrelated processes : the evolution of modern capitalism, partly outlined above, and the bureaucratization of the traditional Left groups and the trade union organisations. *

The degeneration of these organisations is not due to 'bad leaders' who 'betray'. The problem is much deeper. It is due primarily to the overwhelming pressures of capitalist society which eventually transform these organisations into a mirror image of itself. Originally created to overthrow bourgeois society, these traditional organisations have increasingly adopted the objectives, methods, ideology and patterns of organisation of the very society they were striving to supersede. There has developed within their ranks, no matter what the theories, an increasing division between leaders and led. Some of these organisations are caught up in this process consciously and indeed cultivate it, others deny its existence in a cloud of 'radical rhetoric'. This has culminated in the development all the same, of a bureaucracy and bureaucratic cast of mind which can be neither removed nor controlled from below. This structure pursues objectives of its own.

These organisations come forward with claims to 'lead' the working class.

* For another analysis see "The Improverishment of the Canadian Left" by Marjaleena Repo, TRANSFORMATION, Vol. 1, No. 4.

In reality they see the class as a mass to be maneuvered, according to the preconceived ideas of those who dominate the particular political machinery. They all see the objective of liberation as an increased degree of participation in general 'material prosperity'.

The reformists like the NDP claim that this can be achieved by a better organisation of traditional capitalism. The Stalinists, Maoists, Trotskyists and Waffle claim that what is needed is a change in the formal ownership of the means of production along with State planning, which amounts to a kind of socialism from above. Their *common ideology* boils down to an increase in production and consumption guaranteed by the rule of an elite of managers, seated at the summit of a new hierarchy based on 'ability', 'experience', and 'devotion to the cause'. This objective is essentially no different from that of contemporary capitalism itself.

The degeneration is not due to the intrinsic evils of organisation. Nor is it due to the fact that reformists and Stalinists have 'wrong ideas' and provide 'bad leadership', as sundry Trotskyists and Leninists still maintain. Still less is it due to the bad influence of particular individuals : David or Stephen Lewis, Khruschev, or Stalin.

What it really reflects is the fact that even when struggling to over throw capitalism, the working class remains a partial prisoner of the system, and this in a much more subtle way than is usually understood. It remains a prisoner because it continues to conceive of *its* liberation as a task to be entrusted to the leaders of certain organisations to whom the class can confidently delegate its historical role.

The bureaucratised, traditional Left organizations, parties and trade unions, have long ceased to express the historical long-term interests of the working people. The reformist bureaucracy aims at securing a place for itself in the management of the capitalist system as it is. The authoritarian socialist bureaucracy of one sect or another aims at instituting a regime of the Russian or Chinese type where it would itself become the dominant social group.

Despite their periodic conflicts with the ruling class, both reformists and authoritarians whether in political parties or in the trade unions have the effect of perpetuating present class society. They have become the vehicles through which capitalist ideas, attitudes and mentality seep into the powerless class. They seek to canalise and control all manifestations of revolt against the existing social order. They seek to limit the more extreme excesses of the system, the better to maintain exploitation within 'tolerable' limits.

These political and trade union organizations are confronted with an, insoluble dilemma. On the one hand they are as institutions tolerated by established society. On the other hand, they aim at maintaining within their framework a class, whose conditions of life and work drive it to destroy that very society.

The organisation which the majority of exploited and dominated people need must be based on a totally different philosophy and structure and use entirely different methods of struggle.

Apathy and depolitization result from bureaucratic degeneration. The working class organisations have become indistinguishable from bourgeois political institutions.

Apathy and depolitisation result from changes undergone by neo-capitalism. Economic expansion, high employment, the gradual increase in wages, pathological consumerism, mean that for a whole period (which has not yet come to an end), the illusion of progress still affects us. This illusion is deliberately and very

skillfully fostered and manipulated by the system for its own ends.

The programme of reformists like the NDP has been realized in a whole variety of ways. Yet the more we have 'changes' the more the basic features of our lives, like boredom, monotony, purposelessness, remains the same. The political path along which the NDP and the various 'Communist' parties proceed proves its futility. After decades and decades of reform and struggle all that has been achieved in this land of incredible wealth and potential is that commodities can be spread more widely than before. The same social powerlessness exists, and the same economic insecurity prevails. What we have still amounts to charity however bitterly we have fought for it.

Historical experience in Canada has shown that society will only be changed fundamentally through the autonomous and self-conscious activity of the proletarianized class. No stratum, category, party or other form of hierarchical organization can achieve socialism 'on behalf of' the proletariat and in its place. Socialism will only be built through social revolution. Socialism can only be built on the destruction of all bureaucracies. Social revolution does not only mean the abolition of private capitalism. It means the abolition of all dominating and privileged strata in society. It therefore implies the abolition of any social group claiming to manage production or the State 'on behalf of the people'.

(5) THE FORMATION OF A REVOLUTIONARY CONSCIOUSNESS AND OF A SOCIAL REVOLUTIONARY MOVEMENT IN CANADA WILL BE MEANINGLESS (INDEED IMPOSSIBLE) UNLESS IT BASES ITS IDEAS, ITS PROGRAMME, ITS STRUCTURE AND ITS METHODS OF ACTION ON THE HISTORICAL

EXPERIENCE OF THE WORK-
ING CLASS IN THIS COUNTRY
AND IN OTHER COUNTRIES,
PARTICULARLY THAT OF THE
LAST 50 YEARS.

This means that such developments as we describe as constituting the social question must draw the full lessons of the period of bureaucratisation and that it must break with all that is mere ritual or hangover from the past. Only in this way will we be able to provide answers to the real and often new problems which will be posed in the period to come.

A radical analysis of the crisis of modern industrial society and of capitalism is imperative. The essence of the social question as outlined here is that the analysis or critique of the organisation of the economy and of work under capitalism must be at the centre of our reconstruction of the revolutionary movement. We must surrender the idea that capitalism creates rational factories and rational machines and that it organizes work 'efficiently' although somewhat brutally and for the wrong ends. Instead we must express what every person in every region of Canada sees very clearly : that work has become absurd, that it means the constant oppression and mutilation of workers and that the bureaucratic organisation of work means endless confusion and waste.

Where it exists, material poverty must be exposed. But the content of consumption under capitalism must also be exposed. It is not enough to criticize the smallness of the education budget : we must denounce the content of capitalist education. We must denounce and work against the concept of the school as an activity apart from life and society. It is not enough to demand more public monies for housing : we must denounce and work against the prevailing ideas on housing and the way of life they entail.

It is not enough to denounce the present government as representing the interests of a privileged class. We must also denounce the whole form and content of contemporary politics as a business for 'specialists', and the idea that parliamentarianism is democracy. A revolutionary movement must break with electorialism, and on this there can be no compromise. It must show that revolutionary politics are not confined to talk of wages and government affairs, but that they deal with everything that concerns people and their social lives. "Les vrais problèmes sont quotidiens", was the insightful slogan of the 1968 General Strike in France, and with reason.

The confusion about the socialist programme created by the authoritarian organisations of the Left must be exposed. The idea that socialism only means the nationalisation of the means of production and planning — and that its essential aim is an increase in production and consumption, albeit on a more egalitarian basis — must be denounced. The similarity of these views with the basic orientation of neo-capitalism itself must be shown.

Socialism is workers' control and management of production and of society and the localist power of workers' councils and community assemblies. The essential content of socialism is the restitution to people of the control over their own life, the transformation of labour from an absurd means of breadwinning into the free and creative action of individuals and groups (see "Toward a Liberatory Technology" by Murray Bookchin, in the OUR GENERATION pamphlet form), the constitution of integrated human communities and the union of the culture and the life of people.

The libertarian essence of socialism should not be shamefully hidden as some kind of abstract speculation concerning an indeterminate future. The perspective with which we looked at the social question here should be presented for what it is : a prospective for the humanisation of work and of an entire society. Socialism is not a backyard of leisure attacher to the industrial prison. It is not what commodities we can play with during the weekend, even though it might be a three or four day weekend. It is not transistors for the prisoners. It is the destruction of the industrial prison itself. *This means the defeat of American imperialism in content as well as in form.* This is the basis of our position. In an industrial society as developed as our own we cannot separate this question of form from content, so the social question comes first and foremost. The limitations of its resolution by the presence of American domination of Canada are dealt with at that point. We are not third-world voyeurs.

In all local struggles the way in which the result is obtained is at least as important as what is obtained. Even from the point of view of efficiency, actions organised and led by the people themselves are superior to actions decided and led bureaucratically. They alone create the conditions of progress, for this approach alone teaches us to run our own affairs.

In Canada, as in other industrial societies, the mobilisation of youth is essential. Canadian society has lost its hold on the generations it produces. The rupture is particularly brutal in politics. Such a mobilization will be impossible unless the broad outlines of a social alternative for the present and immediate future are clearly articulated. The social movement must help young people in struggle and must contribute towards clarifying and generalising their experience, the objective being the development of skills and a lasting social consciousness and ability to manage social affairs themselves.

Organizing on the regional and local level must be based on the principles of direct democracy and be consciously anti-bureaucratic in manner. This implies a total rejection of 'democratic centralism' and other forms of organisation that encourage bureaucracy. At the local level, and in any regional or large level co-ordination, the principles of autonomy, direct democracy rather than delegation of decision-making, and co-ordination where necessary, should be achieved through delegates elected and revocable at any time by their local groups.

The revolutionary movement should also seek to bring closer together the struggle at the workplace and the broader struggle of other sections of the population, equally deprived of any effective say in the management of the affairs that concern them most. But people, we must remind ourselves, cannot be expected to become participating citizens in their communities actively involved in important social issues, if at work where they spend more than half their day they are beaten down. Nevertheless there are many people who are not part of the regular work force. A large part of educational work should be directed towards these other strata of our evolving society as well as towards new strata of wage earners (various service workers, students, intellectuals).

We have written and spoken at some length on previous occasions about the importance of community work, no matter what importance is assigned to change in the work-place. People who are not part of the regular work force can be organised around questions like housing, transportation, pollution, health, and unemployment. All these issues should be raised within the perspective of community control. The generation of new forms of struggle and organisation is not only profoundly relevant to the socialist future but also capable on a daily basis of eating out the legitimacy of corrupt contemporary institutions in the community. More than a challenge to legitimacy, these developing new social forms, whether they are co-operative housing, radical day-care centres, or community clinics, are on the one hand embryonic attempts at self-management, and, given a sense of economic reality, are also supportive in any community of the revolutionary movement. These networks of community groups can create a sense of cultural change which is indispensable to rooting of any new consciousness in a particular section of a city.

Today, no matter how active young women and men workers are at their place of work, support is essential at home and in the neighborhood. This opens the whole question of co-operative living, new life-styles, communalism. The sterile privatism of traditional radical movements, where after one's daily work, a person goes home to the traditional bourgeois setting does not go far enough. Revolutionary consciousness must be nourished in the whole of one's daily life.

But in the final analysis the similarity between the objects of these new social forms and actions and those of the movement of worker's self-management at the workplace should be repeatedly pointed out, as should the only possible solution to both : the complete democratisation of society through social revolution.

The changes in modern capitalism have done nothing to lessen the contradictions of the system which lie in the field of production and of work, reflecting themselves through the rest of society. These are contradictions focussed in the alienation of the worker. In addition to these contradictions, in Canada, by virtue of the domination of American capital, people here are thrown conflicting signals of identity. On the one hand they are told they are Canadians, and that is supposed to be different from being an American. On the other they are surrounded daily by the values and images of imperial America. Nevertheless this secondary contradiction can only be gotten at by means of the first, that of the objective and subjective condition of working people. Only if people are determined to attain a different way of life, and have a positive alternative in mind, will the struggle by joined. It is simply not enough in Canada to tell working people that we do not want to be controlled by the Americans. Nationalists will use our hostility towards American domination, but towards what end ? To a new bureaucratic society, a state capitalist, or authoritarian socialist society directed by centralising State agencies from Ottawa ? We must not let our desire to break American control distract us from the more fundamental project of breaking the existing social order. This project cannot come after, it must come at the same time, or it never comes.

Even in Québec where there is a tremendous emotional investment in a distinct language, and a largely different culture, the cultural struggle touched a small minority of the proletariat. When this proletariat mobilised itself into the greatest General Strike in North American history on social issues, and realised that one of the limitations of the situation was foreign control, then that question became meaningful. It is becoming clearer in Québec daily, that socialism comes first. But socialism will not be possible without self-determination, that is, the independence of Québec. It is now, when 30,000 people march on May Day in solidarity throughout Québec, that we see the momentum becoming massive.

The subjective undercurrents bending towards nationalism do not exist in Canada. Nationalism's historical role was to bring the bourgeoisie to power. Where the bourgeoisie was only partly in power, and a country dominated by imperialism, nationalism was used to change the balance of power. *Nowhere* have nationalists ushered social revolution. To create a nationalist sentiment ex nihilo in an advanced industrial society is extremely dangerous.

The struggle for freedom, for the social and cultural self-determination of Canada and Québec from external control is one and the same with the struggle against all hierarchy, and this in turn is the struggle against the hierarchy of ideas employed by the bourgeoisie to maintain its world.

The opposition between theory and ideology is no mere academic dispute : it is itself part of the struggle. Thus we do not offer this perspective, the outlines of which we stated here, as mere 'ideas', as just one more contemplative interpretation of our society. Ideas are, after all, alienated desire. We hope with dialogue to clarify theory and to practice this theory in our daily lives.

FOOTNOTES :

1. Gad Horowitz, "Conservatism, Liberalism and Socialism in Canada", *Canadian Journal of Economics and Political Science*, May, 1966, p. 163-5.

2. Gad Horowitz, "On the Fear of Nationalism", *Canadian Dimension*, Vol. 4 no. 4.

3. Mel Watkins et al, *Waffle Manifesto : For an Independent Socialist Canada*, reprint in *Canadian Dimension Kit #3*.

4. *Canadian Forum*, Jan.-Feb., 1972, p. 64.

5. Ibid., p. 54.

6. Ibid., p. 55.

7. Mel Watkins, "Multi-national Corporation and Socialism", in LaPierre et al, eds., *Essays on the Left*, McClelland and Stewart, Toronto, p. 207.

8. Kari Levitt — address to the *Canadian Economics Association*, June, 1972.

9. *Capitalism and The National Question in Canada*, edited by Gary Teeple, University of Toronto Press, $3.95, 256 pages, 1972.

The writers wish to acknowledge debt to Kari Levitt in the first section and to Paul Cardan, especially for the essay "Socialism or Barbarism", in the second section.

Published 1973

DEMOCRACY AND PARLIAMENTARY POLITICS

by Gerry Hunnius

FEW will deny that we are faced today with growing social unrest, insecurity and a feeling of disorientation. The origins of this unrest are frequently sought in specific historical events such as the ban-the-bomb marches of the 1950's, the early civil rights campaigns, the student rebellions and the growth of the anti-war movement centered around the aggression by the United States in Vietnam. Common to all the protest is the refusal of a growing number of people to be integrated into a system without being allowed to discuss and determine its meaning, value or purpose. What is becoming increasingly clear is that the turbulence and unrest in Canada and the United States is not a historical accident but has its roots in the values, policies and structures of our socio-economic system.

The role of democratic theory has undergone fundamental changes which are of importance to anyone concerned with social change. Current elitist theory of democracy is worth looking at because it so accurately describes social reality. Neither the theory nor the reality conforms to the original conception of democracy as an ideal to be striven for. What now passes for democratic theory is little more than the theoretical formulations of the status quo. Because of the misuse of democratic theory, it is important and relevant to review briefly the revision which democratic theory has undergone in recent times. But first let us look at the Canadian reality.

Elite rule in Canada

Until the publication of John Porter's *Vertical Mosaic,* no major analysis of class and power in Canada had come to grips with the realities of elite rule. The pluralist ideology from south of the border was faithfully repeated by Canadian political scientists. Students got their introduction to this ideology largely through the writings of Dawson and Corry. Porter (like Weber) stresses the importance of the bureaucratic nature of institutional power. "Power arises because of the general social need for order." [1] It is distributed through institutional orders. "People in power roles belong to an elite." [2] While Porter admits that the "western" value system of capitalism unifies the elites (winning out over Christianity and nationalism which are irrational), he argues that the exercise of power is limited, "not only because of functional specialization but also because institutional elites compete with each other for power." [3] While Porter strikes a note of optimism when he argues that the competition of elites prevents the emergence of one monolithic "power elite", his general conclusion shatters the liberal notion of Canada as a "citizen-participating democracy". Democracy is absent and the elites are, by and large, not open to recruitment from outside their own ranks. Canada has been incapable in "taking a lead in the changes and experimentation necessary for more democratic industrial societies. A fragmented political structure, a lack of upward mobility into its elite and higher occupational levels, and the absence of a clearly articulated system of values ... are some of the reasons for this retardation." [4] Porter is not optimistic about a change toward a more democratic order in Canada. "Given the complexities of modern societies", he says, "it is unlikely that widespread participation can develop without very great changes and institutional experimentation." [5] The study of Canadian elites is made especially difficult because of the domination of our economy by that of the United States and by the colonial relations of our elites vis-a-vis those of the United States. Since Porter largely disregards this phenomenon, he does not give adequate treatment to the growing nationalism in Canada and its potential for changing the elite structure of Canadian society.

The reality of our democratic system in Canada would seem to be this : our ruling class is substantially composed of the same groups as that of the United States, with the significant difference as George Grant points out, that "the Canadian ruling class looks across the border for its final authority in both politics and culture". [6] The ruling classes in Canada are basically the parties of "corporations, the real estate lobbies, and the rich", [7] in short, those that control what Grant calls, the "private governments (that is, the corporations) and those that control the public government which co-ordinates the activities of these corporations." [8]

The earlier controversy as to whether local communities are ruled by a small elite of business leaders (Hunter) or by several competing groups (Dahl) has essentially been resolved in favour of the pluralist conception of community power. This conception happens to fit neatly into the general framework of the elitist theory of democracy which assumes that a system of competing elites equals democracy.

Harold Kaplan's work on Metro Toronto is one of the few available studies on community power structures in Canada. Kaplan sees the Metro councillors as the area's political elite. Basing his data on a study of the Bureau of Municipal Research (1962), he states that, "despite the growing social diversity of the Toronto area, the political elite was drawn largely from the 'old order' and was much less representative of the groups that entered the community after 1945". [9]

We may question to what extent the councillors represent the political elite in Metro Toronto, but despite considerable changes in their composition since 1962, the overall policy direction in Metro Toronto seems to have changed little. Toronto newspapers frequently pose the question as to whether Metro Toronto is run by the elected politicians or by senior civil servants. In terms of parliamentary politics the answer to this question is, of course, of considerable importance since the entire rationale of parliamentary democracy depends on the ultimate power of democratically elected politicians. In terms of the actual politics which are implemented, this argument loses much of its relevance since the majority of decisions clearly favour the economic elite of a given locality. Robert Presthus has pointed out that while power in a community is frequently attributed to individuals on seemingly non-economic bases, a closer examination of the background of such appointments or elections shows how often such attributions are "honorific legitimations of economic status". "A nice continuity often exists between an individual's official role in service, welfare, school board, and hospital board organizations and his economic role in the community." [10]

While one of the major political myths of our age is the elitist argument that democracy is safe-guarded by the competition between elites, an equally hypocritical influence is the assertion that vigorous local associations, professional bodies and other voluntary associations provide the opportunity for ordinary men and women to participate in their self-government. As Porter and others have pointed out, such associations and organizations are no more democratic than our national and provincial parliaments. They are effectively governed by elites which are in most cases indistinguishable in their make-up and their policies from the larger national elites. [11] The argument of the pluralists that the bargaining among such voluntary organizations culminates "roughly" in the public interest, is open to another criticism, namely that all interests are not equally represented in the bargaining arena. Real competition takes place between a relatively small number of powerful groups and associations. The very fact of their power defines such groups as 'establishment' groups and their bargaining never questions the fundamental nature of the socio-political system. The bargaining power of consumers, welfare recipients, Indians and Eskimos and most workers and employees is no match to that of big business, private developers and government bureaucracies.

Lobbying, Pressure Groups and Democracy :

The belief that lobbying is an objectionable activity which is largely restricted to the United States is one of the many myths of Canadian politics. What is true, as Corry points out, is that pressure groups in Canada operate with less publicity. We know less of their influence and power, and until very recently, few official investigations on this subject have taken place in Canada. Since in Canada the cabinet formulates policy and party discipline usually ensures that cabinet decisions are carried out, representations by pressure groups are usually directed to the cabinet. Another myth, more widely held in the United States than in Canada, maintains that the various pressure groups usually represent competing interests and the end result of such bargaining results in policies which roughly represent the "public will".

Pressures are usually of two kinds : either they come from organized sectional groups and interest, or they are the voice of strongly held and expressed public opinion. Governments as a rule favour the former for a number of reasons. They are easier to control (one can be played off against another if it is in the government's interest), and they usually represent the accepted philosophy of the rulers, i.e. all the major organized bargainers share the basic assumptions of our capitalist society. Individuals and groups who share a less specific and more general view which they wish to be considered or accepted by government, are urged to join political parties which are the one accepted way of combining diverse elements and views within our parliamentary system.

More recently, we are told that the government in Ottawa has begun to worry about "conflict-of-interest, lobbying and influence peddling". Two separate inquiries have been set into motion. Ronald Basford, at that time Minister of Consumer and Corporate Affairs has commissioned a study of lobbying. He said in an interview that there was a growing distrust among Canadians of how things were done in Ottawa. Another study was to deal with possible conflicts of interest among Senators and M.P.'s A case in point was raised by Max Saltsman, M.P. who argued that in the recently appointed Senate-Commons committee to study tax reform, seven of the ten Senators held corporate directorships and "will be faced with conflicts of interest". In the list of briefs submitted to the Carter [12] Commission on Taxation, ten insurance companies are listed as being represented by : "Michener, The Honourable Rold D., P.C., Q.C.' [13]

There have been many instances where the economic elite lobbies successfully, frequently without facing an opponent. Such was the case with the Redevelopment Advisory Council (RAC), a self-appointed group of important businessmen who were asked by Mayor Phillips in 1960 to help encourage development in downtown Toronto. They were given special privileges of information and involvement by Council and have acted until 1971 as an official advisory body to Council. It was not until early in 1971 that a group of citizens challenged this peculiar notion of participatory democracy which gave special status to developers but denied it to citizens' groups. The Citizens' Redevelopment Advisory Council (CRAC) was created. It demanded the same status as the RAC. While the Executive refused to remove the special status enjoyed by the RAC, Council decided that the RAC should not have any status not enjoyed by a citizens' group. The end result was the loss of the special status of the RAC which it had enjoyed for over ten years. [14]

What is significant in the above example is the fact that for over ten years a certain form of citizens' action was given de facto legitimacy by the municipal authorities. The final power to accept or reject collective actions by citizens is seen to rest with our elected representative institutions instead of with the electorate. The Hon. Robert Welch recently made this point very clearly when he stated that "The obvious advantages which individual citizens may enjoy through taking a collective approach to their problems, however, can be meaningful only if government accepts the legitimacy of taking into consideration their collective point of view." [15]

Toronto's Mayor William Dennison has voiced what is probably a representative opinion of how the established order defines participatory democracy. In his recent newsletter, *The Mayor Reports : Some Notes of City Council Issues,* Dennison states that "Citizen participation is what our whole democratic process is about. If citizens had not participated, members of council would not have attained office." Ron Haggart writes that the Mayor dislikes those citizens who attempt to by-pass their alderman and prefers instead responsible groups like the Redevelopment Advisory Council. The efforts of this voice of big business are described by Dennison as follows : "This is the kind of citizens participation that is listened to, appreciated and respected." [16]

Another example of participation within the existing capitalist system is illustrated by Benson's white paper on taxation. A typical response to the politics involved in the taxation proposals was given by John Bird in the *Financial Post* who argues that "Whether one likes or loathes the end product of the Benson taxation program as outlined on budget night, there can be no question that the white paper proposals have been drastically revised. The effect of public representations is clear for all to see. For better, or for worse, this has been a real exercice in participatory democracy." [17]

The fact that this excursion into "participatory democracy" turned out to be a tragedy for the majority of Canadians should not blind us to the fact that within the framework of the rules of the game in our capitalist society, the Benson taxation program is in fact an excellent example of participatory democracy at work. It shows openly and clearly the limitations of meaningful participation by the majority of Canadians. The powerful participate while their servants observe the spectacle of "participatory democracy" for which they will be called upon to labour for the greater glory of the free enterprise system.

While participation by institutions and corporations has usually little trouble receiving de facto legitimacy, participation by citizens is just as frequently denied entirely. One of the arguments used in denying grass-roots participation was recently used by the Prime Minister when he rejected the idea of a plebiscite to determine whether the people of Southwestern Ontario agreed with the proposed site for a second airport (in Pickering Township). Trudeau replied that since Canada had a representative form of democracy he would therefore listen to the views of the M.P.s from the area. [18]

The chances of the isolated consumer winning even a temporary victory are equally slim in the more formalized process of committee hearings. A case in point is the standing committee on health, welfare and social affairs which has been dealing with the Consumer Packaging and Labelling Bill. Initially, the chairman of the committee refused to hear any non-governmental witnesses. After being over-ruled by the committee, a compromise was adopted to allow the committee to hear representatives of organizations but not single persons. Prof. Ziegel of Osgoode Law School points out that this practice "strongly favors trade interests which are well organized and generously financed", and works against consumer interests, "which are poorly organized and chronically under-financed". [19]

The game of pressure groups and power politics is basically the same in all capitalist societies. Despite the occasional victory of citizens' groups or "public opinion", the general rule still holds true that pressure from below (i.e. from the streets) has little chance of success if opposed by pressure from above (i.e. the economic elite of the country and in particular, industry). When the issues are *important*, the response of our political institutions to pressure from above is quick and accommodating, while the net effect of pressure from below is to "find itself in the parliamentary waste paper basket." [20] The militant tactics used by many low-income protest groups is a direct reflection of the general inability of these groups to achieve desired ends by traditional methods of lobbying, discussions, and presentation of briefs.

Concentration of Wealth and Income Distribution ;

One of the peculiarities encountered in Canada is the scarcity of data on the concentration of economic wealth and power in Canada. Apart from the various studies by John Porter and the scattered and incomplete records of the Dominion Bureau of Statistics, relatively little has been published in Canada on this vital issue.

Porter, however, manages to present us with a convincing set of data and analysis which points to a concentration of economic wealth and power in Canada which is not unlike that found in the United States. In 1955, "the top one percent of income recipients received about 40 percent of all income from dividends". [21] From a basic study undertaken by Porter in 1955, he was able to draw up a list of 183 "dominant corporations" in the Canadian economy. In the period of 1948-50, these 183 corporations "were responsible for 40 to 50 percent of the gross value of production in manufacturing, 63 percent of the total value of metal production, 90 percent of railway transportation, 88 percent of the gross earnings of telegraph and cable services, 82 percent of the total revenue of Canadian air carriers, 83 percent of telephone revenues and 60 to 70 percent of the hydro-electricity produced by privately owned companies as well as a large but undetermined proportion of other industries such as industrial minerals, fuels, water transportation, and retail distribution." [22]

Porter then establishes the high degree of interlocking directorships between 170 of the 183 "dominant corporations" (no data was available on the remaining 13) as well as between the corporations and the principal financial institutions. By adding 79 bank directors, who were not directors of the dominant corporations, Porter comes up with a group of 985 men who could be considered to make up the economic elite for Canada. We must add here the fact that "only a small number of Canadians have ownership rights in the vast property instruments that make up Canadian industry". [23] Canada is unique among industrialized nations in that a very large proportion of its productive resources are owned by individuals and corporations outside its borders, largely in the United States. In a very real sense, American corporate capitalism is the major force shaping our society. Porter concludes that a "good measure of control rests with the small group of very rich, or in some cases with their representatives". [24]

Analysis of income distribution is frequently out of date by the time it is made available but we believe that the general pattern established by studies conducted in Canada in 1955 and 1959 is still relevant today. There was little if any change in the degree of income inequality between 1955 and 1959. In both years, "the top 20 percent of income recipients had over 40 percent of the total income". [25] While we do not have adequate data at hand to make a definite statement on the subject, it would seem that the gap between the rich and the poor in terms of income is widening. In 1969, for example, incomes of business executives increased by 10-11 percent compared to an increase of 7 percent for workers. [26]

Given the obvious fact that the distribution of wealth and income in Canada is the result of conscious decisions made by our governing elite, it does say something very loud and clear about the priorities and values of our capitalist system and the small handful of individuals at the top of the pyramid. Class differences in Canada are largely ignored by our academics, politicians, and writers ; yet it remains a fact that in our so-called "classless society", class differences not only exist but "stand in the way of implementing one of the most important values of western society, that is, equality". Porter argues that class differences "create very great differences in life chances, among which are the chance of individuals' reaching the higher levels of political, economic, and other forms of power. The structure of power reflects the structure of class, for class determines the routes and barriers to advancement up our institutional hierarchies. Power is used to perpetuate a given structure of class". [27]

Communications, Socialization and the Status Quo :

It is a more or less accepted doctrine among political scientists today that the ruling elites of every society will attempt to instill in the people, a set of values, beliefs and behavior consistent with the maintenance of the political order. Since it is fairly well established that basic political orientation takes place prior to adulthood, the emphasis of political education and indoctrination centers on young people. It is equally obvious that what *we* do is "political education" or "citizen training" while *they* (e.g. the U.S.S.R., Cuba, etc.) indoctrinate people. While we do not wish to belittle the differences in intensity and method, the purpose of both is the same : to maintain and strengthen the existing social order. Political socialization flows downward from leaders to citizens. It is an important element in the de-politicization of the "masses" who must turn to their leaders (via existing structures and institutions) for political information and education. Thus one reason for the apathy of the masses (one of the props of the elitist theory of democracy) is their manipulation by the mass media. So successful has been this systematic indoctrination, that until very recently few people in Canada and the United States could envisage an alternative to the "good life" which, we are being told every day, is the aim of human existence and which, to a greater or lesser degree, *we* are living now. This subject is of such central importance that we must look at it in greater detail as it applies to Canada.

Long before the "Report of the Special Senate Committee on Mass Media" appeared in 1970, Porter had come to the conclusion that "Canada's mass media are operated as big business. Many of them, particularly in the large cities, are closely linked with corporate enterprise". [28] The amount of capital required to own, control and operate a daily newspaper is so enormous that "only the very wealthy, or those successful in the corporate world, can buy and sell large daily newspapers which become, in effect, the instruments of an established upper class". [29] Ownership and control of Canadian newspapers rests in the hands of a small number of well-established families belonging to the "British charter group". Without exception, they support the existing social order, regardless of their support of the Conservative or Liberal Party. No daily newspaper in Canada supports the N.D.P.

Cautiously, as befits a respected member of the establishment, Senator Keith Davey nevertheless came to about the same conclusion when he described the apparently irresistible tendency for the print and electronic media to merge into larger and larger economic units. This tendency, he argues, "is encouraged by the Canadian tax system, in particular the application of death duties . . ." [30] To put it more directly, this tendency is inevitable under capitalism. The report continues by warning us that this tendency could, (but not necessarily), "lead to a situation whereby the news . . . is controlled and manipulated by a small group individuals and corporations whose view of what's fit to print may closely coincide with what's good for General Motors, or what's good for Business, or what's good for my Friends Down at the Club. There is some evidence, in fact, which suggests that we are in that boat already". [31]

Given the fact that our mass media is firmly in the hands of the corporate elite or their friends, it is not surprising that their content reflects this concentration of ownership. The working class has virtually no voice to speak about the oppression, the monotony and the lack of meaning of factory and office work. As Gorz has pointed out recently : "There are no papers, no movies, no books about factory work and life. The work and life in the factories — and also in the huge office — is something this society doesn't want to hear about". [32] The Canadian Labour Congress has stated in a submission to the Senate Committee on the Mass Media that "in terms of news content and editorial opinion, Canada's daily newspapers tend to treat organized labour at best as some kind of necessary evil". [33]

It is revealing that despite the public opinion poll craze rampant in Canada, no survey had ever been undertaken to find out what people think of the media as a whole. The Senate Committee on the Mass Media undertook such a survey. Here are a few of the results :

— Close to half of newspaper readers suspect that criminal elements influence the news.

— Three out of ten Canadians feel that the media are not sufficiently critical of government.

— About two-thirds of the sample felt that "big business" was to blame for press bias, and four out of ten felt that newspapers serve the interests of advertisers or the government, rather than the public at large. [34]

— Only one in five Canadians believe they are getting unbiased reporting of the activities of politicians. [35]

Shocking as the report on the Mass Media has been, it suffers from a number of severe short-comings which are more or less inherent in any reports which have been requested and are controlled by the spokesmen of the same economic interests they are supposed to investigate. Three shortcomings in particular are of relevance here :

1. Publication, distribution and dissemination of the findings are in effect restricted to a small number of individuals (e.g. why doesn't Information Canada disseminate the findings of such reports ?)

2. Much of the material collected is left out of the final report. This has been true of the Report on the Mass Media as of other similar reports.

3. Such reports rarely question the underlying reasons for the various malpractices and shortcomings they criticize.

On March 10, 1971, Senator McElman, a member of the Special Committee on the Mass Media, delivered a scathing attack on the Irving empire in New Brunswick during a Senate debate on the Davey Report. He stated, "That corporate empire in New

Brunswick operates with the power of a lion, the appetite of a vulture, the grace of an elephant, the instincts of a barracuda and the principles of an alley cat. It is for that reason that I desperately want to see the media of New Brunswick separated from the ownership and control of that corporate collossus. This is an extreme situation, an extremely dreadful situation." [36]

This is indeed an "extremely dreadful situation" but the principles of an alley cat are not the monopoly of the Irving empire. We can see the same principles in operation wherever monopoly capitalism has unfolded itself successfully. To imply that the New Brunswick situation is an aberration due to the monopoly control of much of the province's industrial capacity by one conglomerate, is to confuse the issue. The fact is that the media in advanced capitalist society has a very special relationship to the rest of the economy, i.e. "it is geared to servicing the capitalist economy as a whole, and, if organized in this way, can survive only while it fulfills this function". [37]

Education for What ?

The basic truth about education is summed up by Richard Shaull in his Foreword to *Pedagogy of the Oppressed* : "There is no such thing as a *neutral* educational process. Education either functions as an instrument which is used to facilitate the integration of the younger generation into the logic of the present system and bring about conformity to it, *or* it becomes 'the practice of freedom', the means by which men and women deal critically and creatively with reality and discover how to participate in the transformation of their world." [38] In Canada, the function of the educational system is to serve the purposes of the capitalist market society, to train the required personnel and to do some of the research necessary for technological growth. In Canada, as in the United States, corporate power has deposited the burden of financing this training on the State which helps to explain the rapid growth of the public sector.

We are not here concerned with a presentation of a comprehensive survey of education but rather with brief illustrations of some of the myths surrounding it. The fact that today's rebellion had its beginning in universities, colleges and high schools — the very institutions which are expected to mold the youth of today into the conformist supporters of the status quo during their adulthood — might well have long-range political repercussions. To put it bluntly, the present educational system in Canada does not equalize the opportunities for education ; it functions instead as an agent of social selection and discrimination. Porter shows that the child "born into the lower income family has almost automatically a greatly reduced horizon of opportunity". [39] He adds that "In Canada little has been done to remove the barriers imposed by social conditions on the individual's educational opportunity." [40] A recent study conducted by the Toronto Board of Education comes to the same conclusion, although it refrains from exposing the causes of this phenomenon and draws no conclusions from the findings. The report indicated that children of laborers, waiters and others in low-paying jobs are 24 times as likely to be in classes for slow learners in public schools than children of professionals. The percentage rises to 57 in the case of children whose parents are on welfare. [41]

The class bias in our school system is exposed even more openly in a recent study by an economist at York University. In a table showing the percentage of Grade 12 students who entered university from various secondary schools in Toronto in 1969-70, we can observe that schools like Forest Hill, Harbord, Lawrence Park and North Toronto, send over 60 percent of their Grade 12 students to universities while the percentage drops to 15 or below in the case of Central Commerce, Central Tech., Danforth Tech., Eastern Commerce and Western Tech.-Commerce. It comes as no surprise that the first category of schools named are in wealthier neighborhoods. [42]

The biases displayed in our textbooks are almost unbelievable. In November 1967, the Ontario Institute for Studies in Education set up a study analyzing the content of all social studies textbooks authorized for use in the Province of Ontario. The results of the study were not encouraging. A few examples will explain why the authors felt compelled to entitle their study, *Teaching Prejudice.*

The happy slave is a common occurrence in our school textbooks. Here is one example : "The Virginian treated his slaves as an extension of his family. He was responsible for them and treated them as children, sometimes kindly, sometimes not. It was to his advantage to keep them healthy. They were not, as a rule, intelligent workers . . ." [43]

The liberal ethic of middle-of-the-road "objectivity" is illustrated in one textbook under the caption, "Moderates who stand near the centre are usually those who think over a problem calmly and carefully". The middle-or-the-road position is taught as the ideal position on *all* controversial matters, including such issues as prejudice, discrimination, persecution and human rights. The following textbook lesson, under the above-mentioned caption, illustrates this point. "In most school debates you can divide your class into two camps very early. Try it on one of these topics :

a) Children should have homework

b) Mixed classes make the best classes.

Did you find that some students gave a quick, loud, decided 'Yes', and others voted a quick, firm, decided 'No' ? We call people like those 'Extremists' ; if you were trying to place them on a blackboard chart, they would go at the *extreme* opposite ends. Do you find that some of your classmates see points on both sides ? We call them 'Moderates'." [44] Little wonder that the authors of this Study came to the conclusion that the treatment of critical issues in Ontario textbooks presents a gloomy picture.

It is a mistake to believe that disillusionment with the parliamentary process is restricted to a few radical intellectuals. It is also an error to assume that the elite nature of Canadian society is a secret known only to a few.

In 1964, a survey conducted by the Canadian Institute of Public Opinion (CIPO) showed that 52 percent of the sample chose "big companies" as having the most influence on government. In May 1970, the CIPO found that more Canadians (68 percent) ascribed power to "big business" than to any other group including the prime minister and the cabinet.

The Task Force on Government Information found in its survey that 53 percent of the sample felt that "public officials do not care what people like me think," and 63 affirmed that, "when you walk into a government office you become just a number". A majority in the Ontario survey believe that "once elected, Members of Parliament do not pay much attention to those who elected them". It should be noted that the national survey showed that faith in M.P.s was *highest* in Ontario. [45]

The Elitist Theory of Democracy

An examination of recent theoretical pronouncements on democracy illustrates the tremendous gap which exists today between the popular rhetoric of politicians and public communication on the one hand, and the currently predominant elitist theory of democracy on the other. *We* may believe that men should participate in formulating whatever policies affect their lives but the spokesmen of social science know better. The elitist theory of democracy denies that there can be, in any real sense, government by the people. Raymond Aron states that "it is quite impossible for the government of a society to be in the hands of any but the few ... there is government for the people ; there is no government *by* the people". [46] Compare that with the formulation used by T.B. Bottomore, who argues that democracy depends on ". . . creating and establishing the conditions in which a large majority of citizens, if not all citizens, can take part in deciding those social issues which affect their individual lives—at work, in the local community, and in the nation — and in which the distinction between elites and masses is reduced to the smallest possible degree." [47] What now passes for democratic theory is little more than the theoretical formulations of the status-quo in the Anglo-American democracies. Democracy is no longer an ideal to be striven for, constantly in need of creation ; it has been reduced to a justification of what is. Thus, Seymour Martin Lipset argues that : "democracy is not only or even primarily a means through which different groups can attain their ends or seek the good society ; *it is the good society itself in operation.*" [48]

The justifications for this revision of democratic theory relate directly to the present stress of theorists and politicians alike on law, order and stability coupled with an almost paranoid fear of popular participation.

In contrast to the static and status-quo oriented theory of democracy, the prevailing conceptions of democracy during most of the nineteenth century emphasized its dynamic characteristics. Democracy was seen as a process which was to extend the decision-making rights and powers to groups in society which had formerly been deprived of them. Bottomore correctly points out that this implies that democracy was seen primarily as a doctrine and move-ment of the "lower classes of society against the dominance of the aristocratic and wealthy classes . . ." [49]

Compared to the current static and mechanistic theories of democracy, the nineteenth century emphasis on democracy as a continuing process also implied a greater concern for ends rather than means. The concern for an ideal condition of society gave democratic theory its revolutionary and utopian content. The development of capitalism with the politics of competition and the politics of the market and the establishment of political democracy had a powerful reformist impact on the revolutionary potential of democratic movements.

The coming of universal suffrage coupled with the rapid increase in the size and organizational power of political parties presented the working class with a legitimate channel for political participation. The elitist nature of political parties, the limited extent of popular participation and their very purpose to win political power at all costs, turned this newly won channel for legitimate participation into a reformist tool devoid of any revolu-tionary potential.

The classic example is that of the German Social Democratic Party which, in its 1891 revised programme, stressed the importance of immediate reforms. Socialism was to be achieved by a series of constitutional reforms ; the closer they came to gaining power, the greater the emphasis on programmes as contrasted with desired ends until today the latter have almost entirely disappeared. Such in essence is the history of most social democratic or labour parties in the capitalist West.

Contemporary political theorists are thus sceptical of and hostile to the participative and utopian elements of the so-called 'classical theorists' (e.g. Rousseau and J.S. Mill). The origin of this strong emphasis on stability and the status quo by contemporary political theorists is seen by Carole Pateman in the artifically created contrast between 'democracy' (as defined by contemporary theorists) and 'totalitarianism' as the only two political alternatives available. Two events, according to Pateman, have produced the justification for this currently held view ; the development of political sociology and the rise of totalitarian states. [50]

Mosca, for instance, argued that elite rule was inevitable. In his later writings, he integrated his thesis of elite rule with an argument for representative institutions. The electoral process based on broad-based suffrage does not according to Mosca, conflict with the elitist theory The de jure recognition of power by an elite is always preceded by a de facto monopolization of all political power. Candidates who are successful in democratic elections are almost always members of the ruling elite. [51]

Michels is best known for his famous "iron law of oligarchy" which postulates that the principle of oligarchy is a "preordained form of the common life of great social aggregates". Michels devoted much of his time to an investigation of German Social Democratic parties that were dedicated to democracy within their own ranks. On the basis of his research he drew a number of conclusions about the functions and internal organization of political parties. The need for organization seemed obvious ; and organization, argued Michels, "implies the tendency to oligarchy". "As a result of organization every party of professional union becomes divided into a minority of directors and a majority of directed. [52]

The second event mentioned by Pateman as justifying the current elitist theory of democracy is the rise of totalitarian states. The example most frequently used is that of the Weimar Republic, which, it is often argued, was based on the mass participation of citizens in the political process (a tenuous point at best). The Weimar Republic, it will be remembered, degenerated into fascism. The moral of this argument is that participation of the 'masses' in the politics of the state leads to totalitarian regimes. Little effort is made by those using this argument to look into the nature of this alleged participation of the masses in the Weimar Republic or to enquire to what degree it was voluntary and democratic. Historical evidence of questionable validity was thus used to establish the link between participation and totalitarianism. The emergence of one-party states in a fascist form in Germany and Italy, and in a communist form in the U.S.S.R., further strengthened the credibility and the interconnection of democracy with a multi-party system. The fear of popular participation has been further strengthened by the misuse of carefully selected data from recent large-scale empirical attitude studies which reveal widespread apathy translated by social scientists into a lack of interest in political activity, and authoritarian attitudes. Both characteristics are seen to be particularly strong among 'low socio-economic status groups' (i.e. the masses). The lesson is clear. We are told by contemporary political scientists and sociologists that an increase in political participation by present non-participants would upset the stability of the democratic system as we know it. [53] Rarely do these academic empiricists enquire why people are alienated, why they do not want to participate, and why authoritarian attitudes prevail among 'lower socio-economic status groups.' This political misuse of psychological and sociological data is inexcusable particularly since the more serious studies in this field clearly indicate that these 'antidemocratic attitudes' are directly related to the environment of the community or the workplace. [54]

Pateman points out that there was one further factor which helped contemporary theorists to reject earlier democratic theories which were based, at least to some degree, on the importance of participation. This was the argument 'that those theories were normative and 'value-laden,' whereas modern political theory should be scientific and empirical, grounded firmly in the facts of political life.' [55] This very issue was taken up by Joseph Schumpeter (prior to the availability of the vast amount of empirical data which we now have at our disposal) whose book *Capitalism, Socialism, and Democracy* continues to have a powerful impact on contemporary political theorists. Schumpeter attacked the notion that democratic theory was a theory about means and ends, and argued instead that democracy was a political method for arriving at a political, legislative, and administrative decision. His definition is by now known to every student of democratic theory : 'the democratic method is that institutional arrangement for arriving at political decisions in which individuals acquire the power to decide by means of a competitive struggle for the people's vote.' [56]

Notice how well this notion of democracy as a political method fits into the utilitarian theory which was widely held in the 19th century. Utilitarians argued that "the essence of rational behavior was maximization of individual utilities", and that was seen as the ultimate good. The problem was solved says C.B. Macpherson, "by demonstrating that the way to maximize utilities over the whole of a society was to leave everything to a competitive market economy, upheld by a liberal state". Macpherson concludes that the "justifying theory of liberal-democracy has leaned heavily on this notion of maximization ever since." [57]

Schumpeter's emphasis is clearly and openly on the leaders. The function of the electorate is to produce these leaders (a government) either directly or through an intermediate body. The electorate does not, he argues, "normally control their political leaders in any way except by refusing to re-elect them or the parliamentary majorities that support them . . ." [58] Voters do not decide issues nor do they pick their members of parliament from the eligible population with a perfectly open mind. Schumpeter argued that the initiative lies with the candidates who decide to enter politics (he did not mention the common practice of political parties "selecting" their candidates). Even the limited initiative of voters to accept or reject one of the competing candidates is further restricted by the existence of political parties. Schumpeter was very clear as to what was a political party and what was not. "A party is not", he said, ". . . a group of men who intend to promote public welfare 'upon some principle on which they are all agreed'." [59] Parties will of course use the rhetoric of principles and programmes, "and these principles or planks may be as characteristic of the party that adopts them, and as important for its success, as the brands of goods a department store sells are characteristic of it and important for its success. But the department store cannot be defined in terms of its brands and a party cannot be defined in terms of its principles. A party is a group whose members propose to act in concert in the competitive struggle for political power. If that were not so, it would be impossible for different parties to adopt exactly or almost exactly the same programme." [60] As Schumpeter points out, this happens frequently. What today is said by political theorists diplomatically and cautiously, was said by Schumpeter with brutal clarity. "Party and machine politicians are simply the response to the fact that the electoral mass is incapable of action other than a stampede, and they constitute an attempt to regulate political competition exactly similar to the corresponding practices of a trade association. The psycho-technics of party management and party advertising, slogans and marching tunes, are not accessories. They are the essence of politics. So is the political boss." [61]

To sum up : Democratic politics is not concerned with the realization of ideals but with, "reaping of particular advantages with the limits of a given ethic — an ethic which sets out clearly the rules of the game governing the political jockeying for position and privilege." Ideology, "insofar as it continues to exist as a form in modern society, is nothing more than a cynical propoganda cover for the specific self-interest of competing groups." [62]

At the core of the elitist theory of democracy, as we have seen, is the clear presumption of the average citizen's inadequacies. Thus, democratic systems must rely on the wisdom and the skill of political leaders. Several recent theorists have stated quite categorically that our stable democratic system depends on widespread apathy and general political incompetence. [63] What Schumpeter said about party slogans, advertising and marching tunes was repeated in the mid-sixties by Lester Milbrath who said : "... it is important to continue moral admonishment for citizens to become active in politics, not because we want or expect great masses of them to become active, but rather because the admonishment helps to keep the system open and sustains a belief in the right of all to participate, which is an important norm governing the behavior of political elites." [64]

The Emerging Critique of the Elitist Theory of Democracy.

At first glance the elitist theory of democracy would seem to violate at least two fundamental beliefs of earlier democratic political thought : the equality of individuals and the principle of majority rule. We have seen that the elitist theorists argue that government by the people is, in fact, not possible in our complex industrialized societies, and that the democratic principle can be upheld as long as power in society is open to everyone (at least in principle), as long as elites compete for power, and as long as they are accountable to the electorate at periodic free elections. It is relevant to remember that the elite theories of Mosca and Pareto, and their present-day followers were formulated primarily in response to the "threat" of socialist ideas. In attacking the determinism of Marxists the elitist philosophers created their own determinism, arguing in fact that not only has every known society been divided into a ruling minority and a "ruled" majority, "but that every society must be so divided." [65]

Most of the traditional theories of democracy were largely normative and critical of the societies of their time. They were concerned with human values which they saw as inherently good and desirable : liberty, good government, responsibility, self-realization, etc. The replacement of political ideology with currently fashionable sociological analysis has resulted in a definition of the status quo *as democracy* coupled with a failure to "articulate the criteria on which this judgement is based" [66] The shift of emphasis has been from a concern about the needs and potentialities of the individual to the requirements of the system. [67]

The emphasis on the needs of the system leads Berelson to argue that : "the *system of democracy* does meet certain requirements of a going political organization. The individual may not meet all the standard, but the whole nevertheless survives and grows. This suggests that where the classical theory is defective is in its concentration on the *individual citizen*." [68] Berelson, Parson and other theorists see the democratic system primarily as a system in equilibrium. For democracy to grow, there must be a certain distribution and balance of the various elements and qualities within the system. There must be a balance between active and passive people, between stability and flexibility, progress and conservatism, consensus and cleavage, and individualism and collectivism. Such is the mix which produces the democracy of today.

There are a number of serious problems with this widely held theory. The basic assumption and use "of equilibrium concepts in the social sciences is open to serious methodological criticisms, and leaves its practitioners subject to the suspicion of having based conservatism upon a. pseudo-scientific foundation." [69] Little specific sense can be made of the idea of "balance" without careful quantification of the relevant variables, or the existence of an equilibrium situation which is directly visible and observable, and yet Berelson speaks about the balance among his various qualities where neither of these conditions is fulfilled. [70]

The requirements of such a system are often stated so loosely that it becomes impossible to assess their validity. What, for example, does it mean, that there must be a "nice balance" between consensus and cleavage, reflecting the "health of a democratic order" ? How does one measure these qualities ; how to find out if they are in balance ; how to prove that "equilibrium" is essential for the maintenance of the democratic system ? These and many other essential questions are left unanswered by Berelson and his colleagues.

But when everything is said, the fundamental criticism of the elitist school of democracy is that it has replaced concern with democratic values and ideals by observation of the actual world of politics. Lipset illustrates this approach succinctly when he welcomes, at least for the West, replacement of political ideology by sociological analysis. [71] The good society (i.e. democracy) has arrived — all that needs to be done is to observe it. The observations are typically conducted by "value-free" social scientists using objective sociological tools of research. The stress on *factual* information is seen as the guarantor of objectivity. It does not take much insight to expose this fallacy, as two recent critics have pointed out, when they argue that facts are themselves the product of a particular view of reality seen through our theoretical preconceptions which, "in turn are conditioned by the problems confronting us. And the theoretical precepts which determine the relevant facts of a particular view of 'reality' are not themselves entirely value-free. Social theories, in short, are the result of our concern with specific problems. And social problems, at bottom, are concerned with ethical goals. Social theorists, furthermore, differ in their value judgments and thus differ in their theoretical construction of 'reality'. They differ, that is, in the problems they see or, what amounts to the same thing, they see a given problem in different ways. Consequently they differ as to the facts relevant to a given problem. There is, in other words, a selectivity of facts in the analysis of social problems. Some facts included in one approach are excluded in another ; and even those held in common may, and usually do, differ in the weight given to them and in their theoretical and causal interrelations." [72] The development of more unfettered ways of involving oneself in such analysis flies in the face of this tradition. A democratic society where all individuals are actively involved in the process of decision-making, where democracy is extended to every aspect of life, has not been achieved. We are told that its achievement is impossible ; but to make this assertion valid it needs to be shown exactly how and why "the ideal is rendered improbable or impossible of attainment. This has nowhere been done." [73]

Representative Institutions and the Electoral System

The theory of representative government presents a depressing picture. As one observer has pointed out - there is no agreement on what representation is or means. The range of opinions covers the entire spectrum from those who maintain that every government represents the people it governs to the view that no government can ever really represent. [74]

Representative democracy, or, what is frequently called *indirect* democracy in its present form of parliament and parties, began in Britain and was then exported to the colonies, including Canada and the future U.S.A. Its organized political form is the political party and its purpose is to win seats in parliament. The members of parliament do not normally represent communities. Instead they represent large blocks of voters which generally include sections of actual communities. The principle of choosing "your local representative" has little basis in reality. The local party constituency picks its candidate (frequently only with the approval of, or on the recommendation of, the national office). A sizable number of seats are "safe" seats for one party or another and elected members thus see themselves as professional politicians who can expect to be part of this game for a long period of time — if not for life. As long as the elected M.P. conforms to party discipline, he can expect to be re-nominated. In practice, the elected M.P. will follow in most cases the recommendations of the party leadership. Few parties nowadays pretend to be governed in their policies by their respective national conventions. The only Canadian party which, at least in theory, adheres to this principle, is the N.D.P.

Political scientists agree on very few principles but one of their time-tested arguments concerns the obsolescence of direct democracy. Since our academic mentors are all democrats, this belief in the impossibility of direct democracy in today's complex societies leads them to the belief that we must be governed by popularly elected representative institutions backed up by a competent and non-political bureaucracy. Since representation is seen as essential to democracy, two schools of thought have emerged. There are those who believe that representative democracy is a necessary but unsatisfactory system of government. Advocates of this school attempt to democratize representative government with devices such as the referendum, recall and initiative. The second group, and this is by far the more influential in Canada, believes that democracy can only work through representation. This, the elitist school of democracy, tends to fear the "rule of the mob" and puts its trust in the leaders to prevent the degeneration of democratic rule into the tyranny of the masses.

To sum up : Orthodox political theorists as well as our current political leaders see in representative democracy the perfect, realistic and democratic symbiosis of popular participation and power politics. Whatever version of representation we may wish to analyse (and they range from constitutional democracies to modern totalitarian states) the principle remains the same : "The representative is placed in a special, superior position where he and others like him ... form special groups charged with making state decisions, while constituents arrange themselves into positions of partisanship. Representation, as a form of democracy where ordinary citizens govern themselves, at least nominally, becomes increasingly a hollow rationalization for rigidly hierarchical structures." [75] The contempt for "professional politicians", the feeling of powerlessness and the alienation and anger of an increasing number of citizens can be traced partly to the prevailing structures of *representation* which dominate public and private organizations in Canada and the rest of the Anglo-American democracies.

The credibility gap between the realities of representative institutions and politics in Canada and the material presented to students in the social sciences has never been greater. For over twenty years, the standard text on the government of Canada has been the work by Dawson. This is how Dawson sees the reality of Canadian representative democracy : "The House of Commons is the great democratic agency in the government of Canada ; the 'grand inquest of the nation' ; the organized medium through which the public will finds expression and exercises its ultimate political power. It forms the indispensable part of the legislature ; and it is the body to which at all times the executive must turn for justification and approval." Dawson goes on to argue that the House of Commons speaks, "as no other body in the democracy can pretend to speak, for the people. It presents in condensed form the different interests, races, religions, classes and occupations, whose ideas and wishes it embodies with approximate exactness." [77]

The "delegate theory", which is basically an extension of the principle of direct democracy, sees the elected member as the spokesman of his constituency, as "the necessary human agent through which the voters continually register their will..." [78] The "representative theory", on the other hand, sees the elected member as a free agent who will act according to his conscience and the opportunities available at any given moment.

Criticism of the system of representative democracy in Canada can be divided into two categories. On the one hand there is "legitimate" criticism which usually deals with certain inequities in the application of a given form of representation ; and then there is a more fundamental critique of the entire system of representative democracy which is discouraged by various means. The practitioners of the latter variety are either ridiculed or attacked as advocates of mob rule, totalitarian communism, nihilism, anarchism or whatever "ism" happens to be the favourite target at any given time.

Let us look at a few samples. An example of the "safe" category is the physical boundaries of the constituencies which in Canada have traditionally favoured the rural areas at the expense of the urban. [79] A second criticism frequently voiced deals with the particular form of representative democracy operative in Canada. The candidate with the highest number of votes is elected. This system frequently leads to a situation where an elected M.P. represents a minority of voters in his constituency. On a larger scale, it has resulted in situations where the governing party has a majority in the House of Commons while polling a minority of the popular vote throughout the country. Thus, in 1935, to pick an extreme case, the Liberals polled 47 per cent of the popular vote and elected 73 per cent of the members of the House of Commons. [80]

The more serious criticisms deal with the very nature of the representative system and are applicable, to a certain degree, to every country using the representative model. Inherent in the representative model is the fact that it leads to the rule of the few over the many, the former having greater political power than those they represent. The influence of the voter is restricted to passing judgement, "at fairly long intervals, upon the activities of the minority." [81] Universal suffrage coupled to the representative system allows at best for an assessment of popular opinion on a number of issues. The very fragmentation and lack of permanent organization of the electors does not give them the power to impose their will on their representatives.

Classical parliamentary democracy disappeared a long time ago but the form and structures are being maintained to "stabilize power". One influential critic of parliamentary democracy has pointed out what would seem to be the main political purpose of maintaining the institutions of representative democracy. He argues that the people, who believe in genuine democracy, "are neutralized through an institution which gives the illusion of participation". [82]

Canadians are asked to view the House of Commons as the organized medium through which the public exercises its ultimate political power. It has in the meantime become part of the conventional wisdom that decisions are made by the Cabinet and then, with the aid of the party whip, rubber-stamped by a majority in the House of Commons. An indication of the acceptance of this view is the fact that it is no longer restricted to critical academics but has found its place in the more serious columns of our daily press. Anthony Westell says that it is in the cabinet, "where the executive decisions are made, and the caucus room where the members of the majority party review those decisions and pledge their support..." He continues by stating that : "What goes on in the House of Commons is mostly play-acting. The chamber is a political theatre rather than a forum for debate and decisions." Westell goes on to point out some of the undemocratic realities of our parliamentary system. The daily question period, he argues, is a "performance by actors on both sides, simulating alarm, anger and outrage, between knowing smiles, to win the applause of the public..." Conclusions to debates are predetermined by the fact that the Government can count on the support of the majority in the House. Westell concludes that : "In effect, we elect a dictatorship at each general election, a prime minister and his cabinet commanding enough support to impose their will on Parliament and the public." [83]

Recruitment of Candidates and Local Background of M.P.'s

Recruitment of candidates is controlled by the constituency organizations of the political parties.

The individuals thus recruited are essentially drawn from the upper social strata of Canadian society. Canadian M.P's tend to be members of a profession, usually law. A study of the 25th Parliament shows that although lawyers constitute only a fraction of one per cent of the population, they made up 33 per cent of the M.P.'s. [84] Porter, in his study of the *Political elite* in Canada (i.e. federal cabinet ministers, provincial premiers, and senior judiciary) concludes that 64 per cent of this group were lawyers. Even if we remove the judiciary, who must be lawyers, the percentage remains very high, which leads Porter to state the obvious : "The political elite in Canada is not representative of the population which it leads. [85] Businessmen, both self-employed and corporate executives, were also overrepresented in the 25th Parliament. To sum up : Seventy-six per cent of the sample were in business or members of the professions, "while only 18 per cent of the Canadian population (ages 25-64) of 1961 were so employed." [86]

Representative and Delegate Roles

A central aspect of the difference between delegate democracy and representative democracy concerns the role and function of the elected delegate or representative. The logical extension (in practice) of direct democracy leads to the delegate principle, which, according to Dawson, is shared by few M.P.'s in Canada. Kornberg, however, argues that the largest group of respondents (49 per cent) saw themselves as "delegates-servants" and only a small minority could be termed "trustees" or free agents (i.e. what Dawson calls "representatives"). The rest of the respondents in Kornberg's study (he calls them "politicos") try to bridge the gap between the two principles by admitting the need to consult their constituents while at same time insisting on the need for a certain degree of independence. [87] Kornberg's results are open to a number of objections. The examples he gives indicate that he interprets the "delegate" theory so broadly as to render it meaningless. He cites as a typical example the following response : "It entails being a sounding board for constituency opinion and then making it known." [88] Dawson is more rigorous in his definition of the *delegate* and almost certainly more accurate in his conclusion that the majority of M.P.'s favour the *representative* principle.

The entire process of the selection of candidates, their nomination as well as the absence of a mechanism to *recall* the elected M.P., all argue against Kornberg's findings. It is nevertheless of some interest to speculate about the reason for the unexpected popularity, among M.P.'s, of something approaching the delegate principle. It is likely, we think, that the replies are influenced by what the M.P.'s perceive public opinion to be on this vital question. Kornberg makes the point, which strengthens this assumption, that a majority of M.P.'s (69 per cent) who were not college graduates preferred the *delegate-servant* orientation. They tended to focus on their constituencies more than their college-educated colleagues. [89] Since the M.P.'s without a college education are, at least in their education, more representative of the population than those with a college education, one could perhaps assume that the former's greater sympathy with the *delegate* principle mirrors a similar attitude in the population at large.

Our empirically oriented friends will point out that this thesis is little more than an unproven assumption of ideologically minded critics of representative democracy. There is more to it than that, we think. It is no accident that the loss of prestige in our representative institutions is exhibited most openly by those sections of the population which could be classified as the "disadvantaged". The number of college trained people in this group would tend to be small. Because they are disadvantaged and lack the resources and the power to plug into the "game of representative politics", people in this "category", whether as individuals or as organized groups, tend to have much more immediate concerns centering on their workplace and their neighborhood. They tend to be suspicious and resentful about the lack of responsiveness of their elected representatives. It is from such constituencies that the demand for control over elected politicians as well as institutions originates. Middle class constituencies, on the other hand, tend to be more easily satisfied with traditional methods of playing an advisory role and using more orthodox means of lobbying. They have less need to reject the existing representative system since it operates on the whole on their behalf and in their favour. [90]

Kornberg's analysis of Canadian M.P.'s leads him to make the following points :

— The majority of the respondents showed a high level of political interest, knowledge, participation, and perception of political efficacy.

— Given such backgrounds, one would assume that many of the respondents would expect to play a major role in the policy process.

— One would also expect, Kornberg argues, "that their assumption ought to have been modified by experience in the position, as policy innovation and evaluation in the Canadian House of Commons, as in all Parliaments of the British model, largely are the prerogatives of party leaders." [91]

This, however, is not the case. To the degree that policy-oriented M.P.'s experienced conflict, it was with their constituents and not with their parties. Kornberg gives a number of reasons for this seemingly paradoxical situation.

— Many respondents were strongly attached to their parties before taking office and were thus psychologically prepared to accept the discipline of the party.

— The average M.P. tends to identify his party's policy with his own (whether or not he helps to formulate it).

— M.P.'s learn that their role as a party member entails several relationships including his relationship with the local party organization and interest groups within the M.P.'s constituency. These relationships permit the M.P. to act as a communicator with the gratifying result that his communications are occasionally listened to and accepted by the party leadership.

Given these reasons, Kornberg still tends to believe that the limited role played by back-bench M.P.'s would eventually result in conflict between the M.P. and his party if it were not for the fact that, "the average M.P. is not likely to remain in Parliament long enough to come into serious conflict with his party over an inability to realize policy goals. The high level of attrition characteristic of the Canadian system, although it may be disfunctional in certain respects, helps to insure that most of those who are likely to become disenchanted and frustrated with their party roles are returned to the status of ordinary citizens before that frustration becomes intense enough to threaten the viability of the responsible party system." [92] Kornberg concludes his study with the remark that "once a cohesion norm has been internalized completely the Canadian M.P., with a few improvisations of his own, plays the roles ascribed to him by his party."

We have travelled a long way from the time when *represent-ation* was a concept worth fighting for. Today, in Canada, it has become a thinly veiled, routinized rule by the capitalist elite of North America. The entire complex of liberal institutions, the ostensible purpose of which was to safeguard the democratic tradition, has become a gigantic hoax. The practical application of the elitist theory of democracy is the rule by an elite — the democratic element turns out to be of peripheral significance in the actual decision-making process.

Political Parties

There is general agreement among orthodox political scientists that "cabinet government" functions best in a two-party system. The elitist nature of political parties as well as other unpleasant by-products of the party-system, are explained away in terms which are identical with the attitudes of the elitist theorists. This is what Corry has to say : "It is true that a small group of leaders tries to control the party, but that is a general feature of all human organization, not limited to political parties. Men of good will are not excluded from party councils, but they often exclude themselves because they are too inflexible to make the compromises essential to the gathering of votes. The parties do not frustrate the will of the people, because it is only rarely that even a transient majority of the people is genuinely of one mind about a specific political problem. The parties deceive the public, but so do propagandists of every kind. The deception does not often arise from cynicism but rather from zest for the game itself, a general human trait. It may be said generally in conclusion that the evils in the party system are not peculiar to it but are the outcome of general human frailties. Indeed, it is hard to see how the parties that must woo the electorate with success can do other than reflect its virtues and its vices. Perhaps it is people as much as institutions that need to be reformed." [94]

This paragraph ought to be read over carefully, as it summarizes an attitude of human behavior and institutions which lies at the core of the elitist principle of democracy. It should also be remembered that thousands of Canadian students get their introduction to politics from Corry. Corry justifies the existence of political parties by arguing that they are essential, "as long as we adhere to the rule that ultimate power rests with a diffused electorate..." Political parties, he continues, make peaceful change of government possible, "and thus eliminate the necessity for the armed coup d'etat as a means of changing government, and the counter necessity of ruling by force and terror toprevent such a coup d'etat. [95] Nazi Germany and the Soviet Union are cited by Corry to illustrate what is in store for us if we abandon our cherished party system.

A few general comments can be made at this point to set the record straight. As Downs has pointed out in his *An Economic Theory of Democracy* : "Our main thesis is that parties in democratic politics are analogous to entrepreneurs in a profit-seeking economy. So as to attain their private ends, they formulate whatever policies they believe will gain the more votes, just as entrepreneurs produce whatever products they believe will gain the most profits for the same reason." [96] The comparison is of course no coincidence since the Canadian party system serves the economic elite rather well ; it is, we may say, its legislative arm. It has been said many times before but needs repeating : *The modern party system is a direct consequence of the requirements of capitalist democracy.* [97]

The attempt to rationalize the shocking behavior of our political parties by putting all the blame on general human traits and frailties of people is an idiotic statement which confuses human nature with human behavior, the latter being very much influenced, if not determined, by the institutions, including political parties, of a given society. Nor can the lack of principles in our political parties be explained by simplistic method. As Dawson and Corry admit, the election of candidates becomes a matter of primary concern, equal and frequently superior in importance to the principles themselves. Nor is the situation any better on the municipal level, as one recently elected Toronto alderman has pointed out : "Elections have nothing to do with policy . . . and if policy does manage to work its way into the campaign, are politicians held to that policy, and if so, by whom ? Who at City Hall has followed the policies enunciated in the last election ? What policies were specific enough that the politicians can not weasle out of them ?" [98]

The lack of ideology and of ideological conflict in Canadian parties is seen by many as an essential ingredient of parliamentary democracy. Corry argues, for example, that unless there is a minimum of agreement, "on the ends and purposes of social life", government by consent is not possible. [99] Parties with opposing ideological views will tear the country apart and eventually result in the dictatorship of a one-party system. Not all observers of Canadian politics share this view. Porter, for example, admits that our two major parties are closely linked with corporate interests and that their focus has been to the right. Paradoxically, after admitting the link between corporate interest and the two major parties. Porter continues by saying that the maintenance of national unity, "has overridden any other goals there might have been, and has prevented a polarizing, within the political system, of conservative and progressive forces". However, Porter is uneasy about the lack of a dynamic quality in Canadian politics. He wonders why it has never occurred to any Canadian commentator "that national unity might in fact be achieved by such polarization." [100] Porter's concern is openly expressed in the following statement : "Yet to obscure social divisions through brokerage politics is to remove from the political system that elements of dialectic which is the source of creative politics. The choice between genuinely radical and genuinely conservative traditions could mean a period of creative politics followed by a period of consolidation as conservatives and radicals oscillated in and out of office. That at least would provide a two-party system suitable to parliamentary institutions, the debating of values, and the clarification of social goals. [101] Porter does not seem to be too worried that the radicals would establish the dictatorship of the proletariat and abolish our cherished two-party system. But this utopia does not apply to Canada where political parties have lost whatever idealism they may have had initially and are instead enmeshed in bureaucracy and electoral opportunism. Given the nature of our main political parties and the power of the local and/or national party organization in the nomination of candidates, as well as the power of the parties to discipline their M.P.'s, the lack of choice available to the voter should not surprise us. As one critic has pointed out : "The difference between candidates can only be as significant as the difference between those who *select* the candidates. The interests to which candidates owe allegiance cannot extend beyond the range of interests of their benefactors." [102]

There is little disagreement among observers of Canadian party politics about the fact that our cabinet government tends towards a centralized discipline in the hands of the party leaders. There is little difference between Parliament in Ottawa and the provincial legislatures in this respect. Harry Crowe says about the Liberal Party that it "is a highly disciplined political institution with an extraordinary loyalty and subservience to its leaders. Doctrine is *ex cathedra*. Competing conceptions rarely surface and do not survive. Therefore, one looks to the pronouncements and writings of the leaders." [103]

Few serious observers of our parliamentary system will today deny that our electoral system is proving to be less and less a viable method for responding to public demands. This weakening of confidence in what is the core of our parliamentary system, relates directly, we believe, to the growing awareness that the "average voter" has no influence over the policies of our democratically elected governments. Voters are given the opportunity to choose every few years between two sets of professional rulers, whose policies differ only on matters of peripheral interest to most Canadians.

Both major political parties are wedded to corporate interests. Elections are not the mechanism by which people impose their will on the rulers ; they are, on the contrary, confirmations of the power of the ruling elite. Elections are not autonomous elements to decide on policies ; they only ratify the existing power relationships in Canada which are the result of a political game which has been played outside the parliamentary process.

The real centres of power are located outside of parliament and are not subject to the voter's influence at elections. They remain constant whatever Party is in power. If we were allowed to vote for those who actually control Canada (e.g. the directors of corporations, financial institutions and those who own and control the multinational, largely American, corporations) the phony nature of parliamentary politics would be more easily exposed for all to see. As it is, the voter is left with no choice but to support one of the competing parties. Since the difference between the parties is largely one of management rather than policy it is little wonder that we witness a crisis of confidence in the parliamentary system. This does not mean that these differences which characterize our political parties are meaningless or not worth voting for, but it does mean that the political system has no legitimized avenues for bringing about fundamental social change in Canada.

Agnoli sums up the function of the parliamentary system as follows : "The Parliament is neither master of the people nor law-maker representing the people. It functions more as an acceptable and constitutional instrument for the publication of resolutions which have come about through the cooperation of the state apparatus and social power groupings. It functions as a transmission belt for the decisions of oligarchic groups. *These* (the oligarchies of both economic and cultural groups, the churches, for example) find themselves *well* represented. In this sense Parliament works and functions as a representation of the power structure, and only as such, is it acceptable to bourgeois-capitalist society. Elsewhere, where a drive for emancipation breaks in, the ruling class makes use of stronger means, as, for example, in Greece." [104]

The Multi-party System

The fundamental justification of the multiparty system is the argument that it ensures political freedom. We are told that the very existence of an opposition party defines our political system as a democracy. Since it has become increasingly difficult to prove that our governments are in any real sense accountable to the electorate, the accent of the defenders of our elitist system now rests on the existence of an opposition. We are told that we have a choice — we can vote for this party or that, and we can replace one government by another if we are dissatisfied with its performance. Thus one of the cornerstones of democracy — the principle of accountability — has been replaced by the more-or-less meaningless slogan that the existence of an opposition party guarantees the maintenance of the democratic system.

A political party is founded not to insure freedoms in general, but its freedom to attain power. To attain this goal its has to be organized. The development of a political apparatus and the professional politicians who come to dominate political parties, are tied up with the economic elite with the result that the fragmented individual citizen is left without any real influence in the functioning of the state. His only legitimate channel for political participation is the political party which is dominated by a professional clique and firmly anchored to the economic elite.

The implementation of consensus politics so necessary for the functioning of our political system does not rest solely on the close ties between the professional politicians of our political parties and the economic elite ; it is further strengthened by internal organizational mechanisms which have become an important part of our multiparty system. A characteristic common to bureaucratic system, but particularly prevelant within our political parties, is the development of mechanisms for reducing internal conflict. Cleavages within a bureaucratic system impair its effectiveness in competition with other systems. Conflicts, particularly those originating from competing ideas and policies, are met basically by compromises and mutual concessions, and by "not permitting all of the dissident voices representation in decision-making." This process applies not only to national bureaucracies but also to local governmental and private ones. Daniel Katz describes this process convincingly. "The general pattern for conflict reduction is the narrowing of channels for their expression so that many divergent views are reconciled or silenced at lower levels in the structure. A small unit has to resolve differences among members so that it speaks with one voice in its own subsystem, the unit differences have to be compromised so that the subsystem represents but one position to the higher levels in the structure. This pattern means that many conflicts are handled at lower levels... The example par excellence of this pattern is the two-party system. By the time the wishes of the many interest and factional groups have been filtered up through the hierarchical structure, the party line is not far from dead center." [105]

Many citizen's groups have experienced the conflict reduction mechanism at one time or another either in political parties at the local level, with service agencies, social planning councils or other governmental and non-governmental bureaucracies. It is important to remember in this context that leadership of low-income protest groups is largely composed of people outside the basic power structure of the society. This factor further weakens their influence in the kind of process described above. Katz concludes by stating that the "structure is built to accommodate conflict, to mute its expression and to redefine clashing positions on clearcut issues as moderate stands on ambiguous generalities." [106]

Another significant weapon in the armory of the ruling elite is the use of their power in preventing issues which might challenge the status quo from ever arising. In other words, power can be reflected in so called *nondecisions*. This particular method of manipulation of the democratic process is described by two social scientists in the following words : "A nondecision, as we define it, is a decision that results in suppression or thwarting of a latent or manifest challenge to the values or interests of the decision maker. To be more nearly explicit, nondecision-making is a means by which demands for change in the existing allocation of benefits and privileges in the community can be suffocated before they are even voiced ; or kept covert ; or killed before they gain access to the relevant decision-making arena ; or, failing all these things, maimed or destroyed in the decision-implementing stage of the political process." [107]

What the Canadian multiparty system, as it now operates, has accomplished is to fragment and to emasculate existent or latent class opposition and to incorporate this opposition into parliamentary party channels.

Extra-Parliamentary Politics

Given the nature and internal dynamics of the parliamentary system, it should come as no surprise that the pressure for a more meaningful democratic process (i.e. participation of all citizens in the formulation and executions of policies) takes place outside the traditional channels. The extra-parliamentary nature of this protest is a direct outgrowth of the elitist character of the parliamentary system. Let us look briefly at two such movements of citizens' protest—one Canadian and one European.

Extra-Parliamentary Action-1

The United Farmers of Alberta (UFA), which was organized in the early part of this century, was openly critical of the parliamentary system. The UFA critique of the party system is summarized by C.B. Macpherson as follows : "the worth of any method of political organization is to be tested by its efficiency as an instrument for hastening the destruction of the competitive social order ; the old party system is a method of maintaining that order by dividing, confusing, and ruling the masses, the old parties being subservient to the moneyed interests ; no new party, however democratically begun, can be an adequate instrument for social change, since a party as such is conglomerate, unstable, lacking in principle, and undemocratic. The farmers as an organized democratic force seeking a new social order must therefore reject party organization." [108]

The UFA saw our parties to be inconsistent with democratic control of elected members. In having to appeal to the "general interest" of the entire population, parties necessarily cease to be guided by any principle other than the drive for power (i.e. the full control of the state). The UFA advocated the replacement of the party system by the political mobilization of economic classes (i.e. functional representation by occupation or industrial groups). The theory of group government which they developed was seen to solve the problems of accountability of the elected member to his or her constituents, which the UFA viewed as the essence of the democratic process. [109]

Practical delegate democracy at the annual convention of the UFA operated on simple lines of authority and accountability. The annual provincial convention (the governing body of the UFA) elected the president, four vice-presidents, and the secretary of the UFA. The convention could recall any member of the executive by a resolution supported by three-fifths of those voting. With the exception of the president of the United Farm Women of Alberta, who was an ex-officio member of the UFA executive, all members of the governing body were directly elected by the delegates at the annual convention. [110]

Extra-Parliamentary Action-2

Let us now turn to the recent crisis in industrial relations in Italy, brought about almost exclusively by the pressure and direct action of rank and file workers. Briefly what happened was this :

Unions demanded and achieved changes in the methods of negotiations. The *national contract*, based on industry-wide bargaining, was rejected by most unions largely because of rank and file pressure for participation in the negotiating process. What emerged after 1969 was a system based on a sharp distinction between national bargaining and plant bargaining. The unions also insisted on the right to strike at any time during the life of the contract. Increasingly, rank and file demands began to question managerial prerogatives. Demands for equal wage increases demonstrated workers egalitarianism, and challenged traditional wage policies which were used by management to fragment the workforce through a system of hierarchical categories. In the large Pirelli and Fiat plants the struggle centered around the issues of the speed of the production line and the entire system of piece work. The workers succeeded in setting up *workers' committees* with the authority to control production lines. As the crisis grew, it involved even a non-union organ of representation, the *Commissione Interna* (Internal Committee). These committees, established by law in 1943, have played an important role in the development of industrial relations in Italy. For a number of years the C.I. was the only organ of workers representation close to the workers at the plant level. The unions depended on the C.I. in their confrontation with management.

In coincidence with labour agitation and the eruption of social protest in the late 1960s the C.I. proved to be inadequate as an organ of workers militancy, and its areas of competence (workers safety and health and handling of grievances) were viewed by workers as being too limited. Its essential character became more and more evident - it served as an institutionalized instrument of order within the enterprise. The traditional principle of parliamentary representation, upon which the C.I. was based, became one of the central points of attack by the militants.

The existence of the C.I. was finally undermined by the dramatic rise of the *Comitati Unitari di Base* (CUB), grass-roots councils which grew out of the innovative pressure of rank and file workers. The CUBs functioned as organs of direct worker democracy and thus represented an immediate answer to the workers' dissatisfaction with existing structures of representation within the enterprise. The CUBs were not only the manifestation of a revolt against capitalist management, they were also directed against the traditional hierarchies of the unions. Above all, they were an expression of the determination of the rank and file to take into their own hands the initiative in carrying out the conflict. The CUBs spread rapidly in all major industrial plants in Italy and became centres of discussion, critique and formulation of new tactics of conflict involving the workers directly in decision-making.

The CUBs experience was a short-lived one, however, (by the end of 1969 most CUBs had either ceased to exist or receded into the background), but they occupy an important place in the ongoing development of organized labour in Italy. The CUBs represent the first major organized expression of workers' action based on the principle of direct participatory democracy within the plant and they were the first organs through which there occured a merger between the workers' struggle in the plants and the broader process of protest against Italy's whole institutional network. The CUBs in fact became centres in which students, white-collar workers, intellectuals, and activists from a variety of extra-parliamentary groups converged to assist the workers in carrying out their struggle. The ferment of ideas generated by the militants and leaders of various groups within the CUBs enabled the workers not only to question critically the whole productive setting of Italy's industry, but was also instrumental in shaping their consciousness, i.e., enabling them to see the global implications of their concrete demands. Finally, the CUBs contributed enormously to the goal of a unified workers' movement (a goal which presently is the most debated issue within the Italian labour movement) in that during their daily actions of confrontation the workers transcended individual union affiliations and made the concrete grievances common to all the only rallying point of their actions.

The impact the CUBs had on the labour relations framework can be seen by the way in which the unions were forced to take into account the innovative nature of the conflict as carried out by the new militants, and carefully assess the philosophical and strategic implications of their actions. After an initial period of hesitation, and perhaps surprise, the unions were able to 'recover' and thereafter succeeded in taking over the conduct of the conflict and integrating the action of the CUBs in their own global strategy. The unions' success in their integration strategy has not, however, occurred without they themselves undergoing a process of organizational renewal and decentralization without which they could not have regained their influence on the rank and file. [111]

This reinforces certain lessons drawn from the May 1968 events in France. The most important perhaps is that these and similar less spectacular events elsewhere refute the notion about the integration of the *working class* in capitalist countries. The events in France in particular show that it was not the *working class* which was integrated but the political and trade union organizations which speak in the name of the working class. The events in France, Italy and elsewhere thus demand a fresh look at the relationship between spontaneity and organization in the revolutionary process. These events have shown that small, almost unorganized groups, drawing their support from workplace, university and community, can play an important role as catalysts for revolutionary change.

Concluding Remarks

Returning to Canada, we are faced with following situation: John Porter is probably correct when he argues that elites as well as the mass of the population in Canada are characterised by conservatism to a greater degree than in the United States. [112] We should add to this the statistical fact that the majority of Canadians know perfectly well that the real power is located in the boardrooms of corporations and not in parliament. At the same time a recent study conducted in 1968 has shown that 75 per cent of the respondents perceived voting as the only way people can have any influence about how the government runs things. [113]

This paradox is of course not unexpected. The parliamentary route to social change is the only one we know from experience. It might well be useful to remember that political parties and the representative system as we know it today have not always existed. Political parties, to all practical purposes, appeared during the last century parallel to the rise of the bourgeoisie which organized its parties in the struggle to defeat feudalism. They will have their end just as they had their beginning.

It is not our purpose to offer blueprints on strategy ; nor is it our intention to build a model of a future socialist society. It would seem to us, however, that the critique of existing institutions and politics permits us to eliminate certain strategies and policies as unworkable or undemocratic.

If the parliamentary system has certain inherent qualities which divide the people into rulers and ruled, we should look to different methods of representation and accountability.

If geographical representation fragments the electorate and thus lends itself to the rule of organized elites over the unorganized mass, we should begin to think in terms of an organisational and electoral base which unites the people without the need of geographically based political parties.

If emancipation from above is recognized for what it is — namely a permanent promise held out by the ruling elite "to keep the people looking upward for protection, instead of to themselves for liberation from the need for protection", then we must seek ways and means of strengthening the experience of direct democracy. Freedom and equality cannot be legislated, and cannot be administered by "representatives". Freedom and equality must be taken.

If socialist self-government can only exist if it embraces all parts of society then the "politics of self-government" must permeate every institution and organization in society. We would particularly stress the importance of breaking down the authoritarian decision-making structures in the workplace. As G.D.H. Cole once said : "A servile system in industry inevitably reflects itself in political servility".

The point made by Cole would seem to be obvious and struggles for workers' control and self-management have been central to many socialist and anarchist struggles of the past. Demands for participatory democracy today fall essentially within this tradition. It is only recently, however, that social scientists have begun to be concerned with the effects of the job on the activities of the workers in their leisure time. A recently completed study by Martin Meissner of the University of British Columbia comes to conclusions which we think are of crucial importance to anyone concerned with radical social change. [114]

Meissner has attempted to answer the question whether work affects leisure and more particularly, what effects work in a factory has on the employee's life away from work. The data for his analysis is drawn from a sample of 206 industrial workers in an industrial community on Vancouver Island. The sample was restricted to workers of a large wood products manufacturing company with a number of integrated operations in the community. The sample was further restricted to male union members below the level of foreman. Three possible relations between work and leisure are considered : (1) Workers *compensate* for the constraints [115] (or lack of discretion) and social isolation of the job in their free time ; (2) The experience of constraint and isolation *carries over* into free time ; (3) Life away from work is unaffected by the job.

Meissner was particularly interested in studying the effects of technical constraints on participation in voluntary organization. The findings clearly favour a "carry—over" hypothesis. The study shows that workers who have a chance for social interaction on the job participate more in voluntary organizations. Similarly, work with little discretionary potential results in reduced worker participation in formally organized activities.

The importance of Meissner's conclusion would seem to be obvious. He states : "The design of industrial work creates or prevents opportunities for the development or maintenance of discretionary and social skills. When choice of action is suppressed by the spatial, temporal, and functional constraints of the work process, worker capacity for meeting the demands of spare-time activities which require discretion is reduced. They engage less in those activities which necessitate planning, coordination, and purposeful action, but increase the time spent in sociable and expressive activities". [116]

We have noted before that the core of the prevailing elitist theory of democracy is the presumption of the average citizen's incapacity to govern himself. Apathy and political "incompetence" are seen to be essential ingredients for the maintenance of our stable democratic system. We should not therefore be too surprised if the struggle of workers for democracy and ultimate self-management within the workplace meets with the solid opposition of the owners and managers of corporations and institutions in our society.

The artificial separation of politics from everyday life is one of the means of perpetuating the political emasculation of citizens.

The stress on political parties as the only legitimate avenue for political participation ignores, as we have pointed out, so-called "non-political" areas of life such as the corporations and institutions within which most Canadians spend the bulk of their waking hours. It also ignores the entire voluntary sector with its thousands of organizations and associations. Our elitist system functions best if all the various competing organizations and institutions are hierarchically structured and led by "responsible" elites. Elite accommodation thus becomes the dynamic by which we are ruled and governed. If elite rule in one of the important links in the system (e.g. industry) would be broken (i.e. if the workers were to demand and achieve control and self-management of their workplace) the entire system of elite accommodation would collapse.

As long as "legitimate" political participation is restricted to political parties and the electoral process and political power is shared by the intelocking elites of parties and corporate interests, politics will remain an "alienated force".

Since bourgeois democracy excludes democracy from the basic cells of everyday life (i.e. the workplace and the community) and since nationalization (i.e. state socialism) does not by itself bring about social self-government, it would seem to follow that demands by the left for nationalization must be coupled with massive attempts to introduce self-government on the *micro and macro level*. Social self-government which is restricted to the micro—level will not only leave ultimate power in the hands of national elites and their bureaucracies ; it may, furthermore, degenerate into a system based on autonomous, competitive groups which could exploit and threaten each other as well as society as a whole.

Attempts to overcome the elitist characteristics of the representative model of democracy have frequently led to experiments with some form of functional or occupational representation. The advantages of this form of representation in comparison to the representative model can be summarized as follows :

> The unorganized and fragmented electorate under the representative model is replaced by an electorate which is drawn from occupational and other functional groups which can be expected to have. The members of such functional constituencies are directly represented by elected and recallable delegates, thus eliminating the brokerage function of political parties.

> Representative bodies thus elected would be composed of a majority of delegates who retain their firm links (i.e.

their jobs) within their self-managing structures. They would leave jobs only when the assembly sits. The number, function, and power of professional politicians would thus be sharply curbed and politics as a separate and professionalized sphere of social decision-making would be partly overcome through the 'socialization of politics." [117]

Elected and recallable delegates may actually begin to represent the interests of their constituents in a more meaningful way than presently possible within the representative parliamentary model. (e.g. it is obviously ridiculous to expect a businessman or lawyer, both of which are over-represented in our parliament, to *represent* the interests of the unemployed, the workers, the students, the old age pensioners, etc.)

The necessity (of political parties) to appeal to a wide variety of frequently conflicting interests leads to the dilution of party programmes (see the discussion on the conflict-absorption mechanism above) so that their stated goals become ambiguous and devoid of any political substance. The functional model would allow the formulation of clear-cut policies. Conflicting policies of diverse functional groups would, instead of being suppressed, emerge in the open.

To the extent that it is possible in complex industriel societies, decision-making power will be brought down to the level of the individual within functionally or occupationally oriented collectives.

One conclusion would seem to be obvious from our analysis of the reality of parliamentary politics in Canada. Citizen participation, not to speak of control, in the day-to-day decisions which affect our workplaces and communities is largely an illusion for most Canadians. The New Brunswick Task Force on Social Development, after nearly a year of public hearings, interviews, and community meetings, illustrated this point clearly when it reported that : 'There is a general attitude among the population that 'the government,' at whatever level, exists independently of them, and that government programs do not really reflect the wishes of the people and do not necessarily meet their needs.' [118]

In terms of developing an effective strategy we are convinced that whatever the mix of parliamentary and extra-parliamentary action may be, the struggle within the workplace would seem to be of crucial importance for at least three reasons ;

1. It attacks capitalist power at its source (the parliamentary struggle does not).

2.   If successful, it will avoid the worst manifestations of state socialism.

3.   Since individual self-fulfillment depends (at least partly) on the elimination of traditional authoritarian hierarchies within the corporations and institutions of our society, the struggle within these structures is of concern to every working individual regardless of his or her political affiliation.

Participation in politics in any country has two aspects. One refers to the channels through which citizens exert real influence or control over decisions affecting them. In the second, participation is an instrument through which a regime enlists support for itself and its policies and attempts to create social solidarity through a sense of involvement. The first is real participation from below ; the second, manipulative participation from above. All existing systems exhibit both forms of participation. My argument is simply that the manipulative aspects of parliamentary electoral politics render this particular form of participation useless as a means for real participation (control) from below.

Footnotes

1.   John Porter, *The Vertical Mosaic,* Toronto : University of Toronto Press, 1965, p. 202.
2.   *ibid,* p. 207.
3.   *ibid.,* p. 212.
4.   *ibid.,* p. 558.
5.   *ibid,* p. 558.
6.   George Grant, *Lament for a Nation : The Defeat of Canadian Nationalism,* Toonto : McClelland and Stewart Ltd., 1965, p. 9.
7.   Ian Adams et al, "The Renegade Report on Poverty," *The Last Post,* Vol. I, No. 8 (1971), p. 3.
8.   George Grant, *op. cit.,* p. 8.
9.   Harold Kaplan, *Urban political Systems : A Functional Analysis of Metro Toronto,* New York : Columbia University Press, 1967, p. 199.
10.   Robert Presthus, "The Pluralist Framework," Kariel, *op. cit.* p. 277.
11.   See, for example, John McCready, "Lucky Who ? The United Community Fund of Greater Toronto," *Praxis Notes,* Vol. I, No 1 (1971), pp. 14-20.
12.   Edward Cowan, "Lobbying Causes Worry in Ottawa," *New York Times,* October 12, 1969.
13.   Donald E. Willmott, "Voluntary Associations in the Political Process," prepared for the *Seminar on Voluntary Associations in the Political Process,* sponsored by the Canadian Association for Adult Education, November, 19-20, 1971, (mimeo) p. 42.
14.   John Sewell, "Developers Lose Special Status," *City Hall,* Vol. I, No. 11 (1971), p. 54.
15.   Robert Welch, "Citizen Participation in Community Development," *Address to the First Ontario Provincial-Municipal Conference,* Toronto, April 24, 1970, (mimeo), p. 2.
16.   Quoted by Ron Haggert, "The Mayor's favourite citizens," *The Toronto Telegram,* May 29, 1971.

17. John Bird, "Benson-style 'discuss-it-first' treatment given new bills," *The Financial Post*, July 17, 1971.
18. *The Globe and Mail*, March 30, 1972.
19. S. Ziegel, "Citizens aren't encouraged to help scrutinize new bills," *The Toronto Star*, February 23, 1971 (Letters to Editor).
20. Johannes Agnoli, "Theses for the Transformation of Democracy," *Our Generation*, Vol. 6, No 4, p. 95.
21. Porter, *op. cit.*, p. 5.
22. *ibid.*, p. 233.
23. *ibid.*, pp. 233-241.
24. *ibid.*, p. 118.
25. *ibid.*, p. 133.
26. *OFL Facts and Figures*, Toronto : Ontario Federation of Labour, 1971, p. 23.
27. Porter, *op. cit.*, p. 6.
28. Porter, *op. cit.*, p. 462.
29. *ibid.*, p. 463.
30. *The Uncertain Mirror : Report of the Special Senate Committee on Mass Media*, Vol. I, Ottawa : Queen's Printer, 1970, p. 3.
31. *ibid.*, p. 4.
32. Andre Gorz, "Workers' Control is More than Just That," Gerry Hunnius (ed.), *Participatory Democracy for Canada : Workers' Control and Community Control*, Montreal : Black Rose Books, 1971, p. 21.
33. *Canadian Labour*, Vol. 15, No. 2 (1970), p. 13.
34. *The Uncertain Mirror*, pp. 83-84, and *Good, Bad or Simply Meritable ? Report of the Special Senate Committee on Mass Media, Selected Research Studies*, Vol. III, pp. 26-28.
35. *ibid.*, pp. 26, 48-49, 62 and 77.
36. "Mass Media, Vol. IV. The Irving Monopoly. An Additional Report from Senator Charles McElwan and Others," *The Mysterious East*, May-June, 1971, p. 10.
47. Raymond Williams, "Towards a Socialist Society," P. Anderson & R. Blackburn (eds.), *Towards Socialism*, Ithaca : Cornell University Press, 1966, p. 391.
38. Richard Shaull, "Foreword", Paulo Freire, *Pedagogy of the Oppressed*, New York : Herder & Herder, 1970, p. 15.
39. Porter, *op. cit.*, p. 168.
40. *ibid.*, p. 173. For empirical data to back up this statements, see Porter, pp. 173-198.
41. *The Toronto Telegram*, December 22, 1970, p. 1.
42. "Downtown kids aren't dumb ; they need a better program. A brief to the Management Committee of the Toronto Board of Education from the Park School Community Council," (November 16, 1971). The table referred to above was compiled by Dr. John Buttrick. *This Magazine is about Schools*, Vol. 5, No. 4 (1971), pp. 17-18.
43. Garnet McDiarmid & David Pratt, *Teaching Prejudice : A Content Analysis of Social Studies Textbooks Authorized for Use in Ontario*, The Ontario Institute for Studies in Education, Curriculum Series 12, Toronto 1971, p. 93.
44. *ibid.*, p. 100.
45. Donald E. Willmott, *op. cit.*, pp. 22-24.
46. Quoted in Henry S. Kariel (ed.), *Frontiers of Democratic Theory*, New York : Random House, 1970, p. 130.
47. T. B. Bottomore, *Elites and Society*, London : C. A. Watts Co., 1964, p. 119.
48. Seymour Martin Lipset, *Political Man*, Doubleday, 1960, p. 403.
49. T. B. Bottomore, "The Insufficiency of Elite Competition," Kariel, *op. cit.*, p. 131.
50. Carole Pateman, *Participation and Democratic Theory*, Cambridge : Cambridge University Press, 1970, pp. 1-2.
51. Gaetano Mosca, *The Ruling Class*, New York : McGraw-Hill, 1939, pp. 61-62.

52. Robert Michels, "The Iron Law of Oligarchy," C. Wright Mills (ed.), *Images of Man: The Classic Tradition in Sociological Thinking,* New York: George Braziller, 1960, p. 238.
53. Pateman, *op. cit.,* pp. 2-3.
54. See, for instance, Arthur Kornhauser, *Mental Health of the Industrial Worker: A Detroit Study,* New York: John Wiley & Sons, 1965. Charles Hampden-Turner, *The Factory as an Oppressive and Non-Emancipating Environment,* Cambridge (Mass.), 1970 (mimeo), Centre for Community Economic Development.
55. Pateman, *op. cit.,* p. 3.
56. Joseph A. Schumpeter, *Capitalism, Socialism and Democracy,* London: George Allen and Unwin, 1943, p. 269.
57. C. B. Macpherson, *The Real World of Democracy,* Toronto: CBC, 1965, pp. 50-51.
58. Schumpeter, *op. cit.,* p. 272.
59. *ibid.,* p. 283.
60. *ibid.,* p. 283.
61. *ibid.,* p. 283.
62. S. W. Rousseas and J. Farganis, "The Equilibrium Rationalized," Kariel, *op. cit.,* p. 307.
63. Jack L. Walker, "Normative Consequences of 'Democratic' Theory," Kariel, *op. cit.,* p. 231. See also Bernard Berelson et al, *Voting,* Chicago, 1954, Ch. 14: S. M. Lipset, *Political Man,* New York, 1960, pp. 14-16; W. H. Morris-Jones, "In Defense of Apathy," *Political Studies, ii* (1954), pp. 25-37.
64. Quoted by Walker, *op. cit.,* p. 231.
65. T. B. Bottomore, *Elites and Society,* Penguin Books, 1966, p. 19.
66. Christian Bay, "The Concern with Pseudopolitics," Kariel, *op. cit.,* pp. 174-175.
67. Graeme Duncan & Steven Lukes, "Democracy Restated," Kariel, *op. cit.,* p. 203.
68. Quoted by Duncan and Lukes, *op. cit.,* p. 203.
69. Duncan and Lukes, *op. cit.,* p. 205.
70. *ibid.,* p. 205.
71. Christian Bay, *op. cit.,* p. 174.
72. Rousseas and Farganis, *op. cit.,* p. 311.
73. Pateman, *op. cit.,* p. 16.
74. Hanna F. Pitkin, "The Concept of Representation," H. F. Pitkin (ed.), *Representation,* New York: Atherton Press, 1969, p. 7.
75. Harold F. Gosnell, "Pleasing the Constituents: Representative Democracy," Pitkin (ed.), *op. cit.,* p. 116.
76. Robert J. Pranger, *The Eclipse of Citizenship: Power and Participation in Contemporary Politics,* New York: Holt, Rinehart and Winston, 1968, p. 14.
77. Robert MacGregor Dawson, *The Government of Canada,* Toronto: The University of Toronto Press, 1947 (second edition, 1954), p. 357.
78. *ibid.,* p. 372.
79. In 1947, one Toronto constituency totalled 86,000 compared to the rural riding of Glengarry, Ontario, with 18,732.
80. Dawson, *op. cit.,* p. 370.
81. Bottomore, *op. cit.,* p. 116.
82. Agnoli, *op. cit.,* p. 91.
83. Anthony Westell, 'Public Never Sees The Real Work of Government—MP', *The Toronto Daily Star,* February 20, 1971.
84. Allan Kornberg, *Canadian Legislative Behaviour: A Study of the 25th Parliament,* New York: Holt, Rinehart and Winston, 1967, p. 43.
85. Porter, *op. cit.,* p. 388.
86. Kornberg, *op. cit.,* p. 44.
87. *ibid.,* p. 106-107.
88. *ibid.,* p. 107.
89. *ibid.,* p. 109.

90. See for example, 'Neighbourhood Participation in Local Government: A Study of the City of Toronto,' *Civic Affairs*, January 1970, Toronto: Bureau of Municipal Research, p. 8-9.
91. Kornberg, *op. cit.*, p. 145.
92. *ibid.*, p. 147.
93. *ibid.*, p. 149.
94. J.A. Corry, *Democratic Government and Politics*, Toronto: University of Toronto Press, (second edition), 1955, p. 230.
95. *ibid.*, p. 231.
96. Anthony Downs, *An Economic Theory of Democracy*, New York: Harper & Row, 1957, p. 295.
97. C.B. MacPherson, "Address to the Third Congress of the International Political Science Association", Stockholm, 1955. Quoted by John Wilson, *The Meaning of Socialism; a Community of Friends*, Toronto: The Ontario Woodsworth Memorial Foundation, 1971, p. 18 ff.
98. John Sewell, *The Globe and Mail*, November 12, 1970, (Letters to the Editor).
99. Corry, *op. cit.*, p. 237.
100. Porter, *op. cit.*, pp. 368-369.
101. *ibid*, p. 374.
102. W. Fisher, *Democracy and Social Change*, Toronto: September 1969, p. 2 (mimeo.).
103. H.S. Crowe, "Liberals, New Democrats and Labour", Laurier La Pierre et al., *Essays on the Left*, Toronto: McClelland and Stewart, 1971, p. 210.
104. Agnoli, *op. cit.*, p. 93.
105. David Katz, 'Group Process and Social Integration: A Systems Analysis of Two Movements of Social Protest,' *The Journal of Social Issues*, Vol. XXIII, No. 1(1967), p. 8.
106. *ibid.*, p. 9.
107. Peter Bachrack and Morton S. Baratz, *Power and Poverty: Theory and Practice*, New York: Oxford University Press, 1970, p. 44. The various possible forms of nondecision-making are discussed by the author on pp. *44-46*.
108. C.B. Macpherson, *Democracy in Alberta: Social Credit and the Party System*, Toronto: University of Toronto Press, 1970, *p. 44*.
109. *ibid.*, p. 49.
110. *ibid.*, p. 63.
111. Summarized from Bruno Ramirez, *Industrial Conflict and Industrial Relations in Italy: New Perspectives*, Toronto: 1972.
112. John Porter, "The Canadian National Character in the Twentieth Century," *Cultural Affairs*, Spring 1969, p. 50.
113. George J. Szablowski, *Policy-Making, Bureaucracy and Social Change in the Ontario Government*, Toronto, 1972 (mimeo).
114. Martin Meissner, "The Long Arm of the Job: A study of Work and Leisure," *Industrial Relations*, Vol. 10, No. 3 (October, 1971) pp. 239-260.
115. Three constraints are considered: time (work pacing); space (confinement to work location); function (task dependence and work type).
116. Meissner, *op. cit.*, p. 260.
117. See, for example, Zagorska Pesic-Golubovic, "Socialist Ideas and Reality," *Praxis* (International Edition), No. 3-4, 1971, p. 413.
118. Report of the New Brunswick Task Force on Social Development, *Participation and Development*, Vol. I, Fredericton, September 1971, p. 210.

Published 1972

TOWARDS AN EXTRA-PARLIAMENTARY OPPOSITION IN CANADA

It is of fundamental importance to us where an analysis of a political situation begins. If our political analysis begins with an election, and what is necessary to win it within the present framework and definition of politics, we have taken as central a particular fact which determines all subsequent analysis. Our central interest and what we as a consequence wish to project decides in fact *what* we discuss and *how*.

Alternatively we can start from Canada's general condition : its overall statistical record, its total productivity. We can look at this country as if it were some single entity, to be amended by this percentage or improved by that average. But this description can hide as much as it shows ; it can show a nation-wide income, but not how it is distributed ; or total productivity, but not what is produced. What appears like a neutral analysis has in fact been prejudiced by a camouflaged political assumption : that we are all in the same situation, and have an equal stake and interest in it.

Or again, we can start an analysis from some particular personal careers : the prospects of A in his new administration ; the developing rivalry between B and C ; the character factors, in this speech or that television appearance. The assumption here is that these careers are all important and that policies are merely an aspect of these careers.

Published as an editorial in Vol. 6, No. 4 of OUR GENERATION, 1969.

We are all very familiar with the above approaches; they surround us daily through the commercial press and mass media. In fact, between them, they dominate orthodox discussion, serious and popular. To be interested in contemporary politics is to be interested in these particular approaches. One indication of these approaches is what passes for political commentary on VIEWPOINT every weeknight on the CBC. It is quite difficult to see how things might be otherwise, and how one could start differently. This is how our particular culture imposes its orthodoxy on a politically illiterate society, before any detailed arguments begin. You may go on to differ, at this or that point, but if you accept these approaches to Canadian politics, there are certain things you can never find time to say, or say reasonably and relevantly.

The key to a political analysis is always indicated at the point at which it starts.

We believe we have been dominated for too long by other approaches and definitions, and the consequent politics are both pointless and destructive. We think we have to make a break in order to see the world in our own way, a radical way, that will go to the *roots* of the crisis in this country. Then we can offer this way to others, to see how far they can agree with it, how closely it connects with their lives.

We start our analysis from our situation as revolutionaries amid the present contradictions of radical motion now taking place in Canada and Québec. These contradictions are out in the open, but we must draw attention to them. We say, here and elsewhere that current definitions of radicalism and socialism have failed. We are in fact asking what it means to live in Canada today amid disappearing political landmarks immersed in an urgent reality which we are trying to understand — that is, a particular people in a particular country.

We wish to overcome the unsystematic and fragmented approach to understanding this country and gain an organic overview. What has happened up until now is a bringing together, into a general position of the many kinds of new political and social responses and analyses, around which essentially local work has been done. We stopped talking and writing about 'national' work a long time ago because of its very rootless nature. It was work more often than not without a *base*. Its 'usefulness' was a fiction our society maintains. The consequence of this uselessness has become apparent to many. The positions taken on various questions were fragmentary; they could be taken without real commitment into the simple rhetoric of the 'liberally-minded' progressive party of Canada, the NDP, while the other parliamentary parties used them at will as political footballs. But that NDP rhetoric becomes cant for we are constantly told that nothing can happen without a parliamentary victory.

In the meantime, the fragmented social questions we are concerned about are thrown back at us. So a failure in solving one question is referred to another in an endless series of references and evasions, the staple of all politicians. As a result the character of the general crisis in Canada, of which these failures are symptoms, can never be grasped or understood or communicated. Clearly then what we need is a description of the crisis as a whole, in which not only the present mistakes and illusions but also the necessary and urgent changes can be intelligently linked.

It is our basic contention that the separate campaigns in which we have been active, e.g. against nuclear arms and the cold war, the Vietnam war, Biafra, the recognition of China, the anti-poverty movement, student power, and the other separate campaigns with which we have been concerned run back, in their essence, to a single political *system* and *its* alternatives. We believe that the system we oppose and its injustices can only survive by a willed separation of issues, and the resulting fragmentation of consciousness. The fundamental pivot of our position is that *all* social and political questions — structural and industrial, international and domestic, economic and cultural — are deeply connected ; that what we oppose is in fact a system ; and that what we want to work for is a *qualitatively* different society. An end must be put to the fact that the problems of whole men and women are habitually relegated to specialized and disparate fields, where society offers to manage or adjust them by this or that consideration or technique.

We have had close experience with the different single-issue campaigns. We know and appreciate the dedication and energy that is given to them. We understand the impatience of those who say, ' . . . but let us at least change this small area...'. It is from just this kind of experience, in repeated campaigns, that we set out on this new perspective. We have learned, in the course of following the campaigns through from our different initial priorities, that a new total analysis, however preliminary, is now indispensable. The first stage of this new perspective was gained when we developed from the Campaign for Nuclear Disarmament into a student movement concerned with social change as a means of changing Canadian foreign and defence policy, and have now realized that we must go still deeper into the nature of change in our kind of society. Against the inherent power and speed of the system we oppose, only a systemic position can effectively stand.

Against a discontinuous experience, our immediate political decision is to make new connexions between issues, which means a development in awareness. This is necessary *before* we can solve the problems of political organisation. This may be dismissed by some as merely 'intellectual' work : a substitute of thought for action. Our political culture continually prompts this response . "action not words". But we reject this separation of thought and action, or of language and reality. *If the people interested in social and political change are conscious in certain ways, they will act in certain ways, and where they are not conscious they will fail to act.* Of course it is not enough to simply describe and analyse a general crisis and its particularities ; but unless the new left does, other descriptions and analyses prevail, and the most relevant political life in terms of radical alternatives is pushed back into the margins, and into precarious unwritten areas. Among all the flapping about on the Left in Canada we asked ourselves the question — what action can we take with this journal in the next little while — our answer was to try to establish this practical and alternative view of our world and our society.

We are quite conscious of the fact that *describing* the connexion between social questions within the system we oppose, is not *making* the connexions, or the praxis we support. As a first step we are identifying the facts and reasons for the existing process of incorporation, homogenization, absorption and hence discontinuity. But in spite of this process an unprecedented number of people in Canada and Québec, in many different ways, are still opposing the system. It is clearly not for us as a group of editors, but for all people now in various kinds of opposition, to consider the practical consequences of a radical systemic political analysis. We have tried to initiate the process of political analysis afresh which, if successful, would go far beyond ourselves, though we should still belong to it.

WHAT IS NEO-CAPITALISM ?

Our society has many dimensions, some more central than others. We shall begin at the most central, with an analysis of the socio-economic framework of this society and its significance.

We are in a transitional phase between the old and new capitalism. Often those seeking fundamental change belabour the old definition of problems without understanding their new underpinnings. Radicalism is a tool which allows us to understand the nature of the transitional process. What we will describe further on under the label neo-capitalism should not suggest that all of the old classical contradictions have disappeared. Rather it should be made clear that in order to solve these contradictions we must be aware of the fact that although the point of gravity of the system has not changed, the fulcrum has.

We must first describe that unfamiliar but now crucial phenomenon called in official circles — post-capitalism or the mixed economy — which is in fact a new kind of capitalism, the political dimension of which is referred to as liberal corporatism. It presents crucial problems of recognition and description, and leads our society to political problems of a new kind.

Canada, like societies elsewhere, has adapted and changed in order to survive. This process of change has been the main task of the post-war governments. The leading role of the State has been to initiate the reshaping of an economy in relative decline, structurally imbalanced, backward in many regions, paralysed by a slow rate of growth, by inflation, recession and balance of payments problems : and to create in its stead a political economy based on organised rapid expansion. An essential part of this strategy has been the containment and ultimate incorporation of the trade union movement and other sections of the infra-structure as well as the opposition political parties. An essential prerequisite was the redefinition of what is progressive and what is socialism, and the internal adaptation of the agencies of change — including the New Democratic Party and Communist Party — within some broad consensus. The current crisis is then a phase in the transition from one stage in the political economy to another. It is the crisis which occurs when a system, already beset by its own contradictions and suffering from prolonged entropy, nevertheless seeks to stabilize itself at a more 'rationalised' level.

Neo-capitalism, though a development from free-enterprise capitalism, is — in terms of its essential drives and its modes of operation and control — a distinct variant. It is an economic system dominated by private accumulation, where decisive economic power is wielded by a handful of very large US industrial multi-national corporations in each sector, emulated by those remaining Canadian enterprises. The bureaucratic complexity of corporate structures, the size and scale of operations, the advanced manipulative techniques required to man and control such units, and their pervasive impact upon society at large, are so immense that the allocation of human and natural resources and the creation of compulsive consumption can no longer be left to the play of the market place. What is required according to the prevailing public philosophy is a further rationalisation, such as would enable our kind of society to go over consciously to an administered price system, wage negotiations within the framework of agreed norms, managed demand, and the efficient, and effective transmission of orders from the top to the bottom. The attempts to rationalise injuctions in the Rand Report for example is only one such effort dealing with one aspect of the production process. This integrating and harmonising authoritarianism is among the constant themes uttered before meetings of the Manufacturers Association and the Chambers of Commerce. These efforts would represent, without doubt, a major stabilization of the system. The market place, once the focus of capitalism, is progressively by-passed for the sake of greater management and control, and the consequent rewards of growth. Within this context, it is this shift which makes some kind of *planning* imperative.

Planning in this sense does not mean what socialists have understood — the subordination of private profit (and the direction which profit-maximization imposes on the whole society) to social priorities. The fact that the same word is used to mean different things is extremely significant. It is by this semantic sleight-of-hand that the NDP has mystified and confused its supporters, taking up the allegiance of many to one concept of planning while attaching quite another meaning to what it understands in reality.

What does planning of an economy mean today ? It means better forecasting, better coordination of investment and expansion decisions, a more purposeful control over demand. This in turn enables the more technologically equiped and organised units in the private sector to pursue their goals more efficiently, more 'rationally'. It also means more control over the trade unions and over labour's power to bargain freely about wages. This involves another important transition.

In the course of this rationalization of capitalism, the gap between the corporations and the State is narrowed. The State, indeed, comes to play an increasingly critical role. It makes itself responsible for the overall management of the political economy by fiscal means. It must tailor the production of trained man-power to the needs of the economic system — hence the active influence of this system on the educational apparatus. In the political field, it must hold the ring within which the necessary bargains are struck between competing interests. It must engineer the public consensus in favour of these bargains, and take on the task directly — of intervening to whip it into line behind the norms.

The Canadian work force, of course, can only be expected to cooperate with the system if it regularly gains a share of the goods produced. The *first* promise held out is that the State will be in a better position to manage the inflation-recession cycles which have beset the post-war political economy. The *second* promise is that a stable system will be more efficient and productive, and that, so long as it works, labour will win its share in return for cooperation. When productivity rises, it is suggested, labour shares the benefits. On the other hand, when productivity slows down labour cannot contract out since it has become party to the bargain. This looks on the surface like a more rational way of guaranteeing rising standards of living : it is in fact a profound restructuring of the relationship between unionized labour and capital.

We noted already how the word 'planning' has been maintained, but how its meaning has been redefined. Equally the word 'welfare' has been given a semantic somersault. Free-enterprise capitalism was for a long time the enemy of the welfare state. This has now undergone certain changes, why ? The welfare state, in the US, Britain, and Europe has been introduced as a modification of the system. Like wage increases, it represents a measure of redistribution and egalitarianism, cutting into profits, imposing human needs and social priorities on the profit-oriented system. The various welfare states in the Western world vary in comprehensiveness. In Canada, the comprehensive welfare state is in the foreground of the political program of the NDP.

There is one central difference, however, between this aspect of a neo-capitalist economy and its alternatives. Rising prosperity—whether in the form of higher wages, increased welfare or public spending—*is not funded out of the redistribution of wealth from the rich to the poor.* Redistribution would eat into the necessary mechanisms of private accumulation, internal reinvestment and the high rewards to management on which the whole system rests. Rising prosperity for the powerless class of our society, must therefore come out of the margin of increased growth and productivity.

The *existing* distribution of basic wealth and power remains the same. It is no wonder that the quality of our lives has not changed, and in fact has deteriorated. The new wage claims can only be met by negotiation, out of the *surplus* growth, and controlled by a framework of agreed norms. The norms, however, are not the norms of social justice, human needs or claims of equality : they are arrived at by calculating the percentage rise in productivity or growth over a given period, and by bargaining at what proportion of that is the 'necessary' return to capital, and what proportion is left over for wage increases and welfare costs. In effect, within this new system of bargaining, wage increases must be tied to productivity agreements (not to egalitarianism), and welfare becomes a supporting cast for modern capitalism — not an inroad into or a modification of the system.

This is one of the crucial dividing lines between neo-capitalism and the old, and between organized capitalism and the demands of revolutionary socialism. It means that the rising prosperity of the industrial working class for one, is indissolubly linked with the growth and fortunes of the multi-national corporations on the one hand, since only by means of the productivity of this industry will there be any wage or welfare surplus at all to bargain for.

Therefore a successful neo-capitalist political economy is one in which the people may enjoy a measure of increased abundance and prosperity, what is loosely called 'affluence', provided there is growing productivity ; but it is by definition *not* an egalitarian society in terms of real income, wealth, opportunity, authority and most importantly, therefore, *power*. There may be some levelling of social status within classes ; nevertheless, 'open' capitalist societies, where stratification is not so marked, are still closed systems of power. Free enterprise capitalism created the modern hostile relations of class-society : neo-capitalism, where successfully evolving, seeks to end these conflicts, not by changing the real relations of property and power, but by surpressing all the human considerations of community and equality, in favour of the planned contentment of organised producers and consumers. In this task the system is aided consciously or not by the New Democratic Party of Canada. By continuously avoiding an organic political philosophy that goes to the root of our crisis, that is radical in that it deals with the new problems of our post-scarcity society and which includes questions of the quality and meaning of our lives, the NDP helps perpetrate a fragmented view of society. Nobody profits from this condition other than those who continue to have power in all its centralised, bureaucratic and military sense.

All these factors hinge on a decisive reality in Canada, and that is our relationship to the USA. Our practical dependence on the US, expressed in political and military alliances, confirmed by various forms of economic penetration, and supported by diverse kinds of cultural and educational colonization, makes any attempt at disengagement a struggle from the start. Radicals should not rely in such a struggle, on the counter-force of nationalism, and certainly should not toy with any 'social nationalism'. We have noted with encouragement in past numbers of this journal the emergence in the past few years, throughout the US of a revolutionary movement, which works towards the same internationalist objectives as we do. The elan and courage of this growing movement presents an urgent claim upon us not only for our solidarity but an active strategy of collaboration in the pursuit of this new international radicalism. The development of a similar movement in Québec is also a factor to be celebrated and encouraged.

But, it must be stressed again, no critique of Canada is valid unless it recognizes from the start the fact that this country is a 'branch-plant economy' or a 'client state'. Slipping into the cosy embrace of Moloch we have developed the fine art of a client politics, a client militarism and a client culture. As the old stiffness of the British - embroided class structures of recent times fade, this client apparatus, extensively established in every field, with most of the national communications system safely in its hands, confronts us as an enemy who is very difficult to recognize because the accents and appearance are 'Canadian', though the decisive agency runs back to the corporate powers of the USA.

WHAT IS THE NATURE OF LIBERAL CORPORATISM ?

Towering over the socio-economic structure of our society is a political super-structure surrounded by a chorus attempting to legitimize its values. In the face of the system's twin process of *maintaining* and *developing* our powerlessness and our meaningless lives, how does our political superstructure respond. To us clearly the elaborate procedures and structures of "representative" or parliamentary democracy born in the nineteenth century and embroidered on since stand as ossified caricatures. We live in a society where the majority of people passively consent to things being done in their name, a society of managed politics. The techniques of consultation are polished, but they remain essentially techniques and should not be confused with participation. This 'passivity' or 'apathy' is officially decried, ritualistically, but in fact is generated by the very structures of our society.

It is a fact that in our type of society any conventional opposition group inevitably assumes the values of the system it opposes and is eventually absorbed by it. In Canada as elsewhere this is the fate of socialists and social democrats, supporters of this country's political party of the Left, the NDP. The whole point is that in opposition, there is a profound gap between consciousness and organisation : partly because of real changes achieved through industrialism and technology, and partly because the familiar institutions of the Left have been pressed out of shape and recognition by the society we have been describing.

The perspective of Canada's power elite and its supporting institutions is to us clear. It is to muffle real conflict, to dissolve it into a false political consensus ; to build, not a genuine and participatory democracy, a community of meaningful life and work, but a bogus conviviality between every social group. Consensus politics, integral to the success of neo-capitalism, is in its essence manipulative politics, a politics of man-management, and deeply undemocratic because of its basic and unnegotiable premises. Governments are still elected to be sure, M.P.'s assert the supremacy of the House of Commons, but the real business of government is the management of consensus between the most powerful and organised elites.

The ruling elites can no longer impose their will by coercion as they used to : but neither will they see progress as a people organising itself for effective participation in power and responsibility in a society that can be de-bureaucratized and decentralised by modern technology.

The task of the politicians is to build consensus around each issue by means of bargain and compromise through a coalition of interests, and especially to associate the large units of power with their legislative programme.

Consensus politics is thus the politics of incremental action : it is not intended for any large-scale structural change. It is the politics of pragmatism, of the successful manoeuvre within existing limits. Every administrative act is a kind of clever performance, an exercise of political public relations. Whether the manoeuvres are made by a Conservative, Liberal or a social democratic party like the NDP, it hardly matters, since they all accept the constraints of the *status quo* as a framework.

> *"The difference between Liberal, Conservative and NDP is no longer one of conflicting visions of society. What distinguishes the parties are a great many scattered and random proposals of a technical kind as to how best to finance and manage the welfare state. The difference between the political parties is one of managerial technique—but is this conceivably a difference worth analysing, or deciding upon? It is not a difference that is intellectually liberating or morally compassionate. This is very obviously a serious conclusion to reach and to recommend or at least to sanction. For its implies that the political parties—all of them—are not operating within the province of deep political concern. This is not to say either that objectively 'it makes no difference' who wins an election : it is rather to say that the 'difference' is so slight in degree or lies in such relatively trivial areas that one might very well by-pass the area of electoral politics as being irrelevant to any fresh and profound issue of political circumstance in which such questions might more naturally be confronted."*
>
> *From the editorial 'Canadian Elections', OUR GENERATION, Vol. 6 Nos. 1 & 2.*

The nature of politics is very narrowly defined in Canada and thus has been closed — this in a very special way. In all societies there are always separate sources of power, but in our own the consequences of the negotiations are disasterous. The whole essence of this system is an increasing rationalisation and co-ordination of these sources of power. The states within the State — the high commands in each sector — the banks, corporations, the federations of industrialists, the Canadian Labour Congress — are given a new and more formal role in the political structure, and this, increasingly, is the actual machinery of decision-making : in their own fields, as always, but now also in a coordinated field.

This structure, which is to a decisive extent mirrored in the ownership and control of the public and private media of communication, is then plausibly described as 'the national or public interest'. To the extent that the 'public interest' is defined largely to include the very specific and damaging interests of the banks, insurance companies and combines, it also *excludes* what, on the other side, are called 'sectional' or 'local' interests of the poor, low-paid workers, youth in general, and backward regions. The elected sector—the vote which is still offered as ratifying—gets redefined, after its passage through the machines, as one interest among others : what is still called the public interest is present now only as one—relatively weak and ill-organised—among several elements involved in effective decision-making.

All this has thrown socialists into profound confusion. They have in effect, those who have not turned ideologically to the East or those who have not accepted a libertarian perspective, been absorbed by the system. For neo-capitalism, in the very process of 'surpassing' socialism, in fact takes over many collectivist forms—though none of the content—of freedom. Thus socialists have always believed in planning—and now organised capitalism needs to plan and does. The NDP has opposed the free play of the market—and now organised capital transcends the market in its old form. The NDP supports a strong trade union movement—and now organised capitalism needs a strong, centralised trade union movement with which to bargain. It seems easy to turn and say, as does the NDP leadership : we are making socialism in fact, only we call it something else, and we are all in it together.

What in fact has happened is quite a different matter. Long before the present evolution began in earnest, NDP leaders and intellectuals translated these aspirations into narrow economism—expert planning—and a minimum welfare standard. With the whole end of the spectrum of democratic recovery and power left out, this meant a *critical* redefinition. In this transition period the NDP leadership, already wedded to a very particular concept of socialism, sees its opportunity for power. It is thus making a bid for the job of harnessing and managing the new system : but only partly because of its exhaustion and, more important its faulty perspective. It has been itself taken over, from both outside and inside, by a very subtle process.

"But democracy means parliament", "Elections are politics". Isn't that the usual answer ? At a very formal level it appears that parliamentary democracy is the democracy of today *but it is not*. It offers in fact a congress of representatives more loyal to their political parties than to their constituents. These elected represent-atives will, of course, often quarrel among themselves, and the rest of us may be asked to take sides. But all actual choice will be directed towards the resolution of conflicts within that specific machinery. We then confront a *whole system* which is foreclosing upon democracy, and which is robbing the people of any political culture and identity. *What we face is not simply a question of programmes and ideologies, what we face primarily is a question of institutions.* Consequently we add this footnote, that as long as the present order prevails even a political party with a 'revolutionary programme' contesting from within the electoral system is doomed.

Can we then challenge our political institutions and the political economy and culture that depends on it, given our *systemic analysis* by entering that pre-defined area in order to contest it ? Our answer must be an emphatic no ! And it is not a yes and no. It is a principled no. Otherwise as radicals we will delude ourselves again, for what will look like confrontation turns out to have been another bargain ; changes *of* the system reappear as changes *in* the system ; and the quality of our lives remains the same while the cardinal questions confronting society persist.

The traditional agencies of political change are failing, and so have the older definitions of politics. The political voting ma-chines once considered the means by which humanity would be emancipated have been by-passed in importance and indeed seek to expropriate us from any political identity. Is it not farcical to hear the Conservative leader of the opposition or a Union Nationale government or social democrats talk about the need for participatory democracy. All of a sudden, the politicians who have discovered participation talk glibly about the need for an extra-parliamentary opposition. The capacity of the establishment to absorb the language of radicals while leaving the essentials unchanged is horrific and only deepens the cynicism of the young.

We have no alternative but to withdraw our allegience from

the machines of the electoral process, from the institutions of 'representative democracy' like parliaments, to forego the magical rite of voting for our freedom, and resume our own initiatives before liberal corporatism asphyxiates us. We are now in a period of transition like the system itself, in which we will seek to unite radicals in new common forms of resistance and counter-institution building. As we have explained elsewhere, we wish to create a political movement of people with the capacity to determine their own lives, but a movement that has a cultural reality to it. For this we need common opportunities for education, for agitation, for building, for international discussions, for mutual consultation and support in all active campaigns against injustice.

WHAT IS AN EXTRA-PARLIAMENTARY OPPOSITION IN CANADA ?

The idea of the Extra-parliamentary Opposition (EPO) arose as a result of a lot of people arriving at much of the analysis above. EPO is not a formal organisation but rather a *critical concept* or a *political term of reference*. We shall describe what EPO should be like in Canada, and this is based on the political experience of many people here and in other industrial countries.

The idea of EPO is that a coalition of individuals and groups with a common critique of liberal democracy and a minimum programme choose to act together and separately within such a framework. The range of the coalition is focused on a similar although not identical critique of the institutions of political representation in this country. At one end of the coalition the EPO includes individuals and groups very critical of the functionality and representativity of parliament and electoralism. This part of EPO although it recognizes the necessity of generating a movement for social change in Canada still believes it useful to 'utilize' electoralism by supporting certain candidates on their own merits who while campaigning would also criticize the inadequacies of both electoralism and parliamentarianism. This would constitute the moderate wing of EPO.

At the other end of the coalition, people in EPO would have a principled position against electoralism (especially at the federal and provincial level) and against parliamentarianism and would seek to create revolutionary alternatives to this definition of politics. At the head of this wing of EPO would be the new left student and youth movement which demands that producers should control what they produce using the operational principes of "self-determination", "autogestion", "worker's councils", "participatory or direct democracy". This section of EPO would consist of individuals and groups ranging from revolutionary socialist parties to other revolutionary groups that reject involvement in party politics, electioneering and voting in our prevailing political institutions. They seek to organise new centers of power among ethnic and racial minorities, urban and rural workers, youth, the poor and other groups on a neighorhood and work level.

The two wings of EPO would thus share a basic critique of the political institutions of Canada but will differ as to the implication and application of this critique. There would be a 'creative tension and dialogue' between them.

Our programme for the EPO would include the following :
* *the decolonization and liberation of Canada from the American Empire.*

* *a stand against all Great Power Imperialism and Chauvinism — East or West.*

* *the self-determination of the people of Québec, and for that nation's independence if its people so choose.*

* *the creation of a broad movement for social and political change in Canada to implement the human rights of all people. Further EPO recognizes that Canada's basic foreign and defence policy will not change until certain key institutions and values are also changed, which includes a disengagement by this country from American imperialism on the one hand and the decolonization and democratization of Canada on the other. This task is the burden of a movement for social change.*

* *the cultural autonomy of ethnic and racial minorities and their right of self-determination and the struggle against current attempts of assimilation and institutionalised racism.*

* *for the self-organization of new constituencies presently without a political voice, i.e. the poor, ethnic and racial minorities, youth and students, farmers and industrial workers. This can be done by creating a movement with a cultural reality based on counter-institutions.*

* *the encouragement and help to focus the need for research into Canada's colonialized past and present.*

* *the principle of legal mass action as well as civil disobedience where necessary.*

* *a minimum action programme which is under continuous study and evolution. EPO is not a formal organisation but a common political term of reference of those in Canada who seek genuine change, and a qualitatively new society. EPO will have specific positions on specific issues, i.e. with reference to Vietnam — US*

GET OUT NOW ! or with reference to Czechoslovakia — USSR GET OUT NOW ! etc. These positions are common denominator positions but what is important is common action. Supporters of the concept of EPO in Canada and in other countries will sometimes act both together and separately.

There is no doubt that there is much to be discussed in this proposed EPO programme. It is significant however to note that many groups across the country individually include many aspects of what is suggested above. The striking difference will be having a common campaign on many of these questions which will begin a *systemic* approach to change in Canada, and allow us to emerge out of our *fragmented* existence.

The EPO and its supporters are brought together because of a new awareness that :

* The present system cannot solve the major problems of our society. It pretends that our difficulties are temporary. The present system is not geared to give to the majority of our people : real social security ; meaningful and humane education ; peace and disarmament.

* The present system cannot identify or solve the new problems of our society. It drifts against social change, and substitutes its rising curve on existing lines and inequalities. As a consequence it must absorb or deflect new kinds of demands, in a rapidly changing world. It cannot affect the quality of our lives, and thus cannot provide for the growing demands for meaning in work and leisure, for participation in actual communities, for an urban environment shaped by human priorities, for equality of women, for personal liberation from the routines of living inside the machine. All it can offer is compulsive consumption and its fashionable gimmicks and 'entertainment', and these feed on themselves. In the face of dissent, alienation and apathy, and a growing social and personal violence, it can offer only new manipulation, new forms of control and force, for it cannot conceive what indeed would end this.

* The present system cannot operate with genuinely conflicting political parties and movements, and so it must try to drain these of meaning, which in practice involves taking significance, legitimacy, values and participation away from many thousands of people.

* The present system cannot, finally, stand the pressure of the contemporary world. It is the last dream of a myopic local group : a way of preserving its structures of minority power against a world revolution, with which the needs of its own people, for

peace and freedom, must be eventually ranged. Centered in its dying concepts of what the world should be like, it is being driven to conflict and war, to massive armaments and de-humanization even while it proclaims its own version of life as an endless, mild, hand-to-mouth paradise. This contradiction is already bending it, and will continue to bend it. It is the weak link in its otherwise glassy facade. It is the point where change will begin, and where we must be ready to push change right through, until the system as a whole is dismantled.

In the coming years, the failures of the present system will provoke repeated struggles, on particular issues, representing the urgent needs and expectations of millions of people. We must see each conflict as an opportunity for explaining the basic character of the system which is cheating us, and as a way of helping to change consciousness : to follow our needs and feelings through until they reach the kind of demands which the system can neither satisfy nor contain. What has been the characteristic weakness of those in this country who have sought radical change, namely running separate campaigns in so many different social and political fields, through the EPO can become our strength. We are present in a society where the system and its political leadership have a diminishing legitimacy.

The existing political institutions and party structures are under great strain, and the pressures can be expected to increase. This system and we who have worked within it up until now, were not able to prevent nuclear bombs from entering Canada, not able to disengage ourselves from the Cold War and arms race, from American imperialism in Vietnam, unresponsive to the aspirations of the people of Québec, to the poor, youth and oppressed minorities in our society, unable to do much about the immense human suffering in the world.

We do not intend to make any premature move, which would isolate people interested in radical change, or confuse our actual and potential supporters. At the same time, we mean what we say when we declare an end to tactics and allegiances which are wholly enclosed within traditional organisational forms. If this analysis is right, then radicals must make their voices heard, again and again, among the growing majority of people who feel no commitment to these forms. Already thousands of young women and men who share many of our objectives and whose internationalist conscience and immediate personal concern are more alert than those of their predecessors and elders, stand outside the NDP and refuse to give it the kind of allegiance it demands. The other organisations of the Left represent, in most cases, the same hardening shells of old situations, old bearings, and old strategies. *What matters now, everwhere, is movement.* In the context of such a new awareness, a movement for fundamental social change has a greater chance of emerging. A movement that will have the capacity to both resist injustice as well as build the new society by means of building the institutions and system of institutions of that new society now, thus giving a cultural reality to the new politics. We have indicited elsewhere what the scope and orientation of such a movement as a part of an EPO should be.

To those who say that there is no future without changing the NDP, we reply that we shall only influence it by refusing to accept its machine definitions and demands, and that the real change required is so large and so difficult that it can only come about as part of much wider changes of consciousness, and as a result of manifold struggles in many areas of life. In a seminal sense we must begin afresh.

This statement asks for a response. There are many people who share this general analysis and who have come to a similar position. We invite their active initiative.

LET THE NIGGERS BURN!
Racism in Canada

The Sir George Williams
Affair and its
Caribbean Aftermath

edited by
Dennis Forsythe

From the black point of view, Dennis Forsythe, who teaches sociology at Sir George Williams University has edited a collection of essays by other blacks which include: the problems of the black immigrant, the background to the "Anderson Affair" at Sir George Williams and what happened and the subsequent upheaval in the Caribbean area.

These and other essays in the book contribute to the publication of an important book in the growing literature of social criticism in Canada.

Contributors include: Delisle Worrell, Bertram Boldon, Leroi Butcher, Carl Lumumba, Roosevelt Williams, and Rawle R. Frederick.

200 pages / Hardcover $6.45 / Paperback $2.45
ISBN : 0-919618-16-2 / ISBN : 9-919618-17-0

BLACK ROSE BOOKS No. B4
Library of Congress Catalog Card Number : 73-76057

THE POLITICAL ECONOMY OF THE STATE

Canada / Québec / USA

edited by
Dimitrios
Roussopoulos

This new book subjects the State in our society to a rigourous examination. Both the enormous growth of the State bureaucracy and the myth of its neutrality in social and economic affairs is carefully studied. Rick Deaton in *"The Fiscal Crisis of the State in Canada"*, deals with the whole range of activities in the public sector as well as the enormous growth of the Federal State, while B. Roy Lemoine in *"The Growth of the State in Québec"* examines the new role and function of the State since the "quiet revolution". Graeme Nicholson in *"Authority and the State"* studies the relationship of authoritarian patterns of behaviour and hierarchical institutions which are inter-laced with the State at their highest expression, while John and Margaret Rowntree in *"Revolution in the Metropolis"* submit a major essay that pulls many of the themes of the book together. Finally Lorne Huston comments on the effect of *Local Initiative Projects* and *Opportunities for Youth* grants on citizens groups.

The Political Economy of the State begins an important new approach to the study of government and society which political science has ignored for a very long time.

200 pages / Hardcover $9.95 / Paperback $2.95
ISBN : 0-919618-02 / ISBN : 0-919618-01-4

BLACK ROSE BOOKS No. D8

THE GENOCIDE MACHINE IN CANADA

The Pacification of the North

by Robert Davis and Mark Zannis

The two authors examine the Canadian North thoroughly with a documentation that is impressive. This book will shock. It assesses the impact of such activities as "Project Chariot", "Icefield Ranges Project", the work of the "Defence Research Board", and the Department of Health and Welfare.

The role of the courts, legal profession, the RCMP are all critically observed as to their negative influence on the native people and their economy. The question of 'scientific' planning by various institutions like the Arctic Institute of North America is also examined in the light of the United Nations Convention on Genocide.

300 pages / Hardcover $9.95 / Paperback $2.95
ISBN : 0-919618-04-9 / ISBIN : 0-919618-03-0

BLACK ROSE BOOKS No. D10

QUEBEC LABOUR STRIKES

Arnold Bennett

Since the publication of the widely acclaimed *"Québec Labour"*, the greatest General Strike in North American labour history has taken place. A Common Front of the Confederation of National Trade Unions, the Québec Federation of Labour, and the Québec Teachers Corporation while in a protracted struggle with the Québec government provoked a spontaneous revolt of some 350,000 workers in public service as well as private industry. What are the facts behind this upheaval? What has happened to the labour movement since the General Strike? What does the breakaway CSD trade union represent? What has happened to the growing radicalisation of the teachers union? How has all this affected the whole social movement consisting of the multitude of citizen committees, tenant associations, welfare recipients, unemployed workers, community medical and legal clinics and so on? These and many other related questions are examined in this thoroughly documented book.

225 pages / Hardcover $9.95 / Paperback $2.95
ISBN : 0-919618-1 / ISBN : 0-919618-07-3

BLACK ROSE BOOKS No. D11

ESSAYS ON MARX'S THEORY OF VALUE

by Issaak Illich Rubin

According to the prevailing theories of economists, economics has replaced political economy, and economics deals with scarcity, prices, and resource allocation. In the definition of Paul Samuelson, "economics — or political economy, as it used to be called ... is the study of how men and society *choose,* with or without the use of money, to employ *scarce* productive resources, which could have alternative uses, to produce various commodities over time and distribute them for consumption, now and in the future, among various people and groups in society."

If economics is indeed merely a new name for political economy, and if the subject matter which was once covered under the heading of political economy is now covered by economics, then economics has replaced political economy. However, if the subject matter of political economy is not the same as that of economics, then the "replacement" of political economy is actually an omission of a field of knowledge. If economics answers different questions from those raised by political economy, and if the omitted questions refer to the form and the quality of human life within the dominant social-economic system, then this omission can be called a "great evasion".

Economic theorist and historian I. I. Rubin suggested a definition of political economy which has nothing in common with the definition of economics quoted above. According to Rubin, "Political economy deals with human working activity, not from the standpoint of its technical methods and instruments of labor, but from the standpoint of its social form. It deals with *production relations* which are established among people in the process of production." In terms of this definition, political economy is not the study of prices or of scarce resources ; it is a study of social relations, a study of culture.

Rubin's book was first published in the Soviet Union, and was never re-issued after 1928. This is the first and only English edition. The translators are Milos Samardzija and Fredy Perlman.

275 pages/Hardcover : $7.50   ISBN : 0-919618-11-1

BLACK ROSE BOOKS No. D 13

THE CRISIS OF BRITISH SOCIALISM
BY KEN COATES

After the 1970 defeat of the Wilson Government, the future of the Labour Movement appears more than a little bleak. Rapidly falling membership, financ ' l crisis, widespread loss of morale, serious disputes separating the major trade unions from the political leadership : all these difficulties reflect a deeper malaise. The Labour Party has lost its way. Whatever its future as a political force, whether or not it is capable of resuming office, the socialist basis of its traditional philosophy has become more and more obviously incompatible with the short-run policies which have become the mainstay of its practical strategy. This book assesses the "Wilson years".

.012/243 pages   SBN 85124 0097
                                   Hardcover $9.95

A TRADE UNION STRATEGY
EDITED BY KEN COATES

This book is a translation of the Workers' Control programme adopted by the Belgian trade union movement (FGTB) at their 1971 congress. It is the only book in English that highlights the major advances being made by a trade union centre that has often blazed a path for the whole of European trade unionism. Ken Coates outlines the Belgian situation, M.B. Brown deals with the public accountability of companies, and Louis de Brouckere deals with how workers' control can be set up.

013/149 pages   SBN 85124 023 2
                                     Hardcover $4.95

ESSAYS ON IMPERIALISM
BY MICHAEL BARRAT BROWN

There are four major essays, "A Critique of Marxist Theories of Imperialism", "The Stages of Imperialism", "Imperialism and Working Class Interests in the Developed Countries", and "The E.E.C. and Neo-Colonialism in Africa". The essays are a major intervention into the debate between Sweezy, Jalee, Magdoff and Mandel, among others, as to whether capitalist countries will remain united r their joint efforts to exploit the Third World, or split into warring competitive factions. Barrat Brown argues that both views have limitations.

014/163 pages   SBN 85124 024 0
                                     Hardcover $9.95

IMPRIMERIE GAGNE LTEE g